'FRAGILE STATES' IN AN UNEQUAL WORLD

'Fragile States' in an Unequal World

The Role of the g7+ in International Diplomacy and Development Cooperation

Isabel Rocha de Siqueira

OpenBook Publishers

ISBN Paperback: 9781800647930
ISBN Hardback: 9781800647947
ISBN Digital (PDF): 9781800647954
ISBN Digital ebook (EPUB): 9781800647961
ISBN Digital ebook (AZW3): 9781800647978
ISBN XML: 9781800647985
ISBN Digital ebook (HTML): 9781800647992
DOI: 10.11647/OBP.0311

Cover image: Basket-tray from Sudan (2015). Photo by King muh, https://commons.wikimedia.org/wiki/File:African_Sudan_Art_Basket-Tray.jpg. Cover design by Katy Saunders.

Contents

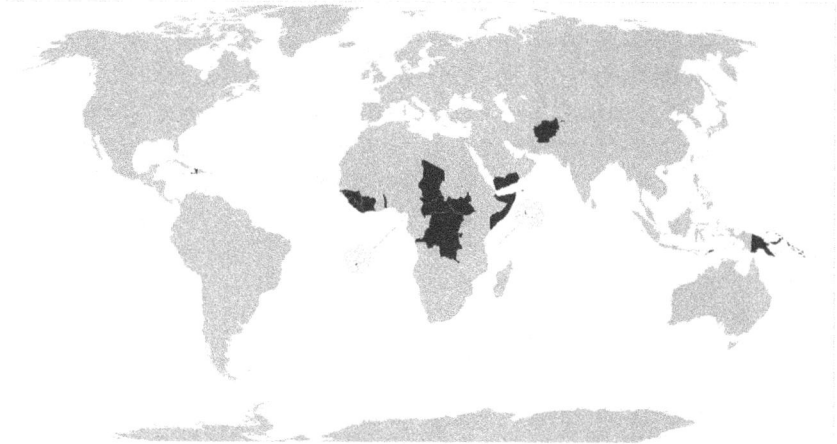

g7+ member countries (2020)

Afghanistan	Liberia
Burundi	Papua New Guinea
Central African Republic (CAR)	São Tomé e Príncipe
Chad	Sierra Leone
Comoros	Solomon Islands
Côte D'Ivoire	Somalia
Democratic Republic of Congo (DRC)	South Sudan
Guinea	Timor-Leste
Guinea-Bissau	Togo
Haiti	Yemen

Figures and Illustrations

Cartoons by Luiz Matheus Ribeiro da Silva (Ribs), June 2020.
Strips by Carolina Avelino Cardoso (Ina), June 2020.
Cartoons ands strips are unnumbered.

Additional Resources

Photo Archive of the g7+ Secretariat

The photo archive of the g7+ Secretariat is available at
https://www.flickr.com/photos/195846664@N05/. The
archive contains photos of people discussed in the book,
as well as of individuals who have played an important
role in the g7+ .

Foreword

The second decade of the twenty-first century dawned with the outbreak of the COVID-19 pandemic, which affected everyone around the world. However, the severity and longevity of its impacts have not been equal for all countries. It has adversely affected conflict-affected countries much more than other nations. The pandemic has highlighted social, political, and economic inequalities that have been present for a long time, and it has revealed the fragility of an international system that has been ruled by a select few countries. The unequal distribution of vaccines speaks very loudly to this reality, despite the fact that no one is safe from the virus until everyone is safe.

As the world started to heave a sigh of relief as the pandemic has started to recede, we have witnessed the Russian invasion of Ukraine, a tragedy familiar to many of us. Although this is not the first war of its type taking place in this century, its impacts are being felt even in the most distant parts of the world. The brunt of the indirect socio-economic impacts of this invasion are very deeply felt in the world's so-called fragile and conflict-affected countries. These impacts have included an economic depression characterised by spikes in inflation, shortages of food and geopolitical tensions that will affect peace and stability in many of these countries. The war in Ukraine and the associated global instability are indicative of the hegemonic nature of world politics and how it has been hindering peace for decades. The world might have been considered peaceful by many standards since the Second World War, but, for a large majority of its countries, it has been hostile, unstable and chaotic, as these places still experience colonization, aggressions, civil wars, natural crises, fragility and poverty.

Many factors are at play. However, the pandemic and the war in Ukraine can be perceived as litmus tests for the resilience and relevance of the global policies and institutions that have been put in place to

    https://doi.org/10.11647/OBP.0311.08

ensure shared peace and stability in the world. These events speak volumes as to how inclusive and effective they have been. As most of the United Nations (UN) members denounce the war on Ukraine, the conflict has continued with greater intensity. While a majority of UN members have called for the COVID-19 vaccines to be declared a global public good, free of patents, the suggestion was met with refusals by the very few powerful nations that produce vaccines and that can use the crisis to amass more power.

The leaders and people of many countries have been struggling to raise their voices about these injustices and others for years now. They have actively engaged in debates and advocacy to reform the current international system, for it to become more inclusive and equal, and hence, more effective. They have faced grave challenges at every step. *'Fragile States' in an Unequal World: The Role of the g7+ in International Diplomacy and Development Cooperation* is the story of some of those individuals. It summarizes their journey within the g7+, a group that was established with the express aim of achieving peace and stability in conflict-affected countries.

Countries such as those in the g7+ are labeled 'fragile', 'failed' or 'failing' states by international development experts and the hegemonic organizations that set the norms. Each of these labels has strings attached that further determine the fate of these countries at a global level, by regulating access to resources determining where and how certain demands might be placed.

The book is not only a history of the g7+ but also an exercise in storytelling that relies on accounts by professionals who have risen to the occasion, coming from difficult trajectories. It provides a counter-narrative and a counter-archive to the stories that one hears in the media, expert reports and assessments. For that alone, it is necessary reading and a small form of doing justice itself.

E.P. Xanana Gusmão
Former President and Prime Minister of Timor-Leste

Acknowledgements

A long time ago, I was lucky enough to decide to study a subject that suddenly became a 'hot topic' in international politics. I had been studying state fragility for a while when I started my PhD and, for those who have been in that position, you might understand how happy I was when the g7+ was founded—there was finally a group of people speaking in the name of countries that had been called fragile for so many years. And because my view had always been more critical towards this agenda and terminology, it was interesting to speak to people who had appropriated the label and were seeking to change the narratives around it. Moreover, I was thrilled that they would generously share their experiences. I never encountered closed doors when I tried to approach them—and this was the very beginning—even when they had their hands full. They were also always keen to listen, which drew my attention more and more. There were bound to be many challenges involved in their work, and many shortcomings and failures, as no one does politics without making mistakes one way or another, but there was considerable potential hovering in the background. It seemed to me, consciously or not, that they were borrowing from the history of other groups that have tried to enter into dialogue with the 'experts', the 'North', the 'donors', and so on, their different names all equally understood in the places I go to conduct my research.

This book is a culmination of these years of talking, listening, observing and trying to understand the people in the g7+. My approach was sociological before and is still sociological now; I was interested in the people and it is they who, I hope, appear in the book. The goal has been to understand the role that 'big politics' (such as decisions related to war and peace) plays in their lives, and how smaller and different ideas come to the fore. When the g7+ Secretariat first mentioned the idea of the book, there was a lot of room to explore its subject, but we all agreed the book should be about 'more human' accounts of big politics. The book also needed to be accessible; that was key for us all. I can only hope I did justice to these notions. On that note, I thank OBP for embracing this project and for believing knowledge should be shared; I'm especially thankful for the patience and understanding of all the editors involved in preparing this perhaps unusual manuscript for publication.

I want to thank, first and foremost, the g7+ Secretariat for the opportunity to receive and recount these stories, and to say I really appreciate the time taken by those who spoke to us, and all the feelings and thoughts that were shared in these conversations. I learned a lot and felt honoured to listen to these personal stories. I also want to thank my team: Beatriz Teixeira, Lucas Manuel Machado, and Tatiana Castelo Branco, for their invaluable help with research and preparation for this manuscript and for the careful comments provided. They fulfil the trust our g7+ interlocutors have placed with the younger generations. Truly, this book is a collaborative effort at offering a brief history of a collective undertaking.

Acronyms and Abbreviations

ANDS – Afghanistan National Development Strategy

ASEAN – Association of Southeast Asian Nations

AU – African Union

CAP – Common African Position

CAR – Central African Republic

CAS – Country Assistance Strategy

D(P)PA – Department of Political and Peacebuilding Affairs

DAC – Development Assistance Committee (OECD)

DPA – Department of Political Affairs

DPKO – Department of Peacekeeping Operations

DRC – Democratic Republic of Congo

EP – Eminent Person

F2F – Fragile to Fragile

FCS – Fragility and Conflict Affected Situations

FCV – Fragility, Conflict and Violence

FDI – Foreign Direct Investments

FOCUS – New Deal principles: Fragility assessment, One vision-one plan, Use PSGs to monitor results, Support political leadership and dialogue

FREITLIN – Revolutionary Front for an Independent Timor-Leste (in Portuguese)

G77 – Group of 77

GDP – Gross Domestic Product

HIPC – Heavily Indebted Poor Countries

HLP – High Level Panel of Eminent Persons on the Post-2015 Agenda

HLPF – High Level Political Forum

IDA – International Development Association (World Bank)

IDP – Internally Displaced Persons

IDPS – International Dialogue on Peacebuilding and Statebuilding (OECD)

IMF – International Monetary Fund

IPU – Inter-Parliamentary Union

LNOB – Leaving No One Behind

M&E – Monitoring & Evaluation

MDG – Millennium Development Goal

MDRI – Multilateral Debt Relief Initiative

MINUSCA – United Nations Multidimensional Integrated Stabilization Mission in the Central African Republic

MSF – Médecins Sans Frontières

ODA – Official Development Assistance

ODI – Overseas Development Institute

OECD – Organisation for Economic Co-operation and Development

PALOP – Portuguese-speaking African Countries community (in Portuguese)

PBSO – Peacebuilding Support Office

PFM – Public Finance Management

PGRT – Poverty Reduction and Growth Trust

PNG – Papua New Guinea

PRSP – Poverty Reduction Strategy Paper

PSG – Peacebuilding and Statebuilding Goals

RMR – Risk Mitigation Regime

RRAs – Risk and Resilience Assessments

RSW – Refugee Sub-Window

SAP – Structural Adjustment Program

SDG – Sustainable Development Goals

TAR – Turnaround Regime

TRUST – New Deal principles: Transparency, Risk-sharing, Use country system, Strengthen capacities, Timely & predictable aid

UN – United Nations

UNDP – United Nations Development Programme

UNOPs – UN Office for Project Services

UNSOM – UN Assistance Mission in Somalia

UNTAET – UN Transitional Administration in East Timor

USAID – United States Agency for International Development

USSR – Union of Soviet Socialist Republics

WB – World Bank

WHR – Window for Host Communities and Refugees

1. A Book about People
The Stories of the g7+

'The fight against injustice cannot but be emotional and it will help mutual understanding if this simple truth is remembered.'[1]

In a traditional Somali story, Igal Shadad is "bound by duty to find a better place for his family and animals: both are under the mercy of a relentless drought. Under such conditions, the [provider] in the homestead is required to travel far and wide until he finds a place with pasture and water... Travelling at night, and away from his homestead, Igal comes across a menacing object on the ground. He cannot surmise or ascertain the real identity of the object, which, to him, looks like a lion, ready to strike. He decides to wait the night out. Finally, at daybreak, he finds out the identity of the object that had rendered him motionless through the night: a tree stump." What the fictional character thought has roughly been transfigured from traditional Somali storytelling into the following: "What I thought of you, and what you actually have become, and what will not be repeated."[2] The story makes one laugh so that one can conquer real fears. At the same time, it recommends that we expect the unexpected and avoid walking in dark nights.

There are many dangers in this world. Some are dangers to one's physical survival—the lion ready to strike; some are dangers to a person's beliefs and the teachings held in one's heart—the indignity

---

1 Remark by Sri Lankan prime minister Sirimavo R. D. Bandaranaike, in the context of the Non-Aligned Movement (NAM), in 1976. Much of the Conference of Bandung's and NAM's spirit, if not the major components, is present in the stories in this book.

2 Ahmed, Ali Jimale (2002). *The Somali Oral Tradition and the Role of Storytelling in Somalia*. Minnesota: Minnesota Humanities Center, pp. 10–11.

https://doi.org/10.11647/OBP.0311.01

of cowardice; and others are a combination of all the small and large challenges that cause one to fail to prepare for these other dangers, or render one incapable of doing so because of lack of skills or resources—the journey in the night with no light.

Igal is a fictional character. How do real people cope with terrible challenges they may face? And how do they learn? What are their real fears? The dangers to body and soul, such as hunger, lack of access to medicines, constraints in access to education, inequality, violence, and conflict are routine, and attempting to tackle the bigger and most vital challenges, such as finding long-term political solutions to such problems, can often feel like travelling in the dark. The world is still highly unequal: The 2022 World Inequality Report indicates that '[t]he share of the bottom 50% of the world in total global wealth is 2% by their estimates, while the share of the top 10% is 76%. Since wealth is a major source of future economic gains, and increasingly, of power and influence, this presages further increases in inequality.'[3] Overall, inequalities within countries have increased, while inequalities between countries have declined, yet 'despite this decline, between-country inequality remains very high in absolute terms: in 2020, it is roughly at the same level as it was in 1900'.[4] The same holds for intangible goods such as peace: 'Since 2008, the 25 least peaceful countries deteriorated on average by 16%, while the 25 most peaceful countries improved by 5.1%', revealing the snowball effect conflict-affected countries know so well, which sees problems compounding each other.[5]

If one is looking to solve problems at this scale, if we are honest and generous, we would probably find there are rarely any heroes, and the villains are often in disguise. Besides, going back to our metaphor, most people don't travel alone, and whether they make many mistakes or only a few, the scope of such errors often depends on their travel companions. But then the story of Igal, used here as a figurative illustration, becomes too complicated. And what is the purpose of this story, anyway? What place does it have in explaining the hard facts of the world? I believe the

---

3   Chancel, L., Piketty, T., Saez, E., Zucman, G. et al. (2022). *World Inequality Report 2022*. World Inequality Lab. wir2022.wid.world, p. 3.
4   Ibid, pp. 56–57.
5   Institute for Economics & Peace (2022). *Global Peace Index 2022: Measuring Peace in a Complex World*, Sydney, June 2022. http://visionofhumanity.org/resources, p. 4.

everyday and personal stories often have an important role to play in understanding political possibilities.

I have no idea how to tell complicated human stories, much less ones that go from individuals to groups of all sizes. And I dislike simplifications. Instead, in the following pages I shall attempt to offer a little bit of what a popular story like Igal's conveys with some *simplicity*, amid a vast field of moral reflections for anyone to explore. It is an ambitious goal, so please bear with me. By the way, I don't appear in the story. But as the hand doing the writing, *I* will unavoidably come up. Please ignore me.

First, the setting:

We are in a world where the key physical threats to human survival—poverty and violence—have been addressed in recent decades by a huge machinery of frameworks, budgetary formulae, experts, modalities of funding and local people themselves (that elusive category). We may call this the development field, but there are also humanitarians and security professionals involved. Actors can generally be divided between development partners (formally known as 'donors') and partner countries (usually, poor and conflict-affected countries), but these are far from settled categories as they vary from context to context. The currency we are mostly talking about here is *assistance* or *aid*, in the form of financial, material and other resources.

Despite all the aid that has been provided to this date, nevertheless, there has been many a dark night for some.

The results of all that investment have been profoundly unequal. Fragile and conflict-affected states[6] still have 3.5 times the percentage of the world's poor 'than would be expected if poverty were equally prevalent everywhere', and that is probably an underestimate.[7] Extreme

---

6   The term 'fragile' is controversial and not used lightly here. I have discussed the terminology extensively elsewhere, see: Rocha de Siqueira, Isabel (2017). *Managing State Fragility: Conflict, Quantification and Power*. London: Taylor and Francis. The term is not used by every representative in the g7+, nor is it used in every context. It is, however, the term that was originally embraced by the group. Today, this is complemented by 'conflict-affected' in most cases, or else only the latter is used. I choose to use both in this book to simplify matters, but a more detailed dicussion is provided in the box on p. 122.

7   World Bank (2018). *Poverty and Shared Prosperity: Piecing Together the Poverty Puzzle*. https://www.worldbank.org/en/publication/poverty-and-shared-prosperity-2018, p. 36.

poverty was considerably reduced between 1990 and 2015, but the rate of reduction has shown signs of decline since 2013.[8] That means the urge to find pasture and water is not only still very much present, but might require even more energy and perseverance.

Reading a summary of current world events might have felt like reading a dystopian novel even before the onset of the new coronavirus pandemic (COVID-19):

> The number of violent conflicts is at a 30-year high, and fragility impacts 28% of the world's population. Only 18% of contexts affected by fragility are on track to meet selected SDG targets [Sustainable Development Goals]. More people are displaced than at any time since the end of the Second World War. The past four years have been the warmest on record and the trend is almost certain to continue.[9]

The pandemic has indeed made these issues even worse, especially for the poor and those affected by conflict: per capita gross domestic product contracted 7.5% in 2021 and per capita income is not expected to reach 2019 levels in fragile states until 2024.[10] Not only that, but vaccination has become another cruel marker of inequality. It is estimated the typical (median) fragile state will reach a vaccination target of 70% of their population by July 2025, 'while the typical extremely fragile context will reach it by December 2034. By comparison, 23 OECD members have already reached the target.'[11]

Now come the characters:

Very recently, it seems 'the global aid system support[ed] some 15,000 donor missions in 54 recipient countries per year—and in some countries this amount[ed] to over 20 official visits per week'.[12] This is a lot of people, missions and official attempts to 'fix' things. The business-as-usual is a crowded space.

8　　Ibid., p. 22.

9　　OECD (2019). *Development Co-operation Report—A Fairer, Greener, Safer Tomorrow.* https://www.oecd.org/dac/development-co-operation-report-20747721.htm, p. 28.

10　Bousquet, F. (2022). *Fragile and conflict-affected economies are falling further behind.* World Economic Forum. https://www.weforum.org/agenda/2022/02/fragile-conflict-economy-states-pandemic-covid19-debt/.

11　OECD (2020). *States of Fragility.* http://www3.compareyourcountry.org/states-of-fragility/covid/0/.

12　Ramalingam, Ben (2013). *Aid on the Edge of Chaos.* Oxford: Oxford University Press, p. 3.

In these visits, on the other side of the proverbial table ('because we [development partners and partner countries[13]] somehow always seem to sit facing off each other'[14]), there are also fascinating characters. Like all characters in a story, they have different personalities, make mistakes and have flaws. In any case, they are the ones who have to find water and pasture more often than not in an unequal world. They are not necessarily so different from the others in donor missions, nor are they bound to be similar to each other. The story does not intend to make them so. But it is a story about them and how that story came to be.

OECD Development Assistance Committee (DAC)

There are 30 DAC members, mostly European countries, but also United States, Canada, Korea, Japan, New Zealand and Australia. To be a member, a country has to demonstrate 'the existence of appropriate strategies, policies and institutional frameworks that ensure capacity to deliver a development co-operation programme; an accepted measure of effort; and the existence of a system of performance monitoring and evaluation.' Those who receive Official Development Assistance (ODA) can also apply to become a member. Non-OECD countries can engage as well, but with limited rights and obligations.

(See: http://www.oecd.org/dac/dac-global-relations/joining-the-development-assistance-committee.htm)

The plot:

Those who can do so ought to shine more light on the dangers lurking in the dark: hunger, poverty, inequality, conflict and so on. Our main characters have been pushing for such light to be shone on a regular basis, so that, when one light goes out, another is readily available, and no family will go without water, or animals without pastures because a person could not travel to look for them; this is about preparedness, and about the unacceptable reality of basic needs not being met when the world has enough resources to do so. Moreover, one should include peace among these needs, for no amount of material resources can provide quality of life without peace.

---

13   Terminology used generally in the field, respectively attributed to 'donors' and 'receivers'.

14   Interview with Hodan Osman, 24 April 2020.

But the world is not prioritizing prevention. Since 2015, there has been 'a shift towards responding to emergency situations rather than addressing the drivers of crises and fragility.' In recent years, only a small portion of the Official Development Assistance (ODA) has gone towards conflict, peace and security—this amounted to only 4% of ODA provided by the OECD's Development Assistance Committee (DAC) to fragile contexts in 2018, for instance.[15]

There are other interconnected complicating factors in the plot. Cooperation means acting together, but recently, multilateralism has been under threat:[16] 'trust in governments and institutions is plummeting and populism, protectionism and exclusive nationalism are on the rise'.[17] In that context, it can be difficult to harness solidarity in order to face complex problems, such as the COVID-19 pandemic, climate change, or the fact that insecurity in some countries often serves the political or economic goals of other governments and companies.

The truth, nevertheless, is that a reliance on external support has always meant being vulnerable to crises and changes in political mood. This is why the characters in this story keep repeating that self-sufficiency is required: as the people most interested in there being fewer and fewer dark nights, they want to have more say in how the light system works.

Now, the point of view:

This is a tricky story to tell. There will be real facts and events and there will be the narrator's perceptions of the people whose stories are being told. That means I will retell the stories that have been told to me and my team, and also add notes of my own. I will mix and combine them in an order of my own devising, to offer something more that can perhaps be extrapolated from these individual stories. In that way, the people involved are presented as very much themselves in their rich individualities, but, most importantly, they are also their brothers and sisters, children, neighbours and colleagues. The idea is to tell *kinds* of stories, to open space to see what certain stories can achieve.

***

---

15   See OECD (2020). *States of Fragility*, Executive Summary.
16   Ibid., p. 32.
17   Ibid., p. 19, box 1.1.

We are used to reading and writing long reports about the technicalities of the lives of the Igals of the world. Those are important too (although there are probably too many of them). Recently, organizations have experimented with quantifying facetime, that is, face-to-face meetings,[18] measuring intercultural dialogues[19] and 'modernizing' narratives in order to harness solidarity in the face of increasing distrust of any multilateral action.[20] These experiments aim to understand the impact of doing things collectively and to learn how to create incentives for such practices. They ask: how relevant is it to spend time together—really, physically together? How important is it, to international development initiatives in general, to speak the same language, share the same culture? How essential is the element of identification for the presence of empathy and the willingness to trust when it comes to negotiating peace, for instance? And yet, if you ask people doing public policy in difficult contexts, a lot of what is done is due to pure and simple joy, which is something that cannot be quantified, nor designed. Much of the joy people find when working with each other comes from deep beliefs and commitments that were passed on in the family and the community, many of which are not seen in reports.

The stories that follow try to offer some of these elements.

Behind the Scenes

I have been working on fragility for some years now, and I closely followed the foundation of the g7+ in 2010, a group now composed of 20 countries who self-identify as fragile states.[21] I have also coordinated the *Independent Review of the g7+* in 2019. During their tenth anniversary, in 2020, the group commissioned this book as a publication meant to talk about the people involved with the g7+. However, as the pandemic

---

18 World Bank (2020). *IDA19*. https://ida.worldbank.org/replenishments/ida19.

19 See UNESCO (2018). *Expert Meeting on "Measuring Intercultural Dialogue: Strengthening data to enhance impact on the ground"*. https://en.unesco.org/events/expert-meeting-measuring-intercultural-dialogue-strengthening-data-enhance-impact-ground.

20 OECD (2019). *Development Co-operation Report—A fairer, greener, safer tomorrow*. https://www.oecd.org/dac/development-co-operation-report-20747721.htm.

21 See www.g7plus.org.

unfolded, other challenges took center stage in our lives, and thus this book has had a long journey to publication..

Above all, it is a book about people. It is not a technical report (for that, see the 2019 review[22]); it is about a political agenda, but we understand that by listening to those who previously worked for, or currently work for the g7+ in various capacities, discovering who they are, how they came to believe in politics and policy, how they feel about their work and the work they do for the group, how their family and communities relate to the work they do and what they would love to see in the next generation, including from their own children. The broader story is about values, commitments, mistakes and challenges at a personal and collective level. It is a story (or many stories), therefore, that probably rings true to anyone who has tried to organize and work in a network of very different people, complete with all the joy and the difficulties this entails.

People have shared many hours of their time and even personal memorabilia with me in the process of researching this book, and it has been an honour to receive them. I have focused on different characters for diverse reasons: sometimes I want to focus on the time they have spent with the g7+, sometimes on how new they are to this agenda, or what they have to tell us about it. Unfortunately, not all those who have been involved with the group can be featured here. Those who *are* featured are not all presented the same way; I let the story guide how it should be told. I could not meet all of the contributors in person, not least because of the COVID-19 pandemic and the restrictions imposed. But as I said, I am not important in the story to come; it is about *their* meetings and exchanges with each other. To some extent, their narratives are personal, but importantly they are also collective and represent what the g7+ stands for, and all the unavoidable shortcomings that entails.

I should also mention that the g7+ works with two official languages, French and English. The conversations were held in those languages, in addition to Portuguese, which many spoke and is mine and my team's mother tongue. Some of the poems and proverbs cited were born in other, indigenous languages. That the book is in English, therefore, means choices were made about how to translate what was said, and

---

22   Rocha de Siqueira, Isabel (2019). *Independent Review of the g7+*, BRICS Policy Center—International Relations Institute (PUC-Rio).

we are aware translations have their limits. This is only one of the many challenges with this book.

In addition, I should say that I am an academic, and this is not what my work usually looks like (but more and more I think academic work should read more like it). The fact that I am writing it means that, after 12 years, there is an opportunity to try and do justice to the incredible life stories that compose the group I have been observing from afar. It is also a reflection of my belief in people and our capacity to thrive. In that sense, it is an attempt to change my own conversations slightly, in order to focus on anything that can help us to create structures that might encourage younger generations to engage with politics and policy with a generous disposition. The worst that can be done, in the setting and within the plot I have just described, is to have people disengage. But how do we offer hope in this context? I believe that the people telling their stories in this book have a lot to say about hope. In fact, their hope is a wonder.

I had a few sources of academic inspiration in mind that served as a guide to the way the conversations were held and how they are reported here. Mostly, I think this book is an exercise in pluralizing voices in an unequal international system. Not only are fragile states not often at the centre of international decision-making, but their civil servants are seldom invited to speak about how they manage their work. This book is not simply an exercise in filling space by reproducing first-hand testimony such as diary entries; it is a way of collecting memories and, through it, making the broader picture of international affairs more complex. As the inspirational sources show, there is a sense in which history is a story told by the experts, by scholars and authorities; it is *one*, while memory opens itself to being individual and collective at the same time, and, therefore, *plural*. In this way, memory also poses a challenge to the idea that there is only one history to tell. Here, such thinking helps us frame the fragments of personal stories into a collective undertaking of pluralization, whereby the notion that there has been a linear, progressive engagement with the poorest people and those most affected by conflict is problematized by several instances when this narrative had to be made to hold together in the face of reality. In this sense, we encounter the anecdotes and struggles of individual lives and, at the same time, through the g7+, we can perhaps see the material, symbolic, and functional roles such groupings can play, as platforms that provide counternarratives, with all the many restrictions an unequal international system and the very nature of politics pose to such endeavours.[23]

Indeed, in that sense, the stories are perhaps more relevant because they express the hope that permeated the search for a voice with the g7+ than because they reflect the capacity of these voices to address inequalities effectively. They reflect certain aspirations and ambitions, which, in turn, are born in a context of possible solidarity. These accounts do not deliver an epical story of underdogs speaking up, but a mundane account of how people found ways to talk about themselves to themselves while believing that the group could lead to some change. By the time the g7+ was founded, after all, there was much criticism about the fact that emerging countries, such as the BRICS, and most developed countries were not exactly demonstrating a willingness to pay the price of a fairer system when it came to fragile states. At one early point in the formation of the g7+, comments made were along the lines of, 'the BRICS have done little to alter the prevailing patterns of marginalization and inequality within the world economy'.[24] It was in this context that the g7+ came to be and why many of the stories recounted express some hope of speaking up to major organizations and the richest governments, but also relief in speaking *with* each other, even if this does not ultimately translate into major political influence or material gains, which is nonetheless—and always will be—a cause of frustration.

When it comes to the angle this book provides, we can say the conversations we had and that are reproduced here were not interviews; they were 'ethical encounters', where my team and I tried to build humble 'relations of testimony', actively hearing instead of listening in 'too literal a way'.[25] For the latter, there are technical reports. One

---

23   See Shani, Georgio (2016). 'Spectres of the Third World: Bandung as a Lieu de Mémoire', in Phạm, Quỳnh N. & Shilliam, Robbie (eds). *Meanings of Bandung: Postcolonial Orders and Decolonial Visions*. London and New York: Rowman & Littlefield, ch. 12.

24   Ibid., p. 147.

25   Amy, Lori (2011). 'Listening for the elsewhere and the not-yet: Academic labor as a matter of ethical witness', in Inayatullah, Naeem (ed.). *Autobiographical international relations: I, IR*. Abingdon: Routledge.

point of interest is how the testimonies invite us to imagine the often challenging and daily bureaucratic work that sustains public policies and politics in these countries. This is not to be romanticized in any way, but to compose a plurality of experiences that often escape the pages.

The Book

The story will be divided in five parts. Together, they tell us of how the g7+ fights to have a collective voice. They also show the paths its members have walked to find their own voices and what they have been doing since. The group and the people feed into each other; they share frustrations and expectations.

Part one is about negotiating skills and what makes a diplomat, even if an accidental one. It tells of the many, *many* back-and-forths one has to endure in politics. The capacity to navigate these turns is often the result of complex historical reconciliation processes that have taken place in a community; it is also intimately connected to the experience of incredibly steep learning curves across generations. These diplomatic practices, to some extent, are instance of 'new diplomacy' or a 'transprofessionalization' of diplomacy, involving the mobilization of new actors, skills, and methods, but also the challenges of 'learning the game'.[26]

Part two focuses on survival. It explores the life experiences that have led the members of the g7+ to develop a profound respect for equality of opportunities and, most crucially, for those who not only survive but see their lives as an opportunity to do something, to help others. Survival imprints a deep feeling of commitment, but also guilt, which can result in a person working well beyond any job description and paying high personal costs to accomplish a mission. These are stories that also tell us about the innards of public administration in post-conflict societies and the difficulties around identity issues and postcolonial relations.[27]

---

26   Constantinou, Costas M., Cornago, Noé, & McConnell, Fiona (2017). 'Transprofessional Diplomacy'. *Brill Research Perspectives in Foreign Policy and Diplomacy*, 1(4), https://doi.org/10.1163/24056006-12340005, p. 6.

27   Nandy, Ashis (1983). *The Intimate Enemy: Loss and Recovery of Self under Colonialism*. Delhi: Oxford University Press and Bombay Calcutta Madras; Zondi, Siphamandla (2016). 'A Decolonial Turn in Diplomatic Theory: Unmasking Epistemic Injustice'. *Journal for Contemporary History*, 41(1), 18–37.

Part three, not coincidentally, is about how to work with passion; this is a difficult *how*. Passion helps bring people closer together; it nourishes solidarity; it empowers leadership. Passion can be dismissed in bureaucratic development work, being supposedly opposed to "the scientific" and liable to lead to failure. But many have denounced this dismissal. This book agrees with the latter position: it is about 'initiatives that rekindle the kind of passions — about inequality, about fairness, about improving the lot of poor and excluded people — that for many were the reasons for getting into these jobs in the first place'.[28] But we need also remember that, unfortunately, passion is easily dismissed as a sign of naiveté or lack of skills. These are indeed real risks and working with passion requires avoiding these pitfalls as much as any others.

Part four is about pride, in great measure, because it is the one element that has brought all of the above aspects together in the past. The history of the people in this book is full of moments of pride, which has been instilled in them from a young age by family and community. The chapter is about the enormous challenges involved in having to learn on the job what others might take years to patiently build step-by-step, which, although hard, is also a reason to be proud and confident later in life. This part of the book, however, is also about the ability to shed some of this pride or stow it away temporarily in order to do things that others might not deign to do, because the prize ahead is not one's own, but a collective achievement.[29]

Finally, the last part of the story is about responsibility and the sense of duty. One thing that everyone in this book has in common is their unrelenting belief in the future, their hope for the next generation and their understanding that they have a responsibility to foster a sense of duty in younger people. There is no room for pessimism, and this itself is a conversation-starter. I have also found both a deep commitment to the

---

28   Jassey, Katja (2004). 'The Bureaucrat', in Groves, Leslie & Hinton, Rachel (eds). *Inclusive Aid: Changing Power and Relationships in International Development.* London and Sterling, VA: Earthscan, ch. 10.

29   For related discussions, see Olatunji, Felix O. & Bature, Anthony I. (2019). 'The Inadequacy of Post-Development Theory to the Discourse of Development and Social Order in the Global South'. *Social Evolution & History*, 18(2), 229–43; Nay, Olivier (2014). 'International Organisations and the Production of Hegemonic Knowledge: How the World Bank and the OECD helped invent the Fragile State Concept'. *Third World Quarterly*, 35(2), 210–31.

idea that one is responsible for keeping one's own house in order, and a belief in the promise of giving back to one's people and community.

In line with that hope in the future, the book ends with some of the promising lines of action ahead: not failing to point to problems and challenges, but sharing in the responsibility of outlining some possible paths forward. This is based on the plans and dreams of the people with whom we spoke. It is important to note that some of the chapter titles, and even the perspective from which the chapters are written and their sequence, aim to offer some advice from one generation to the next in the g7+ countries, as per my interlocutors' own wishes. In a very humble way, the book was commissioned with that in mind, to share how one uses their skills and experiences to fight against a 'poverty of influence'[30] when the ladder has been kicked away.[31]

---

30 Najam, Adil (2005). 'Why environmental politics looks different from the South', in Dauvergne, Peter (ed.). *Handbook of Global Environmental Politics*. Cheltenham, UK, and Northampton, MA: Edward Elgar, ch. 8.

31 Chang, Ha-Joon (2002). *Kicking Away the Ladder. Development Strategy in Historical Perspective*. London: Anthem Press.

2. How to Find a Voice

On Being an Accidental Diplomat for the New Deal

No limiar da sombra de um velho oká
se espreguiçam sons e brisas, rastejes e ondas
e nossas fragilidades todas
aqui se semeiam amores e ódios, intrigas e fleumas
aqui se amantizam lamentos e alegrias
como jogo de bligá em domingo festivo
na sombra do oká o rasto do obô primevo e fiel
como a palavra poema em juramento solene
aqui sob a ramada desta árvore frondosa que dará canoa
e boia e jangada e caixa
de guardar memória
a palavra deslizará como óleo de coco em nossa pele ansiosa
a palavra florirá para depois coagular nas bocas sedentas do dizer
e da palavra sairá a esperança
a força
a redenção
a palavra será seiva
a exsudar-se da árvore mãe
a penetrar na alma de todos os ilhéus
aqui não há desertos nem oásis nem tão pouco
rios despidos de fronteiras
nem rochedos agrestes a encobrir ternuras
aqui há tão somente a sombra deste oká inderrubável e imóvel
imponente e longevo
casto como os silêncios de nossos sofridos e longínquos avós
aqui ficará a Palavra quente e odorífera como o café da manhã
em casa de avó Belmira
e virás então falar-me dos campos acesos de frutos e de almas
de veredas onde jamais se voltarão as costas ao silêncio

 https://doi.org/10.11647/OBP.0311.02

contar-me-ás das ausências em teus portos
teus líquidos abismos de luxúrias e desmaios
contar-me-ás dos perfumes intensos de teus rios
opulência exultada em loucas e abruptas quedas
teus falos a rasgar a virgindade do ôbo
teus agrestes penhascos como espada a perfurar o coração
do impuro
teus magmas incandescentes, teu húmido musgo entre fetos
e lianas
teus suores frios de escravatura e submissão
noites longas de mãos cravadas nas fendas da alma
teu rumorejo se ouvirá a muitas milhas de ti
teu rastrear de folhagem, teu ondular de flor sem norte
em íntimo e libido fulgor com a genuína palavra do poema
ligarás o teu coração ao meu
não esperes pelo sol para te aquecer a terra
nem pela chuva para te fertilizar os campos
nem pelo semeador para te encher de searas
pega no arado das palavras e verás
que elas produzem o pão da nossa vida.

By Olinda Beja,
award-winner author of São Tomé e Príncipe.[1]

---

1   On the threshold of the shadow of an old oká/sounds and breezes stretch, crawls
and waves/and all our weaknesses/here love and hatred, intrigue and phlegm are
sown/laments and joys are softened here/as a sweater game on a festive Sunday/
in the shadow of the oká the trail of the primitive and/faithful obô/as the word
poem in solemn oath/here under the branch of this leafy tree that will give/a canoe
and float and raft and box/to save memory/the word will slide like coconut oil on
our anxious skin/the word will blossom and then coagulate in the mouths thirsty
for saying/and hope will come out of the word/the power/redemption/the word
will be sap/exuding from the mother tree/to penetrate the soul of all islanders/
here there are no deserts or oases nor/ rivers stripped of borders/nor rough rocks
to cover up tenderness/here there is only the shadow of this unmistakable and
immovable oká/imposing and long-lived/chaste as the silences of our suffering
and distant grandparents/here the word will be hot and odorous like breakfast/at
grandmother Belmira's/and then you will come and tell me about the lit fields of
fruits and souls/of paths where they will never turn their back on silence/you will
tell me of your absences at your ports/your liquid abysses of lust and fainting/you
will tell me of the intense perfumes of your rivers/opulence exulted in crazy and
abrupt falls/your phalluses to tear the virginity of the ôbo/your rough cliffs like a
sword piercing your heart/of the impure/your glowing magmas, your damp moss
among ferns/and lianas/your cold sweats of slavery and submission/ long nights
with hands in the soul's cracks/your noise will be heard many miles from you/
your track of foliage, your undulating flower without north/in intimate and libido
glow with the genuine word of the poem/you will connect your heart to mine/

We often forget how much politics depends on people and their individual skills. We like to believe the merit of certain agendas speak for themselves, but most ideas take a huge amount of human and financial resources to move forward from the centres of decision-making. Sometimes, the smallest changes take years to negotiate; more significant ones can require huge machinery. Not many organisations have such resources, so partnerships take place; but even partnerships rely on networking, getting the word out, demarcating one's own priorities and broadcasting them. It makes one wonder how changes happen at all.

Dialogue is difficult; politics is tough. Most people doing it professionally were trained to develop just the right set of skills—rhetoric, networking, the right language, the right text, the right outfit. Some are good at challenging these—geniuses, really, who are full of charisma. But we shouldn't expect everyone to be either one or the other. The heavy lifting of true change-making is done by people who wear formal attire but also hug their colleagues as a standard form of greeting; people who speak the technical language but, wow, can they tell a story.

When you are working with these people or are one of them, it can be scary. You have to negotiate your risks, the push-and-pull of compliance and change, the back-and-forth of diplomatic conversations. Sometimes you will sound naïve, too passionate, too partial about your own ideas, and often you will feel frustrated with the slow pace of things. Someone will always say in those moments, 'The bigger the machine, the slower to move'.

Well, in 2020, the United Nations had 44,000 employees, 40% of which worked in New York.[2] The World Bank, as of 2019, had 12,300 employees, 55% of which worked in its headquarters in Washington, D.C., the rest spread across its 141 field offices.[3] The OECD, in turn, has

---

don't wait for the sun to warm the earth/nor by the rain to fertilize the fields/nor by the sower to fill you with crops/take the plow of words and you will see/that they produce the bread of our life. (Beja, Olinda (2015). 'Prelúdios', in *À Sombra do Oká*. São Paulo: Escrituras. My own translation.)

2 See: UN Careers (n.d.). *Where We Are*. https://careers.un.org/lbw/home.aspx?viewtype=VD.

3 See: Edwards, Sophie (2019). *In decentralization push, World Bank to relocate hundreds of DC staffers*. Devex. https://www.devex.com/news/in-decentralization-push-world-bank-to-relocate-hundreds-of-dc-staffers-95875.

around 3,300 employees in its secretariat alone.[4] As a statistical agency, the OECD publishes more than 500 reports and country surveys every year.[5] These machines don't move fast when it comes to change. So, as suggested by the beautiful poem above, by Olinda Beja, from São Tomé e Príncipe, it is best not to wait for the sun, the rain, or the sower; *'take your words and go'*.

In 2010, when the g7+ was officially founded, the Secretariat was established in Dili, Timor-Leste, and had two Timorese nationals among its members: Minister of Finance Emilia Pires and Dr Helder da Costa, who was also working for the Ministry of Finance. Da Costa would soon become the secretary-general of the g7+, a position he still occupies. The group had the crucial support of then-Prime-Minister Xanana Gusmão and counted on two secondments from the United Nations Development Programme (UNDP) and the Overseas Development Institute (ODI), United Kingdom. One international adviser, officially supporting PM Xanana Gusmão, was also working with the team. The g7+'s objectives were inversely proportional to the size of its secretariat; they included the goals to change the international narrative on state fragility; promote national ownership; exchange experiences of peace processes; and modify donor behaviour. Minister Pires said at the time: 'Fragile states must take the reins when it comes to ways development partners give them official development assistance... For us to better guide our development partners and to contribute to a better management of external aid, we have to take the leadership'.[6]

It all came about in 2008. France and the Democratic Republic of Congo (DRC) hosted a meeting in Accra, Ghana, to discuss statebuilding and peacebuilding. There was a roundtable dedicated to fragile states (roundtable 7, as it became known). Apparently, 'everyone was painting a rosy picture, when Minister Emilia Pires talked, instead, of how difficult things were'.[7] The outburst went along the lines of 'if everything is going well, why are we even here, debating aid effectiveness?'. It must have been refreshing indeed.

---

4   See: OECD (n.d.). *Organisational Structure*. http://www.oecd.org/about/structure/.
5   See: OECD (n.d.). *History*. https://www.oecd.org/about/history/#d.en.194377.
6   By Minister Emilia Pires. See: Crook, Matt (2010). *Development: fragile nations speak up to donors*. Inter Press Service. http://www.ipsnews.net/2010/04/development-listen-to-us-fragile-states-tell-donors/.
7   Interview with Helder da Costa, 14 April 2020.

Of course, people are afraid that problems will reflect badly on them and make it appear that they are not doing good work. If that happens in front of key actors, like donors, it can be a problem. On the other hand, if you don't speak about problems, nothing changes. And even when voices were raised against business-as-usual in the meetings themselves, reports and minutes seemed to be written in a language of their own and appeared to filter criticisms for the benefit of sensitive eyes: 'One meeting in 2003, in which the Timorese prime minister arrived unannounced to angrily denounce the UN's efforts as a sham, was apparently written up internally as: "The meeting was further enhanced by the presence of the Prime Minister, who provided insightful comments."'[8] Because criticism seemed so difficult to communicate, the 2008 meeting in Accra probably did feel like a special moment.

By the time the meeting was held, seven countries that would become part of the g7+ had volunteered to be pilot studies for the monitoring of the Principles for Good International Engagement in Fragile States and Situations, advanced in 2007 by OECD. In this context, the operationalization of the Accra dialogue led to the creation of the International Dialogue on Peacebuilding and Statebuilding (IDPS) in

---

8   Peake, Gordon P. (2013). *Beloved Land: Stories, Struggles, and Secrets from Timor-Leste* [Kindle edition]. Melbourne: Scribe Publications, position 2703.

2008. Timor-Leste volunteered to hold the following meeting of IDPS in Dili, in April 2010. A lot is attributed to the leadership of Liberia, DRC and Timor-Leste leading up to the foundation of the g7+, but in this process the support of the representatives of the other four initial member countries were, of course, crucial. (They were the Central African Republic, Côte D'Ivoire, Haiti and Sierra Leone.) Now, the technical side of that story is well known.[9] But how do we explain to people in the 20 countries that now compose the g7+ and beyond what such stories are made of? Not to romanticize small instances of frankness, but it is not common for whoever has attended meetings such as these to speak up against the anodyne general discourse. How did some people decide to go against the currents, to make certain speeches, to put themselves in uncomfortable positions when it seemed so much easier to just go with the flow? How do changes happen, or are at least initiated or mapped out for future intervention? In terms of beliefs and decisions, what hard, sometimes questionable, choices are made?

Regardless of the difficulties around the word itself—'fragile'—the g7+ played an important role in slowly making certain things evident and, therefore, less easily ignored. As in the proverb from Burundi: 'when a stone sticks out from the earth, it will not destroy the hoe'.[10] It seems it became slightly more difficult to paint rosy pictures about development partners' projects on the ground. At the same time the group provided a platform to think collectively about possible paths forward.

Let us see how this was done. The following is the story of four characters, their accidental diplomatic skills, and how these were put to use.

The Need to Listen

Former minister Olivier Kamitatu of DRC comes from a very politically engaged family. His father was close to Patrice Lumumba, first Prime Minister of DRC after independence in 1960, and one of its founding figures. He soon opposed the regime of Mobutu Sese Seko, leader of a coup that deposed Lumumba, and had to leave the country.

---

9   See g7+ publications in the Bibliography.
10   Kadende-Kaiser, Rose M. & Kaiser, Paul J. (1997). 'Modern Folklore, Identity, and Political Change in Burundi'. *African Studies Review*, 40(3), 29–54, p. 49.

Kamitatu's mother, in turn, was, according to him, one of the first female intellectuals in the country, a teacher in the 1960s. She stayed in the country while Cléophas Kamitatu left for Belgium with the children. He completed a PhD in Paris and returned to DRC in the 1970s after an invitation to work for the government. Kamitatu says his father was very close to the population, had a strong rapport with the territory, and apparently was keen to work for the country again. Kamitatu had stayed in Belgium with his siblings, but returned to DRC in 1990, encouraged by his family. He became a civil servant, but in 1997, when Mobutu was deposed, left for exile after suffering threats. In 1999, however, he returned again and served as the leader of the political branch of Jean-Pierre Bemba's rebellion against Laurent Kabila, Mobutu's successor: 'It's the responsibility of people in power to keep the dialogue open. To take on arms is an extreme moral decision,' he explains.[11] When Kabila's son, Joseph Kabila, later took office and decided to share power with the rebels, Kamitatu resumed his work, this time as a politician. He then became the first president of the transition parliament, in charge of negotiating a new constitution.[12] The new constitution gained 85% support and, in 2006, the country held democratic elections, confirming Joseph Kabila in power. With that, Kamitatu took on as Minister of Planning for the new government.

DRC and the African First World War

What would come to be known as 'Africa's First World War' started in 1996 in DRC and lasted until 1997, when Mobutu was deposed. As many as nine foreign countries intervened. In 2001, Joseph Kabila was assassinated. In 2002, his son, Laurent Kabila rose to power and, soon, the Sun City agreement was signed, resulting in a transition government in 2003 and in power being shared among different parties.

(See: Dunn, K. C. (2003). *Imagining the Congo. The International Relations of Identity.* New York: Palgrave Macmillan)

---

11   Interview with Olivier Kamitatu Etsu, 21 April 2020.
12   For related information, see Dunn, Kevin C. (2003). *Imagining the Congo: The International Relations of Identity.* London: Palgrave Macmillan; Roessler, Philip & Prendergast, John (2006). 'Democratic Republic of the Congo', in Durch, William J. (ed.). *Twenty-First-Century Peace Operations.* Washington, DC: United States Institute of Peace and the Henry L. Stimson Center; Prunier, Gérard. (2009). *Africa's World War: Congo, the Rwandan Genocide, and the Making of a Continental Catastrophe.* New York: Oxford University Press.

Kamitatu says that as he travelled along this rugged path, his convictions were rooted in democracy, freedom, the rule of law and equality of opportunities: 'Our population is composed of young people; they are more than 60%. I have to have faith in politics, and we have to set an example.' Among the people who inspire him are, as is common, Nelson Mandela, in addition to Xanana Gusmão, Cardinal Robert Sarah, President Alassane Ouattara of Côte D'Ivoire, and former South African president Thabo Mbeki. One could say that he admires people with good negotiating skills, but also people who are able to survive political turmoil, for better and for worse. 'In every negotiation, it's necessary to know what the other wants.'[13] He would know, it seems, having survived and having certainly made difficult decisions.

Just before the elections that confirmed Kabila in power, the DRC had hosted a meeting of Ministers of Development in Kinshasa, in 2005: 'an extraordinary meeting, with people who wouldn't normally come to Kinshasa', he says.[14] This was in the context of the 2005 Paris Declaration on Aid Effectiveness.[15] That is part of the reason the DRC was invited to co-chair the roundtable on peacebuilding and statebuilding in Accra, in 2008. In 2010, however, when it came to what would be the first g7+ meeting, in Dili, the baton was passed and Timor-Leste took the lead officially, volunteering headquarters as well as a chair in the person of Minister Pires.

The Aid Effectiveness Agenda

The Paris Declaration on Aid Effectiveness was the result of a high-level meeting in 2005, one of many that would look at the field of development cooperation and include discussions on donors' responsibilities. The meeting in Paris followed up on the declaration adopted at the High-Level Forum on Harmonisation in Rome (2003) and principles discussed at the Marrakesh Roundtable on Managing for Development Results (2004). Especially with the Paris Declaration, buzzwords like harmonisation, alignment, ownership and country systems entered into the conversation. The Accra Agenda for Action (AAA), from 2008, is a continuation of these agreements.

---

13   Interview with Olivier Kamitatu Etsu, 21 April 2020.
14   Ibid.
15   OECD (2005). *The Paris Declaration on Aid Effectiveness.* https://www.oecd.org/dac/effectiveness/34428351.pdf

'It was time to make the g7+ official. Minister Emilia Pires was an extraordinary leader, she had the capacity and enthusiasm, and my government didn't want to go in that direction. The word "fragile" was a problem; I didn't have the support,' Kamitatu says. He supported his successor, just as he demonstrates strong support still for the group, even though he himself is not directly involved anymore. He spoke extensively of the g7+ in our conversation and remembered every turn of event by heart, including all the key words of every goal. Kamitatu might just have a very good memory, but it did strike me as something of note that he remembered so much from years ago. The same goes for the fact that he found plenty of time to talk about it and that he made sure to state, by the end of our conversation, that the group has a lot of important work ahead of it; that is, that it has a future, even if he is not directly engaged. Kamitatu says the g7+ is crucial: 'We need to learn statebuilding and peacebuilding; this is the path. We didn't make this our priority before. It's the mission of our states. This is the great experience we take out of fragility.' Among the things he is proud of, he lists the g7+ and IDPS, and in his career, specifically, the approval of the constitution in 2006. For someone with his trajectory, what becomes clear is the value he places in *institutionalisation*, in finally achieving *formalization and a level of dialogue* (see Annex I).

Well, it is all relative.

For someone who once supported the 'extreme moral decision' of taking up arms, middle- to high-level negotiations in the context of meetings, hard as they can be, might feel infinitely more palatable. Nevertheless, these can sometimes be frustrating and require a perennial state of hyperawareness that may put leaders off or just lead to interminable business-as-usual. All this can be enough to halt change in the international arena. *Trust* is extremely important but neglected in contexts of formal exchanges. To get different parties into an unequal setting and to promote political change, a certain 'collective affective politics'[16] is in order: people need to be able to see themselves in each other, to feel that they are free to speak and share their thoughts, that they have similar stories and something in common. Major organizations

---

16   Phạm, Quỳnh N. & Shilliam, Robbie (2016). 'Reviving Bandung', in Phạm & Shilliam (eds). *Meanings of Bandung: Postcolonial Orders and Decolonial Visions.* London and New York: Rowman & Littlefield, p. 10.

have that simply by nature of their deeply rooted corporate culture, which homogenizes practices. Others need to build a collective another way.

The story of how that started to happen modestly in the case of the g7+ tells us a lot about how significant events in world affairs can seem surprisingly small to begin with. The key aspects are often a few people, some lucky starts, much individual inexplicable persistence, and an equally improbable collective effort.

Trust is the Most Valuable Currency

Let us talk about Siafa Hage, because his first contact with the g7+ offers us a very good insight into how difficult new collective work can be.

Conflict in Liberia

The civil war in Liberia is either divided in two phases or separated as two different conflicts. The first one begun in 1989 with the attack of the National Patriotic Front of Liberia (NPFL) on the border town of Butuo and lasted until the electoral process that conducted NPFL leader, Charles Taylor, to the presidency in 1997. In between, there were at least ten failed peace agreements, new rebel forces entered the conflict, there was fragmentation from older factions, engagement of foreign countries and multilateral regional and global organizations, the assassination of the former president (Samuel Doe, who rose to power in a coup d'état in 1980) and intense violence against combatants and civilians.

The second part started in 1999 with a new configuration of rebel forces led by the Liberians United for Reconciliation and Democracy (LURD) and the Movement for Democracy in Liberia (MODEL) fighting Taylor's regime. The fight ended with Taylor's resignation and a peace agreement signed in Accra on 18 August 2003.

The Liberian Civil War turned 50% of the population into refugees and took at least 250,000 lives (8% of the country's population). The conflict was marked by the existence of child soldiers, ethnic violence and war crimes committed by rebels and government. Liberia has experienced political stability ever since the peace agreement and, on 10 October 2017, completed a democratic electoral process.

(Hegre, Håvard, Østby, Gudrun, &; Raleigh, Clionadh. (2009). 'Poverty and Civil War Events'. *Journal of Conflict Resolution*, [S.L.], 53(4), 598–623.

He was working in the Ministry of Planning in Liberia and his ministry was selected as the contact point for IDPS in the government. Soon he was told to go to Paris for two weeks, to follow IDPS meetings at OECD headquarters. Siafa was there with a fellowship for young professionals and had left his wife and two children behind in the United States to work with the Liberian government for two years, because he 'wanted to do something for his country'.[17]

Liberia had recently come out of a civil war, there was much to do and he felt he wanted to contribute, as a Liberian. In 2011, by the time IPDS called, he had many deadlines to meet; he did not think that being away for long was a good idea. But he was asked to prepare a presentation about GEMAP (Liberia Governance and Economic Management Assistance Program), 'a partnership between the Government of Liberia and the international community to promote accountability and transparency in fiscal and financial management'.[18] He says: 'International organisations were taking over finance and money-making from Liberia, and I was sent to talk about that. I didn't know what to do'. Siafa had finished his MA in Southeast Asian studies in 2006 in the United States and moved to Liberia in 2009 with a Scott Family Liberia Fellowship.[19]

> When I first met Helder and Emilia, I didn't know anything about the g7+. I got there, in Paris, and found out we were hosting the next meeting in Liberia. I had 6 months to organize. It didn't matter if I liked or wanted it, we had to learn and be prepared to host. I heard Timor-Leste had hosted the first meeting and they had been looking for volunteers. Sierra Leone had already signed up to the group; DRC had already hosted a meeting. The commitment had come from our government, so we had to do it. It caught some people by surprise, it was short notice, but we couldn't step back.

The way Siafa speaks of that surprise still evokes the anxiety it probably generated. The environment was new, the work was new, the people were new and there was a huge task ahead about which he had no information: 'Honestly, it was all like drinking water from a hose'.[20]

---

17   Interview with Siafa Hage, 10 March 2020.
18   See Liberia Governance and Economic Management Assistance Program, http://www.gemap-liberia.org/.
19   See Center for Global Development. *Scott Family Liberia Fellows*. https://www.cgdev.org/topics/scott-family-liberia-fellows.
20   Interview with Siafa Hage, 10 March 2020.

I got there in Paris and there were clear friendships already, it was a very friendly environment. But I was working. Half of the time I was paying attention, half of the time I was working on my deadlines. In the first meeting I was trying to understand, but I didn't pay much attention until I found out we were hosting the next meeting. I approached Helder at the end and he said "I will come back to you later" but there was too much going on. Then Donata [Garrasi, IDPS/OECD] said "We will provide assistance, but no funds". And Liberia had not budgeted it. We had to have a meeting and cut from other programs. We came up with 150,000 dollars. Seems little, but our [total] budget was 200 million.

This was the beginning of Siafa's more intensive engagement with the theme of state fragility and with the g7+. It seems this is the kind of character that clearly thrives in such environment and tends to pull his weight. Siafa can keep up a lively conversation with anyone for hours. He says he is an introvert, but evidence testifies to the contrary: his role in IDPS and the g7+ was a social one of keeping people engaged and invested, he says. Siafa is one of those people who seems to genuinely like others: 'You have to connect with people how they want to connect'.[21]

Time passed; he participated in many more meetings. Later, Siafa would become the coordinator of IDPS.

---

21   Ibid.

'After that first one, many people made all those meetings happen in Paris and need to be credited. Bella Bird helped a lot. Donata bent backwards to help with space and resources. We had many meetings after with IDPS and the g7+ meetings would run in parallel'.[22] His words are diplomatic and his assessments tend to make sure people are acknowledged.

'The challenges were respect and learning to be vulnerable with them. How do you get to the point of sharing with each other? I credit Emilia with creating that space: because she was so honest, others could speak up. People in the room were key to success. Having the same people coming to all of those meetings, we didn't have to have people catch up. There was *trust*, a level of participation at all levels; we were able to make progress'.[23]

Be Wary of the Annotated Agenda: Donor Pressures and the Problem of Empty Participation

Siafa's thoughts about IDPS in general in the first meetings after the foundation of the g7+ are clearly positive. Others, in different positions, did not quite feel the same way. And things got more complicated as the meetings advanced.

The meeting Siafa was tasked with helping Liberia convene in 2011, for instance, led to the formulation of the Monrovia Roadmap and showed what the increasingly important negotiations would entail.[24] Siafa's position allowed some wriggle room. That meeting in Liberia, however, was a difficult one for some. The fact that the Monrovia Roadmap would soon give birth to the New Deal for Engagement with Fragile States (hereafter, the New Deal),[25] something at the core of the g7+'s work to this day and also central to IDPS in general, suggests the negotiations taking place were crucial and were not always smooth.

---

22 Ibid.
23 Ibid.
24 International Dialogue on Peacebuilding and Statebuilding (2011). *The Monrovia Roadmap on Peacebuilding and Statebuilding*. https://www.icnl.org/wp-content/uploads/Transnational_monrovia.pdf.
25 See: g7plus.org.

Conflict, Security and Development at the World Bank

'The follow-up document, *Operationalizing the 2011 World Development Report*, suggested the World Bank positioned "fragility, conflict, and violence at the core of its development mandate". It announced the creation of a "center of excellence" on "fragile" and conflict-affected states, the Center on Conflict, Security and Development (CCSD), with offices in Nairobi and Washington, both of which opened doors in 2012. These offices were to guide the Bank in the formation of a knowledge platform on "state fragility" and conflict.'

(Rocha de Siqueira, I. (2017). op. cit., p. 73)

Let us provide some context.

Fragility was becoming a hot topic in 2011. The World Bank's *2011 World Development Report on Conflict, Security, and Development*, for instance, had clearly stated that fragile states were crucial if the development agenda was to move forward.[26] Fragile states had lagged behind with regards to the Millennium Development Goals (MDGs), and the next set of goals would not be accomplished unless more attention was given to their plights: 'We could not achieve the MDGs unless we first achieved peace in our own countries', former Prime Minister of Timor-Leste and Eminent Person to g7+, H.E. Kay Rala Xanana Gusmão, said around that time.[27] Slowly, then, it was accepted that working on fragility was essential for *global* development; it was supposed to be at the core of the new agenda just then being developed, the Sustainable Development Goals (SDGs).

'I knew by then that fragile states were to be key for development. I felt like I was about to ride the wave of the future. I recognized that. So it was not only a focus on national interest, but on personal interest too—for my country and my career,' Siafa explains with frankness.[28]

Well, scholars of diplomacy will ask 'Who can legitimately lay claim to be a practitioner of diplomacy, and how far is the distinction between professional and occasional diplomat helpful?'. I prefer the term 'accidental diplomat', as Helder says, as the 'occasional diplomat'

---

26   See Rocha de Siqueira, I. (2017). *Managing State Fragility: Conflict, Quantification and Power*. New York: Routledge.

27   *Strength in Fragility*. Former Prime Minister of Timor-Leste & Eminent Person to g7+, H.E. Kay Rala Xanana Gusmão, p. 4.

28   Interview with Siafa Hage, 10 March 2020.

usually has a privileged background and acts only occasionally as a diplomat to mobilize his social and political capital. The accidental diplomat has to be diplomatic in the exercise of his other activities.[29]

Now let us get back to the scene.

In Liberia, in 2011, the dialogue was supposed to evolve towards a collective plan. Some would say, however, that donors came up with a detailed document far too soon in the conversation. It looked like it had been completely drafted before the dialogue took place, and the g7+ representatives had around two days to discuss and sign it. The Secretariat used this time to revamp the document. That is when they came up with most of what would constitute the New Deal: The Peacebuilding and Statebuilding Goals (PSGs) and the TRUST and FOCUS principles (see Fig. 1). 'That document [the complete draft] was insane, a lot of pages, complicated jargon... We made it simple and punchy', says a former advisor.[30] The rush to develop indicators for the plan while the PSGs had not even been agreed yet also signalled how much the pace and priorities differed between the parties.

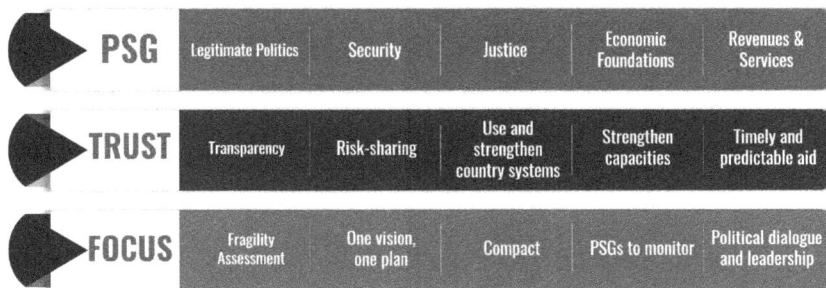

PSG	Legitimate Politics	Security	Justice	Economic Foundations	Revenues & Services
TRUST	Transparency	Risk-sharing	Use and strengthen country systems	Strengthen capacities	Timely and predictable aid
FOCUS	Fragility Assessment	One vision, one plan	Compact	PSGs to monitor	Political dialogue and leadership

Fig. 1 New Deal's PSGs, TRUST and FOCUS. Author's own elaboration.

In the meantime, there was the awkward diplomatic factor: Minister Pires was a minister, but the co-chair of IDPS was a director. That kind of imbalance means a lot in the diplomatic field. Siafa goes as far as to say that his own minister at the time would probably not have accepted this situation. An advisor comments on the fact that people did use to

---

29   Constantinou, Costas M., Cornago, Noé & McConnell, Fiona (eds). (2017). Op. cit., p. 2.

30   Interview with Missy Stephens, 12 March 2020.

refer to Minister Pires by her name, withut using her title, but Siafa says 'she didn't mind, though, she was open to that kind of thing; she cared about the work'.[31] There is a sense in which the professional diplomats have to take pride in the correct protocols, while accidental diplomats can perhaps worry more about what needs to be accomplished at the end of a day's work.

Busan

'In 2011, during the Fourth High-Level Forum on Aid Effectiveness, held in Busan, the group and its main proposals were consolidated, and the New Deal for Engagement with Fragile States (hereafter, New Deal) was proposed under the auspices of IDPS but with the lobby and leadership of the g7+. The meeting in Busan was part of the sequence of meetings previously held in Paris and Accra. It meant much for the South, in general, with South-South Cooperation being acknowledged for its increasing importance in the field.'

(See Rocha de Siqueira, I. op. cit., and Esteves, Paulo and Manaíra Assunção (2014). 'South–South cooperation and the international development battlefield: between the OECD and the UN'. *Third World Quarterly*, 35(10), 1775–90.)

Yet the game changed after the 4th High-Level Meeting on Aid Effectiveness in Busan, South Korea, in 2011.[32] That is when the New Deal was officially launched and signed by many constituencies. The g7+'s and IDPS's profiles were raised. In the IDPS, for instance, soon a European minister would sit at the table and that meant that the dynamic of exchanges and collaborations would change as well:

> After we moved to having a European Union minister as co-chair, things changed, got more formal. The Dialogue became something else, the dynamics changed. We got bogged down with processes after Busan. Our success came to compromise our future. We had an *annotated agenda* in every meeting and would negotiate ahead of time the outcome documents. Pre-Busan, we were able to say important things, like talking about "legitimate politics". I don't think any other documents at the time said that. It came down to our flexibility. Before, conversation would often come and turn the agenda irrelevant, that's why it was so effective.[33]

---

31   Interview with Siafa Hage, 10 March 2020.
32   See *About the New Deal*. https://www.newdeal4peace.org/about-the-new-deal/.
33   Interview with Siafa Hage, 10 March 2020.

The g7+ started to get more and more involved with other debates as well, and it was soon playing UN politics. And that is when the stakes grew higher.

The Search for a Voice

Dr Helder da Costa had started working with the g7+ as soon as it was founded. One of his first assignments, back in 2012, had been to go and brief the G77[34] in the UN about the g7+. For that task, he went with the Deputy Minister for Finance of Afghanistan, Mustafa Mastoor, and then Minister of Finance of Timor-Leste, Emilia Pires. That first assignment was a sign of what was to come in 2012 and after: 'It requires courage to move forward. It's like taking a boat against a storm. You manoeuvre yourself in order to get to your destination. That destination is *recognition*. *Institutionalisation* is the happy end'. 'The meeting with the G77 was frustrating, but I come from a background where I just keep going'.[35]

Brief History of South-South Cooperation

In 1955, the Bandung Conference was held, marking the first time developing countries got together with the goal of having a collective voice, especially as many countries in the South were on their way to independence. This was a milestone in terms of what we call today South-South Cooperation and inaugurated a wave of initiatives to tackle inequality. In 1961, this was followed up with the first meeting of the Non-Aligned Movement (NMA). In 1964, the United Nations Conference on Trade and Development (UNCTAD) and the Group of 77 developing countries (G77) were created. 'Bandung succeeded in two respects; first, it helped forge a common Third-World consciousness that laid the basis for collective mobilizations by the Third World at the UN, through the Group of G-77 and the Non-Aligned Movement (NAM). Second, it underlined the two cardinal principles that would organize Third World Politics in the coming decades: Decolonization and economic development.'

(Rajagopal, B (2003). *International Law from Below — Development, Social Movements and Third World Resistance*. Cambridge: Cambridge University Press, p. 74 and Phạm and Shilliam (eds). (2016). *Meanings of Bandung: Postcolonial Orders and Decolonial Visions*. London and New York: Rowman & Littlefield, p. 163, n. 1.)

---

34   See https://www.g77.org/.
35   Interview with Helder da Costa, 14 April 2020.

In 2012, Da Costa again received a mission. Minister Pires told him to go and organize a meeting alongside the UN General Assembly and gather as many important representatives as possible. Da Costa was wary about this mission. The UN was tough. 'I was generally confident. But for this, I felt less so. I didn't have New York [UN] experience, and it was a big thing. I told Minister Emilia Pires "You're sending me to failure". She said: "Cut the crap, I know you're capable."'[36]

Da Costa arrived around one week before Habib Mayar, who was then representative of Afghanistan with the g7+, working with the Ministry of Finance. He was soon to start working with the g7+ and, soon after, to become its deputy secretary general, but not just yet. Siafa Hage was in New York already; he had gone back to the United States after his two years in Liberia and was working with the permanent mission of Liberia in the UN. He was seconded to help with the task—although he was paid no salary for this assignment at the time, just *per diems* paid by the UNDP. For the two weeks the three of them worked together, they had to get enough guests to confirm attendance.

Habib says it was his first experience with UN politics. He had left Afghanistan as a child, going with his family to Pakistan as a refugee.

---

36 Ibid.

He grew up in Pakistan, became an English teacher and director of a language centre and received an MBA. In 2008, he returned to Afghanistan and was soon working in the Ministry of Finance, where he acted as Aid Coordination Manager for 5 years. The 2012 meeting in New York happened after he occupied that position and before he became secretary general of the g7+.

> I was there in New York as the focal point of Afghanistan for the g7+. By nature, I'm overcautious, careful not to fail things. And that was a tough experience—I had no idea then that I would come to work and do so much with the g7+ and have tougher experiences ahead. We had engaged on the New Deal with the OECD but not with the UN, so it was different.[37]
>
> I was staying in Queens, an hour-long train ride from the UN. For nearly 2 weeks, I had no break, not enough sleep. Thankfully, the Timorese permanent mission in NY helped a lot. Representing Afghanistan as a co-host of the High-Level side event, I was dispatched to NY to help organize the meeting, but there were a lot of anxieties and difficulties. We were supposed to have our President from Afghanistan in the panel but it was a challenge. The Minister of Finance who would step in couldn't come to NY either. Then we had to consider having [the] Minister of Foreign Affairs but we had a hard time securing his participation due to the last-minute changes. I had to rely on support from Mustafa Mastoor (our Deputy Minister) and some personal contacts at the Ministry of Foreign Affairs to get me an appointment with the Minister and finally managed to speak to him once already in NY. Afghanistan was committed to co-host, so we had to do it. The biggest challenge was a kind of dichotomy between Ministries of Finance and Foreign Affairs that exists in most of our member countries. The agenda of aid effectiveness in Afghanistan was in the realm of [the] Ministry of Finance and so this was the ministry that was dealing with donors. But the business of engagement at the UN is with the Ministry of Foreign Affairs. In addition, the Ministry of Foreign Affairs was not inclined to support the country being represented by the notion of "fragility" or "fragile states", for obvious reasons. So part of my challenge in convincing the Minister of Foreign Affairs was to do with this notion of [a] "fragile state". I was worried, but pushy while speaking to him. I didn't realize then, but I was, and my former colleague, who was then working at the Ministry of Foreign Affairs, sitting next to me, kept elbowing me—he told me later— but I didn't realize! To my mind, it was about honouring the commitment

---

37 Interview with Habib Mayar, 23 March 2020.

Afghanistan had made. But we got through, and the Minister agreed. After that, I got a message from the Afghan mission asking me to write the speech. Although part of my routine job at the Ministry of Finance was writing speaking points, I had never written one for a Minister of Foreign Affairs, which would require being diplomatic.[38]

Some scholars of diplomatic theory claim that professional diplomacy has been depoliticized, that it is not so much about 'civic duty' anymore, yet when we listen to accounts such as this the element of duty and responsibility is, on the contrary, strongly present.[39] Habib continues:

> I did, though, I wrote the speech and sent it as a draft. Before sending it to the mission, I had it reviewed by my colleagues at the Ministry of Finance. I had a printed copy in hand during the event, I was listening and checking word by word, and was so surprised when I realized it was not changed though I thought it would need realignment to how messages are conveyed at the UN. I was really happy when I heard.[40]

Siafa also tells us about the day-to-day diplomatic work prior to the event:

> We would go to all [the] ambassadors—we relied on the Timorese mission to talk of them. We would teach [them] about the g7+, explain the objectives and the group. My strength was [speaking] on the phone. Habib was going out, doing advocacy in NY. The first challenge was to get 1 or 2 presidents on board. Xanana and Sirleaf [Liberia] were confirmed, and Xanana used his contacts to get Indonesia.[41]
>
> I didn't know anyone in NY. It was like I was doing *retail politics or retail diplomacy*. It took a lot of perseverance. If one said no, we would simply react like "maybe later".

In terms of structural support, Siafa explains: 'The UNDP helped with resources. For them it was a footnote in their budget, but they knew they needed to keep it discreet. There was already a lot of bad blood [on] the part of the G77. They said we were being used, that the g7+ was a pet group. They didn't understand this was all coming from the countries themselves. There was a disconnect'.[42] We will come back to this 'bad

---

38 Ibid.
39 Constantinou, Costas M., Cornago, Noé & McConnell, Fiona (eds). (2016). Op. cit., p. 9.
40 Ibid.
41 Interview with Siafa Hage, 10 March 2020.
42 Ibid.

High Level Side Event on New Deal:

g7+ Perspectives and Experience

67th United General Assembly

Draft Statement by H.E. Minister of Foreign Affairs

Opening Remarks

Excellencies,

On behalf of the Government of the Islamic republic of Afghanistan as the co-host, it is my pleasure and privilege to welcome you to the High-Level Side Event on The New Deal: g7+ perspectives and experiences. It is a pleasure to see the level of support and the momentum which the New Deal for Engagement in Fragile sates is gaining after it was endorsed in November 2011 during the 4th High Level forum on Aid Effectiveness held in Busan last year. This global recognition is indeed a result of the efforts of the g7+ countries and their partners.

Arena setting:

Ladies and gentlemen, Afghanistan has received generous support over the past decade for its development and reconstruction. There have been noteworthy achievements in the areas of security and economic development since 2001, when we started our journey towards a peaceful and prosperous Afghanistan. We started this journey with weak institutions, poor infrastructure and with almost no formal economy. But despite all these hardships and challenges, we are now equipped with trained national security forces; access to basic health care services has improved; national highways and roads have been rebuilt; and telecoms and other hard and soft infrastructure facilities have been established. Of equal importance, our institutional and public sector reforms have advanced. This was indeed possible with the generous financial and technical support of our development partners.

Excellencies, ladies and gentlemen, despite the tremendous achievements we have had, Afghanistan is one of the g7+ member countries which is lagging behind the goal of materialization of MDGs (Millennium Development Goals). Despite sizable development aid invested in governance and capacity building, we continue to depend on external technical assistance. We can only cover some 60% of our operating expenditures through our domestic revenue. Our private sector is yet to realize its potential to become the engine of growth and absorb an emerging workforce. Our security sector needs to be further strengthened to take over the responsibility of protecting our people after 2014. In view of the perceived reduction in development aid during the decade of transformation, we have taken steps to bolster our domestic revenues and provide essential services to our citizens.

Longer and more sustainable partnership:

Excellencies, sustained international engagement in development of g7+ countries is a necessity. But this engagement shall aim to support nationally owned and nationally led agenda for development. We presented our vision in the 'Towards Self Reliance' strategy paper at the International Tokyo Conference on Afghanistan in July 2012.[1] To fulfil this vision, we have developed our partnership agenda 'The Aid Management Policy' in consultation with our development partners and reaffirmed our commitment to implementing critical reforms and promote accountability and transparency in the Tokyo Mutual Accountability Framework. However, the key milestone of success in our partnership will be the extent to which our partners are willing and able to align their development efforts to our shared strategy. Being mindful of our budding institutional capacity, our partnership needs to be based on mutual trust which could involve sharing the burden of managing development aid and sharing the risks of engagement in fragile and conflict affected environments. This is the only way to reach our common goals. There is, therefore, a need for bold and mutual decisions by all our partners.

g7+ countries and post-2015

Excellencies, ladies and gentlemen:

We are on the verge of 2015, when we will be reviewing our millennium development agenda. The progress made so far across the g7+ countries in terms of achievement of the millennium goals should be an important part of our review agenda and will be crucial in formulating our next steps. Since 2000, and despite the investment of nearly 30% of all development aid in conflict affected countries, we still have a long way to go. These countries are still threatened by conflict, violence and poverty and suffer from humanitarian crises. The next phase of the Millennium Development Agenda should focus more on strengthening the very core of functional foundations which are the pillars of Peacebuilding and Statebuilding. Only then, will we be able to observe the result of our efforts. Drawing upon the context of the g7+ countries, the Peacebuilding and Statebuilding goals should be fabricated in the next phase of our global development agenda.

Excellencies, I would like to conclude by thanking you all for your support for the vision of the g7+ which has been articulated in the New Deal for Engagement in Fragile States. We are confident that with the realization of the New Deal, we can reach a brighter future through our shared efforts.

1　　Transcript from g7+ archives

blood' later in the book, but it goes to show the real need for the g7+ among a group of countries whose people felt that their specific needs were not being considered by middle-income or emerging countries.[43] Siafa adds:

> I was put in charge of making phone calls. At one point, for instance, we heard the UN Secretary General wouldn't be able to come and was sending the undersecretary of DPKO [Department of Peacekeeping Operations] as his representative. We knew Helen Clarke, secretary of UNDP, was coming too, so we didn't know who should speak first, because she outranked him, but he was the envoy of the Secretary General himself. Also, at some point we heard Hillary Clinton might come and, as Secretary of State, she would outrank them all. We didn't have knowledge of protocols, nor any similar experiences. We were learning and doing our best. I was put in charge of certain calls, because I guess, for certain Asian cultures, "*no*" doesn't come easily, and I had no problem with that. Finally, I decided DKPO would speak first. Helen Clarke was a champion of the g7+, still is, and it was fine.[44]
>
> On the day, we had a list of people we had to follow up on, make sure they would be there on time, verify the room set-up. There were staff for some of the tasks, but no one would help with protocol. We made phone calls to let important people know when to arrive, that kind of thing.[45]
>
> At the end we had two presidents, four prime ministers and two ministers in the panel. The room had about 400 people, I think. I know it was standing room only. People were clamouring to make interventions from the floor. The IDPS co-chair was sitting on a folding chair! Some renowned people wanted to speak. We had unexpected important people coming in but managing to barely say two words because the list was full. It was a fantastic experience.[46]

Habib claims 'that event cleared a path for [them]. It helped conveying [their] collective message and also created some doubts on the part of G77 and other groupings that up to that point had the impression that the g7+ was merely lobbying to get more aid. Having Indonesia in addition to traditional donors together with the g7+ in the panel indicated that the g7+ was not a donor-driven agenda'.[47]

---

43 For an overview of current affairs in that sense, see Trajber Waisbich, Laura, Roychoudhury, Supriya & Haug, Sebastian (2021). 'Beyond the single story: 'Global South' polyphonies'. *Third World Quarterly*, 42(9), 2086–95.
44 Interview with Siafa Hage, 10 March 2020.
45 Ibid.
46 Interview with Siafa Hage, 10 March 2020.
47 Interview with Habib Mayar, 23 March 2020.

After that, Habib got an invitation to work for the g7+ in Dili, was encouraged by his deputy minister and, finally, seconded to the Secretariat. He recalls every detail of that period:

> Helder and Minister Pires had asked back in New York whether I would like to work in Dili, but I didn't give it much thought at the time, didn't think whether it would happen or not. Then, my deputy minister got a letter from Minister Pires asking for my secondment. Denmark would fund it through ODI since neither the secretariat nor the Ministry of Finance in Afghanistan could be used as the conduit. As with all transitions, it wasn't smooth. When I left for Timor-Leste in 2013, I still didn't resign from my position in Afghanistan because I was uncertain. Although I had visited Dili in 2012 during the first technical meeting of the g7+, I had very little information about life in Dili. As this would be my first assignment outside Afghanistan, I was excited yet anxious. I arrived a week before a high-level conference on [the] post-2015 agenda hosted in Dili, where the g7+ had a big role. Timor-Leste, represented by Emilia Pires, was selected as a member of the High-Level Panel on [the] post-2015 [agenda] formed by the Un Secretary General to present its recommendations on the post-2015 agenda, what would later be the SDGs. In order to mobilize more voices for the inclusion of a goal on peace among the SDGs, this conference would play a crucial role. In addition, following the conference, there was the second technical meeting of the g7+, since all the focal points of g7+ were invited to attend the conference. There were four other internationals seconded, as part of the preparatory team. I got a desk and computer on my second morning in Dili, but no "job orientation", something I had studied in human resources management books. With only a few days to the conference and the technical meeting, I had to contribute and help with the preparation. But at the end, I was glad I didn't have orientation. It can be limiting. Helder, as my boss, empowered me. When I was being annoying, asking questions, he just said "go ahead".[48]

Avoid Hoarseness: Trying to Keep Up with SDG 16

The search for a voice is not an easy one. One has to decide what voice one wants to have—where one wants to use it and what for—and even with that settled, the strategies to finally find it can be many. If you are seeking to be heard (which means, right now, this is not really happening), once in a room, should you try to be loud sometimes?

---

48   Ibid.

Should you instead speak softly to some, take your time and spread your message around? And then speak loudly when people are more or less ready, or not at all? One way or another, you might end up hoarse with all the speaking done in preparation, so that when you finally find more welcoming ears, your voice is gone.

Part of what makes dialogue and negotiations so difficult for those in less privileged positions is in knowing how to push hard enough to get what you want, but not too much that you might drain your energy (or the patience of others).

In the 'New York bubble', as some put it, the politics of who gets to speak goes far beyond protocols, although these constitute an important threshold—learning the language and how to employ it is a process of working out how to penetrate a monologue: 'Arising from its roots in Eurocentrism, diplomatic theory is a monologue of the West about itself, its heritage, its voices and its archives'.[49] Diplomatic practice cannot go too far with this history.

There is more, however: One needs to know the game, the rules and the players. Some background history is essential too. Usually, countries have permanent missions, career diplomats; different groups have lobbyists, professional advocates with a CV full of the right universities and internships. Perhaps, for many, understanding what is 'hot', what the interests are around a topic and how these interests can change comes as second nature. For representatives of the g7+, what was on the table was an intensive course on *'how to burst the bubble'*, with quick lessons and high rewards involved.

The g7+ is credited with having been key to advancing the inclusion of a standalone goal for peace in the UN 2030 Agenda, the Sustainable Development Goal 16 on Peace, Justice and Inclusive Societies.[50] The interest in having a goal that addresses peace issues in the global development agenda came from these countries' experiences of being marked down in their performance by several international indices, such as Corruption Perceptions Index, by Transparency International;[51]

---

49 Siphamandla Zondi, op. cit, p. 11.
50 See Independent Review of the g7+ (2019) for a detailed account and more information on the SDGs.
51 Transparency International (n.d.). *Corruption Perceptions Index*. https://www.transparency.org/en/cpi/2021.

September 2013 in New York
g7+ Breakfast meeting at the UN

There were donor and g7+ representatives present, in addition to other participants. The conversation regarded peace and security in the context of the new development agenda being negotiated at the UN — the SDGs.

g7+.3: The business of the UN is peace, it is about development, and human rights, and they have never been more needed today to really see and make sure we give everyone this opportunity. In the New York bubble, we are distanced from this but opportunities like this, we cannot forsake, we have to execute the Charter.

D4: It is hard to imagine someone would object to incorporating peace and security to this agenda. [g7+.3] mentioned the New York bubble. I want to ask what it takes to burst that bubble and get peace and security to the negotiation. Do you feel confident about it? Do you feel we are winning? What can we do to support that campaign?

g7+.1: I just cannot understand why would someone object...? My country is the classical example. If we hadn't fought for peace, we would never be where we are. We had thousands of refugees. We had to address the security and instability first. I don't understand, but we need to convince them... Maybe they have been living in this bubble for too long.

g7+.2: No doubt we are puncturing that bubble right now. Peace and stability have a meaning. Before the peace process, 200,000 kids went to school. After that, more than a million. This is peace and security. That is why peace is at the heart of sustainable development, because we have seen it.[1]

---

1   Rocha de Siqueira, I. (2017). Op. cit., pp. 190–91. My transcript of the September 2013 g7+ parallel meeting organized as part of the UN General Assembly. Anonymity protected under Chatham House rules. 'D' stands for 'donor'.

the Fragile States Index, by Fund for Peace;[52] or the World Bank's List of Fragile and Conflict-affected Situations.[53] Some in the countries with low marks feel not enough context is provided, taking into account the

---

52   The Fund for Peace (n.d.). *Fragile States Index.* https://fragilestatesindex.org/.
53   World Bank (n.d.). *Classification of Fragile and Conflict-Affected Situations.* https://www.worldbank.org/en/topic/fragilityconflictviolence/brief/harmonized-list-of-fragile-situations.

many obstacles posed by crises, violence and conflict. These are serious detours, to say the least, taken by any clear development path, and the g7+ countries have always advocated that these should be taken into account by donors, addressed properly—in a harmonized way—and in a manner that was aligned to the countries' own priorities; that is, through country-owned and country-led programs and using country systems. However, there was much resistance to the inclusion of SDG 16 in the 2030 Agenda.

The negotiations that took place in the High-Level Panel of Eminent Persons on the Post-2015 Agenda (HLP) and beyond that forum in the years prior to the SDG's approval saw the g7+ heavily committed, especially in the figure of Minister Pires. She later counted on the support of the African countries, represented by H. E. Ms. Ellen Johnson Sirleaf, then President of Liberia, one of the g7+ founder countries, but this support had to take place through discreet channels and in parallel to the more public efforts of the g7+ itself. This story has been told, to the best of our ability, in the 2019 *Independent Review of the g7+*. Some of what is told there is below,[54] but here I want to focus less on the technical aspects of it and more on the people involved.

In 2012, a meeting involving government and civil society from the g7+, Pacific Island countries and African members of the Portuguese-speaking African Countries community (PALOP in Portuguese) was held to discuss the way forward post-2015. The meeting revealed a common diagnostic: 'We know the well-being of our people depends upon the achievement of outcomes that were not adequately reflected in the MDGs, most notably in the areas of peace and justice and climate change'.[55] With that diagnostic in mind, we can see that having Minister Pires and President Sirleaf both as members of the HLP was an important political opportunity. It was also a big challenge: 'SDG 16 was the most difficult goal of all. It didn't come lightly'.[56]

Having permanent diplomatic missions in New York was crucial, but a lot of the burden was carried by the Timorese delegation, in the figure of Minister Pires, because she was a member of HLP. Siafa, at the time—between the 2012 big g7+ meeting at the UN and taking up coordination

---

54   This subsection includes excerpts from the *Independent Review of the g7+* (2019).
55   g7+ (2012). *The Dili Consensus*.
56   Interview with Helder da Costa, 29 May 2019.

of IDPS—was posted with the permanent mission of Liberia to the UN and, therefore, was supporting President Sirleaf directly. Liberia was co-chairing the HLP with the United Kingdom and Indonesia. Siafa says, of seeing the g7+ acting within the HLP: 'I felt for them. There was a lot that couldn't be shared, so they felt alone. As co-chairs of the HLP, we were responsible for shepherding the entire process and could not be the champion of a peace/fragility goal. We could not play favourites, but we made sure the issue remained on the agenda'.[57] Then Timorese ambassador Sofia Borges was also instrumental, pushing for the adoption of a goal on peace in the diplomatic scene. She, as Minister Pires did, apparently faced quite personal battles to get the message through to the HLP. The g7+ is said to have held position, refusing to negotiate on a lesser goal.

For some, the battle (and the unwillingness to cede) could be traced back to Monrovia in 2011 when, after negotiation, it was agreed that the discussion on peace would be a pillar in the new post-2015 agenda, so that, when a first draft was circulated in the HLP which did not mention peace, the panel was almost disbanded.[58]

Meanwhile, African representatives had been holding regional discussions which involved the same debate around peace and security. The Common African Position (CAP),[59] a key document produced by the African Union that would later be crucial in supporting the approval of SDG 16, was being drafted with a lot of negotiation as well. Nevertheless, when a first draft was submitted to African Heads of States, it did not include anything on peace and security,[60] and it seems that the pressure to go back and include peace in the document came from the Heads of States. There was fear this would not go over well with New York, but a point of convergence was found in the similarities with Agenda 2063.[61] Finally, then, pillar five in the CAP covered peace and security.

57   Interview with Siafa Hage, 10 March 2020.
58   Interview with Paul Okumu, 18 June 2019.
59   African Union (2014). *Common Africa Position (CAP) on the Post 2015 Development Agenda*.
60   Interview with Paul Okumu, 18 June 2019.
61   African Union (2013). *Agenda 2063: The Africa We Want*. https://au.int/en/Agenda2063/popular_version.

Common African Position (CAP) and the 2063 Agenda

'Specifically, the CAP acknowledges 'the importance of peace and security in Africa and in the world, and the inextricable links between development and peace, security and stability' and reaffirms that 'peace and security is essential for the achievement of the continent's development aspirations particularly for countries affected by conflict and those emerging from conflict'. It therefore commits to address the root causes of conflict by addressing:

- economic and social inequalities and exclusion;
- good and inclusive governance;
- the fight against all forms of discrimination;
- ways to forge unity in diversity through democratic practices and mechanisms at the local, national and continental levels.'

The African Agenda 2063 is another key document produced in the continent. Recently, there have been many efforts to map out the synergies between this agenda and the SDGs. 'Agenda 2063 is a people-driven and consultation-led process by the AU on 'The Future We Want for Africa'. The aspirations refer frequently to peace, security and development, including: a prosperous Africa based on inclusive growth and sustainable development; a peaceful and secure Africa; and an Africa where development is people-driven.'

(See: Lucey, Amanda (2015). 'Implementing the Peace, Security and Development Nexus in Africa'. *Strategic Analysis*, 39(5), 500–11, p. 504; African Union (2014). 'Common African Positions (CAP)'; African Union (2015). 'Agenda 2063: The Africa We Want'; and African Union. 'Linking Agenda 2063 and the SDGs', at https://au.int/en/agenda2063/sdgs)

As CAP was being negotiated, Minister Pires was pushing behind the scenes in the HLP and President Sirleaf was articulating the African support, without which she could not stand up for SDG 16 in the panel. In Siafa's opinion, 'without [the African support], there would be no SDG 16, because Africa is huge in the G77. Sirleaf was fighting that battle while Pires fought in the HLP'.[62] For Habib, other regions and countries were key as well.

At the HLP, Minister Pires and the g7+ were facing distrust on the part of emerging countries and the G77+, China in particular, which feared this was an OECD-driven group articulating the agenda of

---

62   Interview with Siafa Hage, 13 June 2019.

donors.[63] There were serious concerns about the consequences of including peace in the 2030 Agenda, especially by some emergent countries whose agenda at the UN had always been marked by concerns with non-intervention and who were wary of what kind of responses the inclusion of a goal on peace would invite.[64]

After negotiations, it seemed the goal would be approved, yet at one crucial point, then Prime Minister David Cameron of the United Kingdom was about to announce the end of a meeting without putting the goal of peace on the table. 'He was saying it was not a priority'.[65] Right then, President Sirleaf raised the point again, then concluded, saying 'you can end the meeting now', Siafa says, with some pride.[66]

At this stage, the behind-the-scenes battles fought by Minister Pires were converging with the approval of the CAP. Once the African Heads of States had signed a document supporting peace and security along with a development agenda, it was much more difficult for a UN panel to ignore it.[67] 'That was how we got the resolution in the HLP. There was a political platform and political clout beyond [David] Cameron', Siafa says.[68] After that, African countries strongly supported Minister Pires's work in the HLP as well.

Right after that victory, however, the g7+ stepped back considerably and was not seen so much in the driving seat of SDG 16-related discussions. It did start participating in the dialogues promoted by one now-key actor in that debate, the Pathfinders for Peaceful, Just and Inclusive Societies, a think tank based in New York.[69] But other than that, there is a general feeling that the g7+ lost its way just after the approval of the agenda: 'They should have declared victory',[70] says Sarah Cliffe, former director of the Pathfinders—meaning they did not.

Habib depicts the general feeling of overwhelming exhaustion well:

63　See Wyeth, Vanessa (2012). 'Knights in Fragile Armor: The Rise of the "g7+"'. *Global Governance: A Review of Multilateralism and International Organizations*, 18(1), 7–12; Pospisil, Jan (2017). '"Unsharing" sovereignty: G7+ and the politics of international statebuilding'. International Affairs, 93(6), 1417–34.

64　See *2019 Independent Review of the g7+*, pp. 52–54.

65　Interview with Siafa Hage, 13 June 2019.

66　Ibid.

67　Interview with Paul Okumu, 18 June 2019.

68　Interview with Siafa Hage, 13 June 2019.

69　See: https://cic.nyu.edu/programs/SDG 16plus.

70　Interview with Sarah Cliffe, 19 June 2019.

Honestly, I sympathize with this feeling. I think, we tend to be humble. Maybe we didn't have the capacity to follow up closely on the process. We should have helped strengthening coordination among permanent missions of g7+ countries in New York by consolidating our group [around the SDG 16 after the approval]. We were uncertain about how it soon was becoming a trend and that some actors that had resisted inclusion of a goal on peace then tended to become champions of SDG 16. The SDGs became too universal and, of course, they are, because it is a universal agenda. But implementation is and should be local. We need to ask what implementing SDG 16 and, particularly, peace means for each country. For instance, making peace in a certain country might be in the realm of the Security Council; in another, it might mean addressing internal conflict; and in others addressing urban violence. We have to become more fluid, to adapt to each context. Yes, I think we should have claimed our victory on SDG 16, protected it, so it is not manipulated. We should have continued our engagement in conversations on indicators. But it is also true that we couldn't catch up with the pace that the discourse was going on with. We agreed in 2016 to report jointly on priority indicators, which we selected;[71] it became very challenging due to lack of data. However, we engaged through the HLPF [High Level Political Forum] every year to highlight and share the g7+ perspective on SDG 16, even when it was not being reviewed yet.[72]

UN High-Level Political Forum (HLPF)

The High-Level Political Forum (HLPF) is held annually at the UN Headquarters, in New York, since 2015, with the purpose of monitoring the progress in the implementation of the 2030 Agenda. As part of the 2-week-long forum, a few countries volunteer every year to offer a review on their progress in relation to selected indicators through Voluntary National Reviews (VNRs).

(See: https://sustainabledevelopment.un.org/hlpf)

The pressure to come up with methodologies, indicators and so on for SDG 16, the PSGs, and 'fragility' in general was something that both reflected the group's successful lobbying in the post-2015 negotiations, and its difficulties in preserving some of that stamina, building upon the political capital they had just acquired and continuing to focus discussions on their own priorities as much as possible. It goes to show

---

71   See *2019 Independent review of the g7+*, pp. 79–80.
72   Interview with Habib Mayar, 22 May 2019.

September 2013 in New York

g7+ Breakfast meeting at the UN

There were donor and g7+ representatives present, in addition to other participants. The conversation regarded peace and security in the context of the new development agenda being negotiated at the UN.

D3: Good that 18 countries accepted to take part [g7+ members then]. We are taking stock of the MDGs here, so how can we use this to make sure the MDGs will be met and that then we should have a special view on fragile states? Because none of the fragile states have reached any of the MDGs. We were hosting one of the thematic consultations of the pot-2015 precisely on conflict and disaster and for us this is a very dear task to make sure that peace and security will be finally included in the new goals with very specific indicators, so that it can be measured and results can be delivered.

g7+.1: Just to remember that we are dealing with people. Our governments are people. They [donors] walk in as if you can control everybody, as if we are homogeneous, as if we are... We are people; we have our own conflicts inside. If the national government need[s] to show some win-win, that means someone has to support this, otherwise they will lose credibility in the eyes of people. I consider myself as donor, because I am the Finance Minister, not the Foreign Affairs Minister, although some people think I am... At the Ministry of Finance, we are afraid of disbursing money just like that. We have to buy time... sometimes you have to divert... At my ministry, for example, I have no systems in place... and procurements were giving me a headache, because I had people saying 'hey, I defended the country, now you come here with your beautiful Western ideas and put all these systems... I don't know how to read and write and you don't give me any projects. On top of that, it is my money', they would say. Then if you don't have the political tools to fight back... I gave the procurements to my prime minister and the donors said 'you can't do that, you're the Finance Minister, you have to have the procurement rule on you'. I said 'no, he has the political leverage; he is allowing me to set up systems quickly'. Now I have set up the systems, now I can take it back. I needed time. All these combinations, you need to understand. The understanding is very important... we are just normal human beings.[1]

---

1   Rocha de Siqueira, I. (2017). Op. cit., p. 185. 2013 UN General Assembly, g7+ parallel meeting with donors. Anonymity protected under Chatham House rules.

that there is a high price to pay for the steep learning curve one needs to go through in order to burst the New York bubble, having not been professionally groomed to do so from one's formative years. The next time the g7+ planned to achieve something big within that bubble, that experience was a powerful propulsor. One may say skills were sharpened throughout the years, especially after that episode with SDG 16. The challenge of the stamina, however, remains.

Have your People in the Room: Seeking UN Observer Status

Let us skip forward a few years to another instance when the g7+ plunged into UN politics.

As we saw, having permanent missions in New York was extremely helpful in organising the 2012 meeting and in getting through with the advocacy for SDG 16. In these cases, the Timorese mission in New York was crucial. Slowly, the g7+ Secretariat came to the conclusion that investing in *institutionalising* the existence of the group in the UN would be an important stepping-stone to further advocacy. That meant applying for *UN Observer Status*.[73] An organisation with UN Observer Status may participate in the sessions and workings in the General Assembly and maintain a mission at the UN Headquarters.

Before it was granted, Da Costa listed to us a number of benefits that he believed accrue from this status:

> It would give us a voice in the UN politics. In practical terms, it means we can organise a side event along the UN General Assembly, either independently or in partnership with other organisations, for instance. We wouldn't have a vote, but we would have the right to intervene, especially at the UN General Assembly. Most important, we would be able to follow UN politics from close [up], especially the discussions on sustaining peace, and to disseminate all this among members. Also, in regard to the Leave No One Behind motto of the 2030 Agenda, we are behind for the deadline, and we could keep people aware, so they don't leave aside our plights. At the end, the status can elevate our work internationally.[74]

---

73 United Nations (2020). *How do organizations and non-member states get observer status in the General Assembly?* https://ask.un.org/faq/14519.

74 Interview with Helder da Costa, 14 April 2020.

Habib explains the idea came out of the Secretariat towards the end of 2018. 'But it felt so difficult, if not impossible. At the time, not every member had ratified our charter yet. The only country member that had ratified the charter was Afghanistan. We had no representation in New York. Also, the membership was not so consolidated yet'. A ratified charter is a requirement for the application.

Habib continues:

> The Secretariat had no knowledge of the process and we didn't know which door to knock on at the big UN system, but the Timorese mission in New York again helped a lot. They put a document together with the contact of the legal team and entities at the UN. We conducted an initial mission and met with the UN entities and the missions from g7+ countries.
>
> Following the agreement by the members to apply for the Observer Status, the permanent mission of Sierra Leone, as the chairing country in the Sixth Committee, sent the request to the UN in July 2019 to include the agenda item in the 47th session of the UNGA. Given the very short time, because the debate would begin in 2 months at the Sixth Committee, we were not even sure if the item [would] be included in the agenda, let alone about getting the Observer Status. But thanks to the Sierra-Leone mission, we got the confirmation that the item had been considered and was to be included in the agenda.

Habib was asked to go to New York to lobby for the necessary support. In two months, the g7+ should have mobilized support from UN members, the idea being to get them to co-sponsor the resolution, or at least make sure no member opposed it. The Sixth Committee is the main entity where legal matters—such as that of granting Observer Status—are debated, so it represented a critical milestone. Habib explains how it felt for him: 'The fate of our resolution would be decided in the Sixth committee of the UN. Every member appoints its expert on legal matters for this committee. All of them are either lawyers or expert on legal matters and I am not an expert in this field. Considering the slow pace with which things that require consensus often happen at the UN, I still thought our application for Observer Status would be sitting at the UN for a long time'.[75] As scholars of diplomacy know well, much of what goes on at the UN and other major organizations smells and tastes

---

75   Interview with Habib Mayar, 23 March 2020.

like improvisation because it is. Major agreements can be facilitated by individuals who happen to know other people. Moreover, backstage talks matter more than formal documents will ever reveal. Yet, one should not underestimate the role historical relations of power play in situations like these: it takes time to learn to improvise and be informal. One should not be fooled by the game of conversations on the sidelines; it takes political and other kinds of capital to be able to participate in these with some ease.[76]

In preparation for the process, Habib speaks of how anxious he was: 'It was a huge responsibility on my shoulders and I was so scared. I think it's my Afghan mentality: If someone gives you a mission and you fail it, it's a source of shame. I took it personally. It was silly of me, maybe'. He explains even the basic action of meeting people was a challenge because he had no UN credentials for a long time. He would often call a friend who works at the UN, for instance, and wait outside, then go in with him or her and conduct his meetings at a cafeteria or delegates' lounge. The politics within the UN is notorious for such 'narratives of absurdity'. Liminal actors, that is, people who are not quite diplomats but act like them, often find alternatives spaces and opportunities in order to hold the necessary conversations.[77] These are made more challenging still when it comes to what some call 'fringe diplomatic actors',[78] which one can say is the case with representatives of fragile states.

The rest of the time, Habib was conducting searches online on everything from the history of all the countries he would have to approach in the Sixth Committee in order to get their individual support, up to the intricacies of UN politics and alliances. After all, he was not a diplomat and he had not been working in New York or with the UN, so all this background knowledge had to be acquired at top speed and in a do-it-yourself fashion.

---

76 See McConnell, Fiona (2017). 'Liminal geopolitics: The subjectivity and spatiality of diplomacy at the margins'. *Transactions of the Institute of British Geographers*, 42(1), 139–52; Constantinou, Costas M. & Opondo, Sam Okoth (2021). 'On biodiplomacy: Negotiating life and plural modes of existence'. *Journal of International Political Theory*, 17(3), 316–36.

77 McConnell, op. cit.

78 Ibid., p. 9.

UN Observer Status

Legally speaking, neither the UN Charter nor the Rules of Procedure of the General Assembly address the question of observers. In practice, the General Assembly has adopted resolutions granting observer status to various organisations and entities.

Procedure:

1. A member state or a group of member states request the inclusion in the agenda of the General Assembly.

2. The Sixth Committee considers the application before submitting to the plenary session.

3. The General Assembly decides on the resolution to grant observer status.

'With the status of permanent observer, the g7+ will have a direct voice in the UN on agenda of sustaining peace and conflict prevention. The group will contribute directly to the work of the General Assembly every year. Most importantly, it will be a platform for g7+ to speak with one voice on conflict, fragility and resilience and become even stronger in advocating for the Sustainable Development Goals (SDGs) 16 on peace, justice and strong institutions. Moreover, the status will allow the g7+ to attend and contribute to the UN conferences on other thematic areas that related to peacebuilding and statebuilding.'

(See Rocha de Siqueira, Isabel (2019). *2019 Independent Review of the g7+*; g7+ Newsletter April 2019)

I found out that there were about ten similar applications submitted. They were all from intergovernmental organisations and their applications had been pending for years. I was looking at examples to see whether their goals were similar to ours. I checked their websites. I also did research on the diplomatic history of the main countries I would have to approach. In order to have the support of the P5 [the countries with permanent seats at the Security Council — USA, France, UK, Russia and China], I learned that I couldn't lean too much on one or another country or I would alienate the other. Like with the US, Russia and China or their allies I had to keep the balance. Another country which is extremely critical in the procedures of granting observer status is Cuba. We had to rely on a colleague from Timorese mission to reach out to the Cuban expert in the Sixth Committee'.[79] In order to make appointments with

---

79   Ibid.

non-g7+ representatives, the g7+ had to rely on either fellow missions of g7+ who might have some contacts or on the blue book of the UN.

When we, that is, myself, colleagues from Sierra Leone, and Timorese missions finally met the representative of Cuba, she was supportive and indicated that since g7+ fulfils the criteria, we would not have any issue. In addition, she gave us some good advice on advocating for it.

Securing an appointment for meeting the UN diplomats is another challenge, given their busy schedule. Habib explains that in some cases, he had to spot the country representatives at the UN and approach them there:

> I would sit at the Sixth Committee either behind the representatives of Sierra Leone, Timor-Leste or Afghanistan. You either have to be with a mission or sit on the second floor. During the session, I would check the plaques of the country I would want to meet, identify who the representatives were, then approach them, give them my card and ask whether I could speak to them for 5 minutes during the break of after the meeting. That's how it happened with Russia, for example. Even before coming to NY, I had already spoken to an American friend in Dili who happened to have worked at the UN on Afghanistan in 1990s and who promised that he would help putting me in touch with a former Russian diplomat to the UN who could further help in identifying the right person at the mission to talk to. Anyway, I managed to speak to the Russia's expert during a lunch break of one of the sessions. I was anxious and careful. The briefing memo that I had prepared included references on the New Deal, which is of course endorsed by the OECD members. And I had had to manoeuvre where to start from. So I started by asking whether she had seen the resolution and of course she had, and then I briefly mentioned the purpose of the g7+ and how we would support a universal goal of peace and stability in the UN. After a few minutes, when I let her react, she said "Fine, we support you". I couldn't believe, as I had thought that Russia would give us a tough time. When I think how that was possible, to get such support, I guess it's due to our emphasis on country ownership, which is a dear notion to many members of the UN.[80]
>
> No country opposed our application which was the minimum we required for approval. For instance, China reacted to our first communication saying "ok, we just need to be sure whether the g7+ has had a stance on Taiwan that would be against Chinese interest". And finally, China co-sponsored the resolution as well.[81]

---

80   Ibid.
81   Ibid.

This point is one that Habib kept repeating as he told the story:

> For other organisations, I guess they would greatly rely on the respective missions of their members, to get the process going. But the missions of g7+ countries didn't have enough manpower. We studied the processes beforehand to see what was necessary. I even thought it was like a competition, so I thought it was good to keep things quiet. I was learning and tried to be spontaneous. When I would speak to representatives of non-g7+ countries, I tried to explain how the g7+ would support the basic goals of the UN and yet bring benefits in terms of the specific interests of each of the members with that global goal of peace and stability. I had realized that successful negotiation at the UN depended on how you would make coalitions. But given the radical division among nations and their foreign policies, it is tough to position yourself as neutral yet supportive of a global goal that is being perceived differently by different actors in global politics. More often, diplomats at the UN would want to hear about what is of interest in line with their respective foreign policies. That's why I often had to form a narrative founded on a humane aspiration rather than on purely national interest, to break the moulds. And the humane aspiration is peace; that is at the core of g7+ mission.[82]

Da Costa speaks of how they got inspiration from the Community of Portuguese Language Countries (CPLP), the Pacific Islands Development Forum (PIDF) and others. And Habib explains some of these were instrumental to get support for the Observer Status: 'We didn't speak with specific countries much. We got support from the CPLP members through countries like Timor-Leste and Portugal. The critical ones would be countries like Brazil, which also, to our surprise, co-sponsored our resolution'.[83] After all, Brazil and other emergent countries had been resistant to some of the agenda that was supported by the g7+, such as SDG 16, the peace goal, as da Costa and others tell. As Da Costa explained, the G77, of which Brazil is a member, had seen the g7+ with some suspicion, as a donors' project. Now, that had clearly changed. In addition, 'Gambia supported the resolution on behalf of the African countries and Samoa for the Pacific Islands'.[84]

It is striking that Habib knows the list of 31 supporters by heart. The non-g7+ supporters were Angola, Brazil, Canada, China, Cabo

82 Ibid.
83 Ibid.
84 Ibid.

Verde, Cuba, Finland, the Gambia (on behalf of the African group), Korea, Mozambique, Norway, Portugal, Romania, Samoa, Sudan and Sweden. Among the g7+ members that were present and supported the resolution, there were Afghanistan, Burundi, CAR, Chad, Comoros, Guinea, Guinea-Bissau, Liberia, Sao Tome and Principe, Sierra Leone, Somalia, South Sudan, Timor-Leste, Togo and Yemen. And finally, the UN General Assembly, in its meeting on 18 December 2019, passed a resolution granting Observer Status to the g7+.

'We couldn't believe it. We succeeded in getting support for our application in less than six months! Everyone was surprised'.[85] An official celebration note was published in the g7+'s March 2020 newsletter, calling this a 'historical milestone in the journey of g7+'.

As the Secretariat knows well, now comes the stamina challenge. Da Costa has been asking himself:

> How can we lift our game in New York? How can we make ourselves more visible?'.[86] Some of the costs to be incurred are well known: 'It costs a lot. We have been discussing different scenarios within the Secretariat and the group. The usual path would be to ask development partners to fund one of ours to be based in New York. There are organisations that can potentially host us. In any case, we need now an exercise [in] public relations for a campaign that is going to be at the global level. We bring the development perspective; now we will need diplomacy to back that. We also want to bring in more people next year to help the Secretariat.[87]

The accidental diplomats in the g7+ achieved quite a lot against the odds. Now they might need support, but that they have gone so far says a lot about their skills and the way they were encouraged to develop them. As in other cases in diplomacy, we should perhaps consider the g7+ both in terms of it being 'a means to an end (international recognition) *and* an end in itself (a parallel system)', in which case, there is considerable ambivalence about its 'transformative capacities', something that requires a nuanced analysis. As an exercise in practising diplomacy within the confines of the 'grey spaces', there is much that can be garnered from such experiences and that can furnish future endeavours.

---

85 Ibid.
86 Interview with Helder da Costa, 14 April 2020.
87 Ibid.

Nevertheless, the ambivalence also means that, as discussed in the 2019 review and often heard pronounced by partners, in the aftermath of each international diplomatic and advocacy victory, the g7+ representatives seem to have to get to grips with the more existential question of how to translate all that *back* to their countries and to people's lives.

One should be proud to have overcome difficult obstacles through a self-taught process, developing the right skills and language and demonstrating astonishing levels of perseverance. But no one, not least these g7+ representatives themselves, fails to ask the difficult question *'what is it all for?'* at the end of the day, as so many people do in various jobs. The trick is in constantly asking what can be done for the people on the ground. As a former affiliate said, 'the results can't be meetings. And results are not outcomes'.[88]

All these stories show that conflict and crises pushed a generation forward without much guidance. By surviving complicated periods in the history of their countries, they also grew up facing a generation gap and in their thirties, they were in for an incredibly steep learning curve. On the one hand, this was probably scary, and it involved personal commitment to a level that clearly impacted family life, as we will see later in the book. But, on the other hand, having slightly older supervisors, being their own supervisor or not having any guidance at all meant that they felt pushed, empowered and trusted to more or less the same degree; all of that, combined with some of the factors we will see in the following chapters, converged and resulted in the development of some surprising professional paths and acute levels of political engagement. This is not secondary to major political goals. It is something to be understood, harnessed and experimented with by the next generations and campaigns to come.

Around 2010, the experienced international advisor who was supporting the g7+ said things were tough, really tough. Nowadays, looking back, she says 'I didn't think we were going to make it, those first two years'.[89] The fact that those closely involved in taking the first major steps thought it all felt too much, too quick, and yet they kept going, is a major lesson.

---

88   Interview with Peter Lloyd, 30 March 2020.
89   Interview with Missy Stephens.

How to find a voice: on being an accidental diplomat

4. One needs to listen

5. Trust is the most valuable currency

6. Be wary of the annotated agenda

7. In the search for a voice, avoid hoarseness

8. Have your people in the room

Lo and behold that
Good sense is better than prowess.
(Somali proverb)

3. How to Use your Survival Skills (to Survive Monitoring and Evaluation)

On Patience, Opportunities and Cooperation

'Salton ku si mindjer

Un mindjer sai pa ba panha salton na roda di mar. I tchiga, i panha salton manga del, i fia na korda. I bin panha un salton e fia na korda. Mindjer di salton sai, i odja si omi, i ba tchora djanan la na metadi di tarafi. I na tchora, i na tchora, i fala si omi ku panhadu, i na tchora. Salton fala si mindjer: "Ka bo tchora. Ora ku bo sinti nha tcheru na iassadu bo ta tchora, ma tementi N ka iassadu inda, ka bo tchora". Mindjer ku panhal i ditanda gora korda e ba laba kurpu. Salton salta, i kapli na corda e miti dentru di koba. I fala si mindjer: "N tarda contau. Tementi bo ka na sinti nha tcheru na fugu, sibi cuma N ka muri."'

(Story from *Contes Créoles de Guinée-Bissau*.)[1]

---

1   The Grasshopper and his Wife
    A woman went out to fetch grasshoppers by the sea. She came in, picked up a bunch of grasshoppers and stuck them in the net. She picked up grasshoppers and stuck them in the net. The wife of the grasshopper went out and saw her man and went to cry in the middle of the mangrove. She cried and cried, saying that her man had been caught, and cried some more. The grasshopper said to her, "Don't cry. The moment you smell me roasting, you cry, but as long as I'm not roasted, don't cry". The woman who had caught him put the [fish] net on the floor and went to bathe. The grasshopper jumped and slipped off the net and into a hole. He said to his wife, "Didn't I tell you! As long as you don't smell me in the fire, you know that I haven't died yet".' My translation from Portuguese.
    See Honório do Couto, Hildo & Embaló, Filomena (2010). 'Um país da CPLP'. *Literatura, Língua e Cultura na Guiné-Bissau*, 20. Brazil: Thesaurus Editora, p. 118.

    https://doi.org/10.11647/OBP.0311.03

How does one survive war, violence, multiple crises and crushing disappointments? Today, the World Health Organisation estimates that more than 264 million people of all ages suffer from depression globally.[2] In the wake of COVID-19 and isolation measures worldwide, one of the major concerns everywhere is the increasing incidence of mental illness from 2020 onwards. Moreover, multilateralism, globalisation and cross-border solidarity face serious political challenges. Therefore, it is perhaps a good time to ask whether there is a fundamental difference in between generations, geographic regions, personal background, collective histories, social structures and family traditions in terms of what a person needs in order to survive and overcome adversity. And what about what is required in order to go beyond survival, to try to change the very conditions within which one was born? Most importantly, how can we learn from those who attempt this?

The pandemic is estimated to have forced more than 100 million people into poverty, 'causing the first increase in global poverty in more than 20 years'.[3] And in the face of COVID-19, the United Nations 2020 progress report on the SDGs had already cautioned that from 2000 to 2015, 'close to 90 million people were pushed into extreme poverty due to *out-of-pocket medical expense*'.[4] This is a grave challenge and one that relates to basic rights and human dignity. It can be made worse as the world dives into an economic recession—data shows that the economies of fragile states, already more vulnerable, have already contracted by 7.5%, while global food prices have risen 23.1%.[5] At the same time as the pandemic has undoubtedly caused immense apprehension, some countries in Africa considered the least developed or most fragile at the beginning of the COVID-19 outbreak have managed to somewhat limit the spread of the disease, thanks to decades of experience fighting other contagious diseases like Ebola. In the African continent, leading

---

2   See World Health Organization (2020). *Depression*. https://www.who.int/news-room/fact-sheets/detail/depression.

3   See United Nations (2021). 'Time for action' to support most fragile States: Guterres. https://news.un.org/en/story/2021/10/1102752; United Nations (2020). *Progress towards the Sustainable Development Goals: Report of the Secretary-General*; Agenda items 5 (a) and 6 (ECOSOC), p. 4.

4   Ibid, p. 7, my emphasis.

5   See World Economic Forum (2022). *Fragile and conflict-affected economies are falling further behind*. https://www.weforum.org/agenda/2022/02/fragile-conflict-economy-states-pandemic-covid19-debt/.

thinkers have called for this moment to be seen as one of opportunity too: 'Health systems need to be transformed, raw materials should finally be processed locally, and the economy should be more diversified', said Senegalese scholar, writer, and musician Felwine Sarr, the Cameroonian political scientist Achille Mbembe, and the Nigerian winner of the Nobel Prize for Literature Wole Soyinka in an open letter. This reflects an attitude that the glass is half full, that moving forward does not always depend on the economic and financial resources available: 'Africa is anything but a helpless continent'.[6] This, I think, is a message that resonates everywhere among g7+ member countries. The experience of surviving and striving through different crises is, as our current times show, a highly valuable asset.

From the beginning, the g7+ has emphasised the message that no one knows a situation better than those who have lived it: the true 'experts on fragility are the citizens of fragile states themselves'.[7] The crises, abrupt changes, violence, and conflict each country has faced are different; however, one might say there are important survival skills that these 'true experts' have in common, skills that are at the core of what a former affiliate calls a certain 'strategic patience'[8] and in the ability to see and seize opportunities.

Much of this can be said to be based on previous encounters with national processes of justice and reconciliation. Whenever such processes take place, negotiations about the terms of reference are extremely difficult; the methods—often involving truth-telling[9]—are painful and involve further sacrifices, and the results are ones that, by nature, do not completely compensate those who have suffered, because this is impossible. The process is usually intended to restore peace somehow, even if not necessarily in a redistributive or punitive way. The challenging combination of tough negotiations, painful methods, and unsatisfactory results seem to fortify some in these societies with the capacity to adapt to incredibly difficult situations. This might be different for younger

---

6   See Schwikowski, Martina (2020). *Coronavirus: How Africa is bracing for pandemic's impact*. DW. https://www.dw.com/en/coronavirus-what-the-world-could-learn-from-africa/a-53259048.

7   g7+ (2013). *Note on the Fragility Spectrum*, p. 2.

8   Interview with Peter Lloyd, 30 March 2020.

9   da Costa Guterres, Francisco (2017). *Reconciliation between Timor-Leste and Indonesia: A Forward Looking Model*. g7+ Foundation, p. 3.

generations who have not lived these experiences first-hand, but some ingrained desire to try and carry on seems to remain with survivors— an 'undercurrent of resentment [that] become[s] relief',[10] a feeling that seizing moments of 'normalcy' should be a rule. With this comes hope, sometimes inexplicably. As in the traditional story from Guinea-Bissau quoted above, *nothing is burnt until one can smell burning*—a tough and perhaps cruel message, and yet also a hopeful one.

Find Yourself Something Sacred and Go Beyond Survival: Valuing Peace and Solidarity

When Habib was living in Pakistan as a refugee, you might remember that he was teaching English. Well, some of his former students had gone back to Afghanistan to become translators for foreign groups working there after 2001, including US contractors. At the time, his reason not to go and make more money in his home country was simple: 'Serving merely as interpreter with US and NATO troops, something I was capable of at that time, was not a big service to the nation'. In addition, 'being an interpreter with the international troops would mean taking part directly in war and hence killing', Habib explains, adding that 'income from a source that involves bloodshed is not halal'. His family was poor, he needed the money, but he also needed to feel he was doing something worthy.

The sacred does not need to be about religion, although it is usually present, one way or another—from religious teachings in one's childhood to the general influence of one's national history. I guess the sacred is, nonetheless, always something that guides a person's path, something to hold dear and close to one's heart, not to mention a line beyond which one is determined not to go. For Siafa, whose stories you might also remember, being together with others had this quality; it was something he lost in part when he had to flee to the US during war in Liberia, but something he says his mother and eldest sister strived to preserve.

Those who lack something sacred can become hopeless when facing difficult situations, because a guiding force will be missing, something fundamental. Not that the sacred is always clear; it can become difficult

---

10   Ibid.

to delineate sometimes, as life changes. Nevertheless, this is the one thing that seems to propel most people forward, even amid war and crises.

It is a beautiful fact that for many of the people in this book this guiding force was family. We heard from almost everyone we spoke with in the g7+ that their parents were determined to ensure they had a quality education, even when they had not had one themselves, so their children could have choices. And we heard of many siblings who protected, supported and kept families close.

Abie Elizabeth Kamara, Deputy Director of Development Assistance Coordination at the Ministry of Finance and Economic Development in Sierra Leone, told us of her six siblings, three brothers and three sisters. Her parents were illiterate and lived in a rural area, 60km from Freetown, but they were committed to getting their children the best education possible. Her eldest sister went first to Freetown to do her secondary education. Soon after leaving school, she was working in the Ministry of Foreign Affairs and she led the way for Abie, who speaks of her sister with much tenderness and gratitude. The path she forged was incredibly important: of Abie's six siblings, all except two went on to complete their secondary studies and three went to university. Abie went further still, to Dakar, Senegal, with a scholarship from the Commonwealth Secretariat, to do her Masters in Economic Development and Planning, at the African Institute for Economic Development and Planning.[11]

Abie came back from Dakar in 1998 to find her country in war. At the time, the fighting had not reached Freetown, but one year that changed. In 1999, she found herself having to leave her home in a hurry. The conflict was getting close; everyone was leaving. While rushing out in despair, she had to throw her small son from the window of a two-storey building, to be caught below. Leaving the building meant crossing the city with bodies everywhere and going without food for days. This is all she says about it, though. War is not something she wants to dwell on. 'You're asking some personal questions', she says, sounding more confused than upset. How could I not? How can those experiences not feature among all the stories that strongly shape one's character? How can they not be fundamental to understanding the work she does as a civil servant and the strength it takes? Yet, she says, the little she does,

---

11   IDEP is a subsidiary and training arm of the United Nations Economic Commission for Africa (ECA).

is enough—her pause meaning as much as the story she has just told. 'Time to move on', she seems to say. (Of course, it might simply be the case that this was not the time and place to talk about it, but that is also significant: we were discussing her current work and her passion for it, and there is so much she can say about that instead.)

With Helche Silvester, who works at the g7+ Secretariat in Dili, the memories of war trigger other kinds of conversations, about reconciliation and the ability to live together:

> When the Indonesians left, Timor-Leste was in ashes. I was six years old, just starting primary school, so I was young, I didn't really understand the context. I witnessed a lot of house burning and had to leave school. We couldn't stay in Dili. My mom was a teacher and my dad was an Indonesian policeman. They both had to work until the day people went to cast their referendum votes [in 1999]. A day after the referendum result was announced, my mom's distant cousin was shot by Indonesians. The nuns transported him to the clinic at the Motael Church, but he was bleeding a lot and he passed away. After this funeral, my dad had to leave the country because he was an Indonesian policeman. And my mom took me to the mountain together with her family, that's where we sought refuge for more than three weeks. We lived in the jungle, surviving eating plants and food that grew near our camp. My mom lost an uncle then too. A few days after our departure to the mountain, someone came to check in my grandparents' house, where my uncle grave was, and they saw that the grave was partly damaged and the fresh flowers that we had laid before were crushed. Apparently, the Indonesian military went to my uncle's grave to see whether we had really buried him. I think they did this because my grandpa was a radical, he was with FREITLIN [the guerrilla force].[12]

In 1999, after much international pressure, the United Nations, Portugal (the former colonial power) and Indonesia (the then-occupier) came to an agreement to hold a referendum so that people in Timor-Leste could vote for independence or autonomy. The result was 78% in favour of independence, and a wave of violence ensued: 'The retreating Indonesian military, feeling humiliated and betrayed by both its government and the people of Timor-Leste, did little to stop the carnage, or actively participated'.[13]

---

12 Interview with Helche Silvester, 05 March 2020.
13 Da Costa Guterres, Francisco (2017). *Reconciliation between Timor-Leste and Indonesia: A Forward Looking Model.* g7+ Foundation, p. 2.

A few difficult years followed and, surprisingly, they culminated in a reconciliation process that has been widely acknowledged as a successful one. 'To avert the country descending back into violence, it was considered essential to promote reconciliation with restorative justice and discourage any retaliation by the victims of the 1999 violence against the pro-autonomy supporters'.[14] It was very telling that the institution inaugurated for this purpose was to be called the Commission for Truth and Friendship.[15]

When I asked Helche whether her mother's family got along well with her father, considering he was Indonesian and her mother's side of the family included rebels and had lost loved ones after the referendum, she says, 'The level of forgiveness was bigger than the hatred'.[16] Indeed, she says her father being an Indonesian was never an issue. 'For us, in Timor, the peace is the most important thing, even with our problems. It helps us understand better what is going on in other countries. Helping others achieve peace is something we hope we can do more. We [the g7+] are more relevant than ever. People need to forgive each other; it's the only way they can find peace'.[17]

Conflict and Crisis in Timor-Leste

'The UN Transitional Administration in East Timor (UNTAET) was established to allow for a smooth transition between the referendum, which decided for independence, and the coming elections.' It operated between 2000 and 2002. 'After 2002 and the end of the UNTAET, the country was thought to be on the right path to development. At the very end of the mission, many spoke of its relative success, although this opinion changed considerably in the following years. However, a violent crisis in 2006 forced the government to call for troops from Portugal, Malaysia, Australia and New Zealand, for which Timorese representatives are said to have been deeply 'ashamed'. The call was just over a year after the last peacekeepers had left the country, and the civil unrest left 15 percent of the population displaced again.'

(Rocha de Siqueira, I. (2017). Op. cit., pp. 75–76; Nicolas Lemay-Hébert (2011). 'The "Empty-Shell" Approach: The Setup Process of International Administrations in Timor-Leste and Kosovo, Its Consequences and Lessons'. *International Studies Perspectives*, 12(2), 190–211.)

---

14   Ibid. p. 1.
15   Ibid., p. 3.
16   Interview with Helche Silvester, 05 March 2020.
17   Ibid.

As to what Helche would like to pass on to her two-year-old son, she is quick: 'I want my son to keep the family bonds. We care a lot; we have a lot of solidarity. It's just like the g7+. It's just being human. Always help people; [solidarity] has a deep meaning. This is a value I want my son to hold on to'.[18]

For those who have gone through war, it seems on the one hand that it is about life, about simple survival; but on the other hand, sense is made of it only by passing on the message, helping others to survive too.

Nevertheless, hard lessons can be taught in many ways. They are not always about war, strictly speaking. Political instability and coups can be profoundly destabilizing, not only in terms of one's individual life, but also in terms of any long-term professional plans and ambitions. Antonio Co, from Guinea-Bissau, has recently retired after almost 40 years as a public servant. In a country that has seen ten coups or attempted coups since the 1980s and has had eight prime-ministers since around the time the g7+ was founded, a civil servant in a supervising position needs to excel at adapting and carrying on (the last coup attempt took place on 1 February 2022).[19] In recent years, Antonio has been promoted and demoted many times: 'We would know of who was in charge by following the decrees that said who were those being dismissed and those being nominated. We were always being made to change things, but so we did'. Antonio is very calm when talking about all these changes. When I what is proudest of in his life, his answer says a lot about the value stability acquires in these circumstances: 'I am proudest of the fact that all my children were educated and that I live in a planned neighbourhood. I worked all my life with planning, I studied planning and now I live in a planned neighbourhood'.[20] After the back and forth of living through many coups and much political instability, it seems one places great value in seeing a plan to its conclusion. Perhaps this is stability in a way. And seeing things through is one's own contribution to peace.

Antonio left his house for the capital to study when he was very young—aged 14—because that was where he could complete his education. He took a technical course on Economic Planning and

---

18   Ibid.
19   BBC News (2022). *Guinea-Bissau: Many dead after coup attempt, president says.* https://www.bbc.com/news/world-africa-60220701.
20   Interview with Antonio Co, 06 March 2020.

worked for three years in the capital before going on to do his bachelor's degree in Cuba. 'I learned Spanish and I liked the weather; it was similar to Guinea-Bissau', he sums up. However, his next degree would be earned under very different conditions. 'There were no universities in the country at the time, so we had to leave to study'. He seems to have lived most of his life as a young adult abroad, away from his family, in different cultures at a time when there was no possibility of easy communication with his home. For his Masters in Economic Sciences, he went to the former USSR and Ukraine for six years, one year of which was dedicated to learning Russian, which he says was very difficult, but he managed. He shared his student flat with people from the USSR itself, Laos, and Guinea-Bissau. Yet, one of the biggest challenges was the temperature: 'I left the 30 to 40 degrees of Bissau and moved to -36. It was *tough*'.[21] (Of all the times he described a challenging situation, his emphasis on the cold weather was notable and sounded almost funny.) To clarify and emphasize, the years were 1985 to 1991, in the USSR. This was a historical moment in the Cold War; one can only imagine what Antonio experienced there. Indeed, one can *only* imagine. After all of his experiences at home and abroad, it is not surprising that he does not

---

21   Ibid.

waste words and tends to answer our questions with only a few pieces of information.

Foreign Student Exchange Programs During the Cold War

The was an increasing number of African students in exchange programs within the USSR as the Cold War progressed.

'The Soviet government reestablished its foreign student exchange programs in 1956 after a two-decade suspension. Along with renewing cultural exchanges with the West and the hosting of the Sixth World Youth Festival in 1957, the foreign student exchange programs were an element in the Soviet Union's effort to fight the Cold War on the cultural front. The opening of the People's Friendship University (UND) in Moscow in 1960 for students from Asia, Africa, and Latin America was pivotal in this endeavor. The number of African countries with students in Russia rapidly increased from ten in 1958 to forty-six in 1968. The 1959–1960 school year had a mere seventy-two students from sub-Saharan Africa, increasing to 500 in 1961, and then to 4,000 by the end of the decade. Of the 17,400 foreign students in the Soviet Union in 1970, 20 percent originated from Africa.' In 1989, there were 27,433 African students in USSR.

(See Guillory, Sean (2014). 'Culture Clash in the Socialist Paradise: Soviet Patronage and African Students' Urbanity in the Soviet Union, 1960–1965'. *Diplomatic History*, 38(2), 272–73; and Katsakioris, Constantin (2019). 'The Soviet Union, Eastern Europe, and Africa in the Cold War: The Educational Ties'. *Working paper series des SFB 1199 an der Universität Leipzig*, 16, p. 17.)

When we asked Antonio how he survived being away from home, he speaks of music and friends: 'I had taken many cassettes of Guinean music with me and we had meetings with the other students'. And when I ask what he took from these experiences, he says: 'There was a sense of cooperation, of being part of a bloc'. These are similar to the words he uses to describe his impressions of the first meeting of the g7+, in 2010, in Dili: 'There was a sense of helping each other and that we were together in a unified front'. He was sent by his minister to Accra in 2010, just before the meeting in Monrovia, with freedom to engage however he saw fit, and he recounts how he eagerly enrolled Guinea-Bissau to become 'one of the first member countries': 'It drew my attention because those were poor countries, countries with few resources, but... people are responsible for their destinies. We first need to know what we want and then we can have one voice'.[22] With that, he has initiated an unusually long engagement with the g7+, since positions tend to rotate often, having been the focal point for 10 years. Since he retired, months previously, no one had taken up the position as of the end of 2020, although he was confident that someone would (and they did).

Antonio offers a valuable lesson in the matter of surviving and striving: 'The young generation has freedom as an advantage, access to a lot of information, new technologies. We wrote by hand! But before, if you missed school, the teacher would come to your home. Today, the freedom can mean things escape control a bit, so sometimes people step out of their paths'.[23] Maybe, because he had few options when he was growing up, the ones available were sacred and he made the most of them. The challenge lies in how to pass that feeling on to younger generations without restricting the important opportunities they should have. There is a delicate balance there, between making sure people value what opportunities they have while not losing sight of the fact that they should multiply, in the present and in the future. All this is not meant to be anecdotal or theoretical; this is an important question for all those in conflict-affected and poor countries, since keeping the younger generations engaged in the lives of their communities there is perhaps an ever trickier and more necessary task than elsewhere.

Have Patience But Be Strategic About It: The Symbolism of Fragile-to-Fragile Cooperation (F2F)

When you believe in something, it can feel personal, and it can be discouraging to realize others do not. How can they not see what you see? But if you believe enough, if something is sacred for you because of what it offers now or what it can achieve in future, then it is usually advisable to keep a long-term perspective, accept that the journey will involve losing sometimes, not to mention repeating yourself to different people, showing the benefits of the plan over and over again. Not everyone can afford to be patient, not everyone knows how, so there is a lot to be said for those who can put patience at the service of strategy.

---

22   Ibid.
23   Ibid.

'In the g7+, they have strategic patience. I think the Timorese are good at that. They fought for independence for 25 years. And they were determined to survive. They survived in the mountains!'[24] If we consider that, at the end of this long process, there was reconciliation, the path is even more remarkable. Individually, most people in the g7+ have had to be stubborn to get to where they are and do the work they do. But we are talking here about something more than stubbornness, because, of course, many people are stubborn in many places. What is interesting is that, along with stubbornness, there is key strategic thinking too. *Just as life was not only about survival but about doing something meaningful, so it is not enough to have patience, but having patience in order to achieve something.*

When former Prime Minister of Timor-Leste and Eminent Person of the g7+ Xanana Gusmão says, 'We did not fight for our independence just to lose ownership of our development',[25] then just as for the g7+, at stake is the ability not to be discouraged by the slowness of change, nor to settle comfortably halfway through the journey—both equally important.

So what were the strategies at play? And what do the members of the g7+ have to be patient for?

Abie, the focal point for Sierra Leone, says what she has had in mind is 'the responsibility for millions of people living in poverty', for which reason, she declares that her work 'was and *is* very fulfilling', even if sometimes it is also frustrating. Her engagement with the g7+ started in 2012, after the major changes brought about by the meeting in Busan. The first meeting Abie attended was in Dili, at the beginning of 2013: 'I was sceptical, also a bit ignorant about the g7+. But I heard Helder speaking, he provided the energy, and the issues resonated with our problems. I became so engaged with the g7+ that soon people at the ministry were calling me "Abie, the g7+". I worked under four ministers; not many showed interest at first. But this is my passion and it drives them to pay attention. Sometimes in a meeting, they hear me. I soon became synonymous with the g7+'.[26]

---

24   Interview with Peter Lloyd, 30 March 2020.
25   g7+ (2016). *Strength in fragility: "We are writing our own history"*, The emergence of the g7+ group from our own perspective, p. 5.
26   Interview with Abie Elizabeth Kamara, 19 March 2020.

Abie describes how she went about convincing people within the government of the merit of being part of the g7+: 'I always said "you may not want to be called fragile, but look at the priorities [the g7+] established, these are all issues we struggle with." That was how I pitched to the ministers'.[27]

Fragility Assessments

The g7+ created Fragility Assessments as part of the FOCUS principles of the New Deal. The goal was for member countries to measure themselves. A Fragility Spectrum was proposed, not as a template for monitoring, but as something open for construction. 'The fragility spectrum is intended to put fragile states themselves — their governments and civil society — in the driving seat in terms of articulating what fragility has looked like, and continues to look like, in their experience and how to move to the next stage of resilience. Fragility is experienced differently in different country contexts as well as in different stages of a country's path to resilience. These differences should be reflected in the strategies designed to support transition out of fragility.' Based on an open Fragility Spectrum, the Fragility Assessment, in principle,

- is a diagnostic tool, drawing on local knowledge, to facilitate a self-assessment process;

- enables a more nuanced approach to the PSGs;

- aims to track incremental progress, and to assist countries in the development of their own targets and goals, while at the same time providing an overview of the overall path towards resilience;

- can help governments, civil society and donors to focus their attention on context-specific indicators — as opposed to the common indicators;

- offers an opportunity for the understanding and monitoring of fragility to be determined by fragile states themselves.

However, as shown in the *2019 Independent Review of the g7+*, implementation of the Fragility Assessment has been difficult, because it requires buy-in across the government, which is hampered by the fact that the g7+ still operates mostly within Finance Ministries and by the frequent changes in some governments. In addition, there are too many templates circulating and capacity is limited.

(See: g7+ (2013). *Fragility Spectrum*, pp. 5–6; Rocha de Siqueira, I. (2019). *Independent Review of the g7+*.)

---

27   Ibid.

Abie ended up coordinating the first g7+ Fragility Assessment, in 2012 (see Annex III). 'Sierra Leone was the first country in the g7+ to do it. We didn't have much capacity. UNDP provided assistance, sending two consultants. We went all over the country. People understood fragility differently: "it's when you're hungry...", "it's when you're sick...", "it's when your country is dependent...". The challenge is that people expect the money to go towards the problems they listed. At the time, 60% of Sierra Leone's budget relied on international assistance'.

It can be hard work, pitching what you believe *and* doing a lot of extra labour to show its value in practice: 'It is additional work, it takes passion to keep things afloat. It takes determination, but it's our responsibility. *We have to have patience.* Sometimes I get frustrated and think of [handing things over] to another person, but then the focus will change, it will not be the one I have'. Frustration sometimes comes not only from others resisting your passionate appeals, but when the thing you are fighting for pushes you so far that you feel like no one is an ally: 'Sometimes I do want to address things quickly as soon as someone asks it to be done. But it doesn't always depend on me, and you can't give ministers an ultimatum, you can't push. Sometimes, working with the g7+, they need something quick, like a go-ahead on a speech, but I'm doing [this] all on the side and I can't push people. Sometimes, pressure and deadlines like this make me want to give up. And then people here also say I only talk about the g7+'.[28]

At this point in the conversation, she quickly begins to reminisce: 'At that first meeting of the g7+, I was really inspired by Helder and Emilia. I saw the passion, I saw the commitment of that country to help others. I was so convinced. Then I get frustrated. And one day, I get a call from Helder, he will say: "No, my *sister*..."'.[29] That is where she stops for a second, at that word, 'sister'; it seems to mean a lot to her. She goes on then, '... he says "these issues are important." And Emilia kept in touch too, even after she left Freetown after the meeting, in 2014'.[30]

It was also in 2014 that some countries in Africa faced the Ebola virus. Out of four countries affected by the disease in the first months, three were g7+ member countries: Guinea, Liberia, and Sierra Leone (the

---

28   Ibid.
29   Ibid.
30   Ibid.

OH, MY SISTER...
THESE ARE IMPORTANT
MATTERS...

disease would eventually reach nine countries in total). 'In the spirit of solidarity, and understanding from experience how crises such as these can set back hard-won progress, Timor-Leste donated USD $2 million to the Governments of Guinea, Liberia, and Sierra Leone under what would be called by the g7+ the Fragile-to-Fragile cooperation (F2F). In line with New Deal principles, Timor-Leste channelled the funds through the national systems of the three recipient countries to address the Ebola epidemic'.[31]

The g7+'s initiative was perceived as a response to the slowness of traditional donors. In 2014, Habib wrote an article commenting on the situation: 'Although there have recently been some pledges to help these countries fight Ebola, the initial slow move to help Ebola-affected

---

31   g7+ (n.d.). *7 Things to Know About Fragile-to-Fragile (F2F) Cooperation.* p. 3.

countries is shocking. With such a severe crisis at hand, one would have expected a more rapid response from the international community'.[32] This was clearly a case when waiting patiently for the 'international community' to react was not an option. At the same time, the g7+ initiated an important strategy of mutual support in the form of F2F, which, with all its limitations, seems to be highly valued by those involved.

At the time, the president of Liberia had called on the international community to come up with 'actions rather than theories to stop these countries experiencing such human tragedies'.[33] Non-Governmental Organisations were also denouncing the slow response of the international community: Médecins Sans Frontières (MSF), the main organisation (and, for a long time, the only one) on the front line, said in their 2015 report on Ebola that 'the international effort to stem the outbreak remained inadequate [in the first months of the epidemic in 2014], with MSF teams seeing gaps in all aspects of the response... Large-scale international assistance was finally deployed towards the end of 2014, when case numbers also began to decline'.[34] MSF had raised the alarm in March 2014, being called alarmists. In June, the situation was catastrophic, but again, international leadership was not up to the task. In September, a doctor from the organization did what was unthinkable before: instead of steering well clear of politics, they gave a speech to the UN Security Council.

Finally, then, and for the first time, the UN created a *health mission* to be sent to the region. However, the international response was still slow and limited, as a report shows, and people were terrified.[35] Timor-Leste's symbolic help came in September and October. Meanwhile, the MSF report states that '[i]n December, the international response was striving to deliver what had been promised three months before'.[36]

---

32 Mayar, Habib Ur Rehman (2014). 'The Journey Towards Resilience Continues: g7+ Priorities to Confront Ebola, Implement the New Deal and Influence the Post-2015 Agenda'. *Journal of Peacebuilding & Development*, 9(3), 122–26, p. 123.

33 Ibid.

34 MSF (2015). *An unprecedented year: Médecins Sans Frontières's response to the largest Ebola outbreak.* https://www.doctorswithoutborders.org/latest/unprecedented-year-msfs-response-largest-ever-ebola-outbreak.

35 MSF (2015). *Pushed to the Limit and Beyond: A year into the largest ever Ebola outbreak.* https://www.msf.org/ebola-pushed-limit-and-beyond, p. 7.

36 Ibid., p. 15.

It is not only a matter of what was done when but rather, it seems, why more was not done before, when major international actors had been called upon to intervene and had all the means to do so. When one case appeared in the United States and one in Spain the disease was considered an international security threat: 'The lack of international political will was no longer an option when the realisation dawned that Ebola could cross the ocean'.[37] Unfortunately, that cruel realization is unavoidable in the daily business of international cooperation: 'Letting [people] die, I want to stress, is not a counterfactual'.[38] By brief comparison with the situation at the time of writing, data on vaccination against COVID-19 showed that, in January 2022, 67% of the population in richer nations had been fully vaccinated, whereas only 8% in poorer nations had received their first dose.[39] Although several countries and organisations have pledged support to poorer countries,[40] this inequality is shocking and evident in several instances. When the COVAX Facility finally delivered several doses of immunization to poor countries at the end of 2021, for instance, 100 million doses were rejected by these governments due to an imminent expiration date after having been rejected by other countries. The fact that many countries are donating doses to COVAX Facility that have a very short shelf life has been a huge problem. That delay in action is now resulting in existing shots being thrown away. The Facility is also late to invest in storage capacity in poor countries.

In the case of Ebola, until June 2016, 'a total of 28,616 Ebola cases ha[d] been reported in Guinea, Liberia and Sierra Leone, with 11,310 deaths', and 'there [we]re over 10,000 survivors of Ebola virus disease'.[41]

---

37 Ibid., p. 11.
38 Li, Tania Murray (2010). 'To Make Live or Let Die? Rural Dispossession and the Protection of Surplus Populations'. *Antipode*, 41(1), 66–93, p. 66.
39 Guarascio, Francesco (2022). *Poorer nations reject over 100 mln COVID-19 vaccine doses as many near expiry*. https://www.reuters.com/business/healthcare-pharmaceuticals/more-than-100-million-covid-19-vaccines-rejected-by-poorer-nations-dec-unicef-2022-01-13/.
40 World Bank (2021). *Global Community Steps Up with $93 Billion Support Package to Boost Resilient Recovery in World's Poorest Countries*. https://www.worldbank.org/en/news/press-release/2021/12/15/global-community-steps-up-with-93-billion-support-package-to-boost-resilient-recovery-in-world-s-poorest-countries; United Nations (2021). *"Time for action" to support most fragile States: Guterres*. https://news.un.org/en/story/2021/10/1102752; International Monetary Fund (IMF) (2022). *COVID-19 Financial Assistance and Debt Service Relief*. https://www.imf.org/en/Topics/imf-and-covid19/COVID-Lending-Tracker#CCRT.
41 See World Health Organization (n.d.). *Ebola outbreak 2014–2016*. https://www.who.int/emergencies/situations/ebola-outbreak-2014-2016-West-Africa.

Abie remembers all this well: 'When we had Ebola here, I felt so proud of being part of the g7+. These are the benefits you get. I saw Fragile-to-Fragile cooperation at work: two million dollars from Timor-Leste, from a fragile state also! If they're so interested, why wouldn't we be? I remember they said: "We provide what we can because we have to make sure fragile countries help one another"'.[42]

Now we see the experience of fighting Ebola at that time was crucial to the current efforts against COVID-19 (and of course, this was not only the case with F2F funding).

With Antonio, in turn, F2F came as an endorsement of his choice to patiently engage with a group that, when he enrolled Guinea-Bissau, was still in its infancy.

In 2013, Guinea-Bissau's government requested support from the g7+ to organize elections. 'Timor-Leste established a Support Office focused on administration, finance and logistics in Guinea-Bissau and provided a Technical and Advisory Support Team to the voter registration process'. In addition, Timorese personnel helped organise training, conduct education campaigns to encourage voting, and prepare polling stations, among other activities. Consequently, the organisation of elections ended up costing $6 million instead of the $40 million estimated by international donors.[43]

> For me, fragile-to-fragile cooperation seems disinterested, a win-win process. It was based on historical relations between the countries, as in the 70s, Guinea-Bissau supported Timor's independence from Portugal. We treat ourselves as brothers. There is cooperation because the realities are similar, both coming out of conflicts. Besides the resources they offered in 2013, the cooperation served to raise special awareness among the Bissau-Guinean people: "If Timor-Leste managed it, we can." Because we *could* compare to Timor-Leste's experience just about ten years before. This motivates us. It is also a matter of trust and self-esteem.[44]

Antonio is definitely among the most positive voices and always speaks of F2F and the g7+ with admiration. Here, what is important is what the

---

42   Interview with Abie Elizabeth Kamara, 19 March 2020.
43   2019 Independent review of the g7+, p. 71.
44   Interview with Antonio Co, 11 June 2019.

experience meant for those professionals, what it delivered in terms of means, not as an end in itself. After all, two million dollars is a meagre sum in terms of international cooperation, for instance, but what people in the g7+ say about their brief experience with F2F is more valuable for the kind of motivation it provides on a daily basis to those who often feel disconnected and abandoned by other partners.

During the 5th g7+ Ministerial Meeting held in Lisbon, in 2019 (see Annex IV), a member of Parliament from Timor-Leste took the microphone to say a few similar words: 'It's not about being a big or small donor. We are fulfilling our role. We are only independent because the international community helped. We are aware of that, that's why we want to help. Peace in Timor-Leste is not for political consumption, it is faith. Peace needs to come from ourselves. It's in the language and the attitude'.[45]

Antonio recalls proudly: 'I visited Timor-Leste five times; I even met the president. I felt the warmth of friendship', he says, with what sounds like deeply felt camaraderie.[46]

Nevertheless, *strategic change can never be born out of the achievements of one person only*; part of the difficult task of the group, and the goal set by most of its members for themselves, is to translate these personal victories and the political will they display in the g7+ into substantive changes on the ground. In any case, it seems some '"kinship producing, world constituting" elements'[47] are present that, *if not directly transformative on the ground, cannot be dismissed either, as they offer the possibility of effecting structural changes, even if limited*. Change, even in initiating something like F2F, take time; structural changes take a lot of time and a lot of patience.

In terms of keeping public policy going at challenging times, such moments are less about the resources available and more about burying the sense of helplessness that these professionals have fought against so often. It is about kindling people's sense of strategy as well as their patience, to offer a vision of what can be.

---

45   David Dias Ximenes, at the g7+ Ministerial Meeting, 26 June 2019, Lisbon.
46   Interview with Antonio Co, 11 June 2019.
47   Muppidi as cited in *Meanings of Bandung*, p. 9.

Seize and Multiply Opportunities for Yourself and Others: The Paths Towards Greater Equality

'The kind of opportunity I had in Afghanistan I wouldn't have had anywhere else'.[48] This is how Naheed Sarabi describes her path so far. She is young and her first contact with the g7+ was in 2019, when she was also appointed co-chair of the group. Before moving forward with this story, it is important that we pause here, because, among the many challenges faced by the g7+ and, therefore, of significance when trying to finish this book, was the takeover of Afghanistan by the Taliban in August 2021. That represented a tragedy for many, and, while it is beyond the scope of this book to report on the terrible losses of that period, it is important to mention that the impacts have been huge. While the 20 years of democracy were not without troubles for Afghanistan, in August 2021, the dreams of many young people were shattered. While Afghanistan has undergone regime change by force before, the new generation could never have imagined such a change as this, according to Habib. Education for girls and women, for instance, was at first forbidden, then allowed so long as classes are not mixed, which effectively curtailed the right to education of many girls and women, as there are not enough female teachers available. After the takeover, the international community has frozen assets and suspended access to donor funds and emergency loans. Estimates are that nearly 900,000 jobs have been lost already, and, with food prices on the rise, many families are in extremely vulnerable situations.[49] In general, 2021 was an extremely testing time for the g7+: in addition to COVID-19 and the rise of the Taliban in Afghanistan, three of the 20 member states have seen coups or attempted coups: Guinea-Bissau, Guinea and Chad.[50]

In the face of such events, we do well to remember that solutions were found before and others can, hopefully, be found as well.

The speed with which Naheed was appointed co-chair of the g7+ testifies to her skills and character, but also to the existence of a certain

---

48   Interview with Naheed Sarabi, 03 March 2020.

49   Human Rights Watch (2022). *Afghanistan: Events of 2021*. https://www.hrw. org/world-report/2022/country-chapters/afghanistan; United Nations (2022). *Afghanistan: 500,000 jobs lost since Taliban takeover*. UN News. https://news.un.org/ en/story/2022/01/1110052.

50   Mwai, Peter (2022). *Are military takeovers on the rise in Africa?* BBC News. https:// www.bbc.co.uk/news/world-africa-46783600.

pattern, present in the life of a generation that has faced particular challenges, of nurturing opportunities. It is a good time to remind oneself that this can be done. These countries have faced conflict and instability before, and while it is horrible to live through them yet again, there is knowledge to build back from.

In 1996, Naheed and her family left Afghanistan as refugees and went to Pakistan like so many other families, staying there for a few years. In her family, girls had always received an education. Her mother was a lecturer in a medical institute. But by the time they left Afghanistan, unlike the opportunities her two brothers would have, home-schooling was her only option—which was another reason why her family migrated. Later, in 2001, many Afghans went back to their home country, but Naheed stayed behind in Pakistan to finish school. They always went to visit, though; her father did not want the children to feel disconnected from Afghanistan. However, going back to a relative's wedding, for instance, meant crossing the Camel Path and walking around 30 minutes on foot on unpaved roads. At one point, during one of those visits, Naheed asked her mother why they had to go to Pakistan. 'We had it better than other refugees, but it was still being a refugee', Naheed explains, justifying the question she posed to her mother. 'My mother said, "Next time you can stay if you want" but I had seen two women being whipped and I knew women had a difficult time under the Taliban', she says.[51] The family was determined that everyone should have the best education possible: 'My family was middle class and all were well educated even before the war. My paternal grandfather had been in the army and studied engineering in the Soviet Union'.[52]

That is why, perhaps, when she finished her studies in Pakistan, she did not consider finally joining her family back in Afghanistan; she knew conditions for her would still be challenging. She decided to go to college in India. Naheed says she missed her family very much, but that whenever they spoke on the phone, her mother never told her to 'come back'. When I asked her about what she feels she sacrificed staying away from her family, she says simply, 'I know that what is a sacrifice for some is a privilege for others'.[53]

---

51 Interview with Naheed Sarabi, 03 March 2020.
52 Ibid.
53 Ibid.

LIFE IS AN IRON. THE MORE YOU HIT IT, THE HARDEST IT IS. IF YOU ARE SOFT to it, IT'S SOFT.

She adds 'I remember my grandfather used to say something... I'm not sure I can translate well to English but it was something like that: "Life is like an iron; the more you hit it, the hardest it is; if you're soft to it, then it is soft"'.[54] His meaning, it seems, was that one needs to embrace opportunities, sure, but difficulties sometimes too, as a key part of a learning process. Fighting and resisting sometimes might make life unbearable. There is an incredibly sensitive balance in that.

She then went on to get two other degrees: an MA in Development Management from Ruhr University-Bochum, in Germany, and an MA in Applied Economics from Western Michigan University in the United States. When she returned to her country in 2010, it was as a volunteer intern, because she wanted to have experience in applying what she had been studying. 'I like to do hands-on work, something practical, and to see the practical solutions. I started as a volunteer in the Ministry of Finance, following the ministerial retreat that was discussing the National Development Strategy, which was under construction. Then they invited me to join the Ministry. I did, and after two or three months, I was promoted to manager. In 2011, I became acting Director, taking

---

54   Ibid.

care of the development of 22 National Priority Programs. So in between 2010 and 2013, I went from intern to director of Afghanistan National Development Strategy (ANDS)'.[55] Soon she would become the Deputy Minister for Policy in the Ministry of Finance. That is a very steep learning curve.

When Naheed started as a volunteer, the Ministry of Finance was working hard on reporting implementation of Afghanistan's first Poverty Reduction Strategy Paper (PRSP) to the World Bank and the International Monetary Fund (IMF). It was also a key step in terms of fulfilling obligations towards the Enhanced Initiative for Heavily Indebted Poor Countries (HIPC) and the Multilateral Debt Relief Initiative (MDRI). These were all crucial factors for pacifying donors.

> I was very aware I was part of the first generation that was participating in government right after the war. There were very few women working as first- or second-rank civil servants. By the time I became a director, I was the only woman at MoF in senior rank, and very young. At the beginning nobody listened to me; it was a big challenge convincing people of new approaches, but I eventually made myself heard. Yet sometimes I doubted I could deliver. When I became a director, there was no one at middle-level for two to three years. Sometimes I got agitated, nervous before a meeting, but then I calmed down when it was time to speak, and I realized I was in a position of power.[56]

As Naheed says, there were many challenges for the new generation, which were surely at times overwhelming considering what was at stake: 'I wanted to contribute to reconstruct my country. You see the changes so much more. That compels you. Of course, there are many challenges and sometimes you feel things don't change,' she concedes. Naheed was the only national in her team at the beginning: 'I had the mentoring of international colleagues and my bosses. I had a lot of respect at the time from my superiors; I guess I even took it for granted. They gave me leverage and encouragement. We didn't have that many women willing to come back, but I also had the skills and could deliver. Yet, things could have been different if it were today; there are many more educated women now'.[57]

---

55 Ibid.
56 Ibid.
57 Ibid.

Naheed recounts: 'I would often stay until late in the office, like 9pm, which was very unusual for a woman, maybe not rare, but unusual. I was very interested; I worked hard'.[58]

Debt Relief

The World Bank's website says of the HIPC: 'The World Bank, the International Monetary Fund (IMF) and other multilateral, bilateral and commercial creditors began the Heavily Indebted Poor Country (HIPC) Initiative in 1996. The program was designed to ensure that the poorest countries in the world are not overwhelmed by unmanageable or unsustainable debt burdens. It reduces the debt of countries meeting strict criteria.' As of 2022, 37 countries have benefitted from HIPC and Multilateral Debt Relief Initiative (MDRI) programs and around $100 billion in debt have been relieved. 'To be eligible for the HIPC Initiative a country must:

- Face unsustainable debt situation after the full the full application of the traditional debt relief mechanisms (such as the application of Naples terms under the Paris Club agreement).

- Be only eligible for highly concessional assistance from the International Development Association (IDA) and from the IMF's Poverty Reduction and Growth Trust (PGRT).

- Have established a track record of reform and sound policies through IMF and World Bank supported programs.

- Establish a track record of reform and develops a Poverty Reduction Strategy Paper (PRSP) that involves civil society participation.'

For Afghanistan, at Completion Point, in 2010, the HIPC assistance in nominal terms was estimated at US$1.3 billion. 'Upon reaching the completion point under the enhanced HIPC Initiative, Afghanistan will also qualify for additional debt relief under the Multilateral Debt Relief Initiative (MDRI). Debt relief under the MDRI from IDA would reduce nominal debt service by US$38.4 million over a period of 33 years.'

(See: World Bank. 'Heavily Indebted Poor Country (HIPC) Initiative', at https://www.worldbank.org/en/topic/debt/brief/hipc; World Bank (2010). 'Islamic Republic of Afghanistan. Enhanced Heavily-Indebted Poor Countries (HIPC) Initiative - Completion Point Document and Multilateral Debt Relief Initiative (MDRI)'. For a critique, see: George, Susan. 'How the Poor Develop the Rich', in Rahnema, Majid and Bawtree, Victoria (1997). *The Post-Development Reader*. London & New Jersey: Zed Books, ch. 20.)

---

58   Ibid.

Unfortunately, as of the beginning of 2022, the interim cabinet of Taliban included no women and no ministers from outside its own ranks.[59] Sadly, Naheed has left the country.

In 2019, when Naheed attended the 5th g7+ Ministerial Meeting, in Lisbon, it was her first contact with the group. Habib, as a fellow national, not to mention deputy secretary-general of the g7+, briefed her at the airport. Afghanistan was the logical option for g7+ deputy-chair, so, on the last day, Naheed was appointed, the chairing being confirmed with H. E. Dr. Francis Mustapha Kai-Kai, Minister of Planning and Economic Development of Sierra Leone. Naheed admitted she had not had the chance to act much within the g7+ when we spoke, but, commenting on her lessons from that first meeting, she said, 'The one thing I always say is that we can't fall for the victimization narrative; this happens, I saw some of it there. But for me, I always think "Count your blessings, think of the changes *you* can bring"'.[60] Tellingly, she finished the conversation saying she wanted to act more and be of use to the group. It is even more painful now to look back at these words, considering she will no longer be able to attend the g7+ as the deputy chair or representative of the country. It remains to be seen what the future holds.[61]

For Abie, the g7+ offered a similar opportunity. She had earned it by supporting the g7+ and lobbying for her government's engagement from within her ministry. In 2014, her minister, in turn, convinced the President to host the 4th IDPS meeting: 'This involved costs, of course. We had IDPS ministers, civil society representatives, the g7+ members. It was challenging, but it was fun', she recalls. (Why shouldn't it be?) She continues: 'There were many challenges managing the logistics. Ebola was in the outskirts of Freetown and donors were sceptical. Some people didn't want to come. We had to secure visas on arrival'. A while after that, her minister became IDPS co-chair and g7+ co-chair representative and she became Adviser to the Minister on the g7+ and IDPS, which she says is a chance a woman does not get often, in her experience. She has been a civil servant for more than 25 years: 'Women

---

59   Human Rights Watch, op. cit.
60   Ibid.
61   Al Jazeera (2022). *Taliban delegation holds talks with EU, US diplomats in Doha*. https://www.aljazeera.com/news/2022/2/16/taliban-meets-with-eu-us-in-bid-to-unlock-funds-for-afghanistan.

Poverty Reduction Strategy Papers (PRSPs)

In 2002, the World Bank changed its discourse towards a renewed focus on outcomes and results and the monitoring of progress towards the MDGs, as part of an increased focus on poverty reduction. For this purpose, the Bank created the much-debated Poverty Reduction Strategy Papers (PRSP), which, together with the existent Country Assistance Strategy (CAS), would provide a refined analysis of a country's initial scenario, allowing for better planning and monitoring of progress.

The CAS was already in use to determine risks, goals and indicators for each project, with an overview of the country's situations. The PRSPs were supposed to add an element of ownership, since the strategy for poverty reduction would be aligned with the country's own priorities and plans, as stated in national strategic papers. The PRSPs would have three pillars: prioritising public actions; managing resources with efficiency, transparency and accountability; and establishing M&E of progress.

In terms of the many critiques directed at the template, the PRSPs were accused of being an expansion and repetition of the Structural Adjustments Programs (SAP) of the 1980s. Moreover, critics accused the World Bank and IMF, with whom the Bank partnered for the PRSPs, of imposing priorities rather than obeying the ownership principle that the PRSPs were supposed to follow—the PRSPs were accompanied by a 1,260-page sourcebook.

There were other important obstacles to 'true ownership': Malaluan and Guttal point, for example, to the issue of language, as most PRSPs were not translated into the local language and, thus, were inaccessible to most local communities and NGOs, and made work more difficult even for senior officers.

(See Rocha de Siqueira, I. (2017). Op. cit., pp. 94–95; International Development Association (IDA) (2002). 'Additions to IDA Resources: Thirteenth Replenishment. Supporting Poverty Reduction Strategies'. Washington: World Bank; Malaluan, Jenina Joy Chavez and Shalmali Guttal (2003). 'Poverty Reduction Strategy Papers: A Poor Package for Poverty Reduction'. *Focus on the Global South*; Cornwall, Andrea and Karen Brock (2006). 'What do buzzwords do for development policy? a critical look at "participation", "empowerment" and "poverty reduction"'. *Third World Quarterly*, 26(7), 1043–1060.)

often have to do 10 times the work men do to be acknowledged, and sometimes at home, this is difficult. So it was a good opportunity'.[62]

---

62   Interview with Abie Elizabeth Kamara, 19 March 2020.

At this point we can stop to consider Siafa's words in one of our conversations: 'Maybe we need less speaking and more action. I learned a lot about how people actually behave. Dealing with politicians, for instance, they are often charismatic, but do they live extravagant lives? Asking questions like this, observing what people *do*, that's how I was brought up and what I learned from experience'.[63] Bearing that in mind, it is telling then, even if that is *all* we can conclude, that there is a certain pattern to the stories some people in the g7+ told us, a pattern of mutual respect and a common concern with seizing and multiplying opportunities as a mission

Helche, for instance, after a crash course on the g7+'s activities when she got the job, in 2015, says 'I learned a lot from them. I travel sometimes with Helder and Habib; we go to the US four or five times a year. I learned a lot about how they negotiate. And they push me to the limits of my creativity. The first newsletter I produced, they helped me directly. Habib and Helder have been very supportive'.[64]

In 2017, she was 19 weeks into pregnancy with her first baby when she travelled to Washington, D.C., where she would meet Habib, who was flying from New York. 'I guess I had been sitting for too long because of the flight. When I came to the queue for passport control, I fainted just before it was my turn and was taken to hospital. I had no one in Washington, D.C., in principle, but I remembered a friend from college in Australia and that her parents lived there. I called and his mother came to collect me from hospital. In the meantime, I talked to Habib over the phone. He was so nervous and worried', she laughs softly.[65] This is what she remembered when I asked her about what it was like being a mother in the middle of all the travelling and the extremely challenging work. She is completely at ease speaking of Helder and Habib, with whom she shares a one-room office in Dili.

'Later on, when I had already had my son, I used to travel and always tried to pump breast milk. For example, before boarding a plane, I would talk to the stewards to ask if I could store the milk in the fridge, which they all gladly agreed to do. It helped, keeping the milk frozen, same when I was in transit. I just wanted to make sure my son received

---

63   Interview with Siafa Hage, 10 March 2020.
64   Interview with Helche Silvester, 05 March 2020.
65   Ibid.

exclusively breastmilk for his first 6 months before shifting to a formula. It used to drive Habib nuts; he used to say, "You do too much, you don't need to search all this". It was funny', she laughs again; they seem to be good friends. Helche continues: 'My husband has his own business. And because I'm the only child, by custom, we live with my parents. My husband is very supportive, that's how I manage. It's worth it. Working with the g7+ opens my view to the world. I started reading about what's happening in the world, in our member countries', she says excitedly.[66]

It might be considered an achievement in itself to offer opportunities to people, like our characters in all these stories. But they themselves would not consider it nearly enough if these did not translate into as much positive change as possible in their own countries. Nevertheless, in times when basic equality in many places is under attack, it is a very good message indeed, to *walk the line*. What else can be harnessed from all these examples of survival, patience and dedication? And what are the possible pitfalls?

Make Changes and See Things Through

Survival is a key skill, especially after war, violence and all kinds of crises. This is, to varying degrees and with many differences among them, something people in the g7+ seem to have in common. This is certainly something to be valued, understood and harnessed, not least because current times present unique challenges in every aspect of life. But, as Siafa cautioned, 'it can't be just about surviving. It's about what you do with it'. He continues: 'I remember a friend wrote when I was in the US. We were children and he was mentioning the war in the letter...I still keep it. It means a lot to me'.[67] (See Fig. 2.) This is the same reasoning Naheed emphasised when she spoke about the need to think about how one can change things. The bottom line seems to be that surviving is about strength; it requires skills and purpose; it requires, as we suggested, making something sacred and fighting for it, as a guiding force. Siafa again suggests that 'surviving always leaves behind some guilt about the ones who haven't survived'.[68] Perhaps the key is in doing

---

66   Ibid.
67   Interview with Siafa Hage, 10 March 2020.
68   Ibid.

good in response to that guilt and moving forward, not alone, but with others.

Indeed, the lesson here might be to value one's own opportunities by really seizing them, but also helping to multiply them and making structural changes so that having opportunities is a *tendency*, reaching as many people as possible. With that in mind, there is much that can be explored in terms of mentorship within and outside the g7+, as we will see ahead.

This is the very nature of an anti-victimization narrative. However, going beyond the position in which you find yourself requires patience. This brings us back to the survival skills of our characters: if patience is a must for anyone to survive, one requires the driving force of *strategy* in order to overcome passivity—not *just* surviving, but doing something with one's life. The old universally known idea that 'nothing worthy comes easy' holds true here, especially when it involves politics.

It would be cruel to say that surviving is easy or that patience is basic; they are not. That only makes the fact that these characters are insisting upon building something—and something in common—a point of merit, especially after witnessing a sequence of setbacks. Nevertheless, this needs to be constantly reiterated: patience can only be a *means* to something of political relevance, not an end itself, not an endless practice.

Just as Antonio taught us, *seeing things through*, finishing them, is its own form of peace and stability.

How to Use Your Survival Skills: On Patience and Opportunities

1. Find something sacred and go beyond survival.

2. Have patience but be strategic about it.

3. Seize and multiply opportunities for yourself and others.

4. Make changes and see things through.

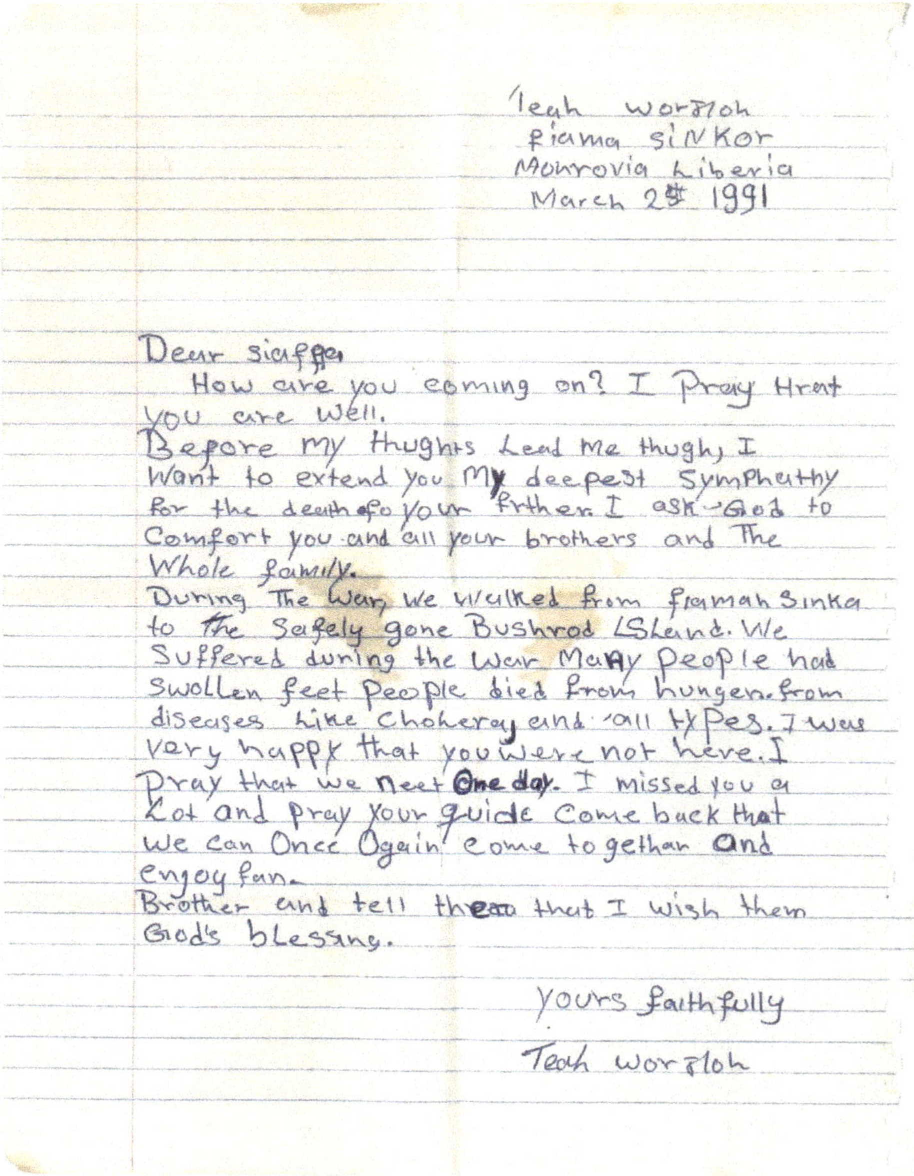

Teah Worloh
Plama Sinkor
Monrovia Liberia
March 2nd 1991

Dear Siaffei
    How are you coming on? I pray that
you are well.
Before my thoughts lead me though, I
want to extend you my deepest Symphathy
for the death of your brthen. I ask God to
Comfort you and all your brothers and The
Whole family.
During The war, We walked from Plamah Sinka
to the Safely gone Bushrod Island. We
Suffered during the war Many people had
Swollen feet people died from hunger, from
diseases like Choheray and all types. I was
very happy that you were not here. I
Pray that we meet One day. I missed you a
Lot and pray your guide Come back that
We can Once Ogain come togethan and
enjoy fun.
Brother and tell them that I wish them
God's blessing.

                    yours faithfully
                    Teah Worloh

Fig. 2 Letter from an 11-year-old friend that Siafa Hage received while already
living in the US.

4. How to Work with Passion
On the Value of Doing Things Together

In the Land of the Fisherman
Finding bait is a worry that torments me
But I only have enough for me, and I am young
But truly, I only have enough for me, and I am young
And to be alone in a canoe is to be powerless....
—Song from Comoros Islands.[1]

This is how Missy Stephens, an international advisor who spent quite a long time supporting the Timorese leadership and the initial work of the g7+, describes her expectations about the group at the very beginning: 'I had been around a lot, supporting international processes, the Millennium Development Goals... and I could see there was a big disconnect. It was clear [that] all that was not helpful. When the g7+ was being created, all I could think was "If the g7+ doesn't happen, nothing will", because their existence was a microcosm of everything that was going on with development. The first two years were painful, I didn't think the group would make it. And I thought all the time, "If they [donors] would only listen! The people who know are the ones who survived. If donors would listen, development might have a chance'.[2] She was later responsible for inviting over Peter Lloyd, a renowned Australian war correspondent, to lead the group's communication team.

This was all news to Peter: 'I had no idea what the g7+ was about. But then I realized it was about social justice. It was social justice in action.

---

1   In Said Ahmed, Moussa & Walker, Iain (2011). 'Two Fisherman's Songs'. *Wasari*, 26(2), p. 60.
2   Interview with Missy Stephens, 12 March 2020.

    https://doi.org/10.11647/OBP.0311.04

I didn't go in with that impression, but that's how I left'. Nevertheless, in our conversations, Peter's was perhaps the most critical voice, and this says a lot. Peter finished his contract frustrated by the lack of more robust changes. I think it is important to start with that, even if it sounds oddly negative, precisely because working with passion is vital for certain lines of work, but it has its own difficulties. Although Peter suggests that changes on the ground, and structural transformations, did not happen as much as he would have liked, nevertheless at the end of our conversation he says that the worst that can happen is for the g7+ to adopt the managerialism he sees elsewhere: 'Managerialism is toxic. We need to have a conversation about *values* in those rooms'.[3] The reason I start with Missy and Peter, who are not part of our main cohort of characters, is that, being born into American and Australian cultural codes, theirs is a peculiar position when they speak of what the g7+ is *not* and *should not* be: more business-as-usual.

Along with the promise of alternative solutions and the constant passionate undertone is always the fact that 'alternatives' and passion are bound to fall short in fulfilling their promises. Yet, without that, there might be no changes at all. I find it useful here to remember what a long-time critic of business as usual once said: 'The world needs to build all possible strategies that allow [us] to lay down the ground for change...That change will not come if we simply wait for developed countries to solve their problems, forgetting about the interdependent and unequal nature of the international economy'.[4] To build 'all possible strategies' when these are so often insufficient or even stillborn requires considerable motivation and courage. But then, the world is full of good intentions and little change. How do we judge which alternatives are worth a passionate investment?

When the g7+ was established, its overall ambitions were big: 'The g7+ was formed to work in concert with international actors, the private sector, civil society, the media and the people across countries, borders and regions to reform and reinvent a new paradigm for international engagement'.[5] Moreover, the specific goal with which the g7+ was

---

3   Peter Lloyd.
4   Acosta, Alberto (2018). *O Bem Viver*. São Paulo: Editora Elefante, p. 218 (my translation).
5   g7+ brochure (English version).

founded was 'to stop conflict, build nations and eradicate poverty through innovative development strategies, harmonized to the country context, aligned to the national agenda and led by the State and its People'.[6] That meant that the group wanted to both achieve important changes on the ground—especially since member countries had been suffering heavily with poverty, conflict, and violence—and to fundamentally modify donor behaviour, making cooperation in international development more equal and changing the narrative around 'fragility' to focus more on taking ownership of issues and on national leadership.[7] Even if one were to narrow these objectives down to a few practical and specific issues or targets, they would still be very difficult to attain.

Anyone trying to address the many obstacles to peace and happiness (it seems this word applies better than 'stability') in the 20 g7+ member countries will have to be driven by some kind of strong purpose, and will require support, peer-learning, an exchange of experiences and much solidarity, at least on the part of those whom one considers 'brothers and sisters' in their common trajectories. Indeed, there are many things one normally does not do alone. Being in a room full of 'international experts', for instance, can be a lonely experience, so one would be grateful for reinforcements, a sympathetic face pushing one to intervene, or to break protocols or expectations, if necessary. 'It happened often: when one of them [g7+ representatives] got into a room for a meeting, it would be *one* of them and dozens of donor representatives. We were always fighting to make it more even', Missy recalls.[8] This is coming from a former advisor to the g7+, but it is widely acknowledged by others as well, including inside major organisations. A World Bank senior officer once told me of a situation that arose when she lived in in Timor-Leste: 'Once I asked: "Do you really want that matrix?". The person said: "There are twelve donors here, it's easier if I just agree"'.[9] That same officer later left the World Bank, disappointed at living through many situations like this, and went to work in civil society.

---

6   Ibid.

7   Rocha de Siqueira, I. (2019). Op. cit.

8   Interview with Missy Stephens, 12 March 2020.

9   This is an excerpt from Rocha de Siqueira, I. (2017). Op. cit., p. 123. Anonymous interview conducted in 2013.

In general, the overall feeling when the g7+ was founded was not only that the solutions presented by 'experts' were often ineffective, but that their attitude needed a major overhaul—from micro-practices to larger agendas. Former Prime Minister of Timor-Leste and Eminent Person of the g7+ Xanana Gusmão, even with all his diplomatic experience, said at the time: '[I]t has been our experience that aid delivery can be inflexible and process-heavy, resulting in funds being spent in the wrong places and not able to be used to prevent emerging conflict that threatens the State. We have also had to deal with development "experts" seeking to impose their supply-driven or template solutions with little regard for our culture, our context and the reality of our country'.[10]

Facing that reality, all the people we spoke with in the g7+ listed the biggest achievement of the group as raising a unified voice for conflict-affected countries on the international stage. In second place is usually

---

10　Gusmão, K.R.X. (2011). 'Opening Speech', g7+ Ministerial Retreat, Juba, South Sudan, 18 October 2011 quoted in *Strength in Fragility*, p. 1. On the issues of partnership, participation and ownership, see Crewe, Emma & Harrison, Elizabeth (1998). *Whose Development? An Ethnography of Aid*. London and New York: Zed Books; Mosse, David & Lewis, David (eds) (2005). *The Aid Effect: Giving and Governing in International Development*. London: Pluto Press; Mosse, David (2005). *Cultivating Development: An Ethnography of Aid Policy and Practice*. London: Pluto Press; Edelman, Marc & Haugerud, Angelique (eds) (2005). *The Anthropology of Development and Globalization: From Classical Political Economy to Contemporary Neoliberalism*. Malden, Oxford, Victoria: Blackwell Publishing.

the sharing of experiences among countries that have much to learn from each other. Herman Kakule Mukululuki, Director of External Resources Coordination at the Ministry of Planning in DRC, for instance, indicated that one of the g7+'s main realizations was the very fact that fragile states have been grouped together in solidarity in order to debate their common challenges.[11] This perceived feat, in fact, has a double aspect to it: not only is the g7+ said to have unified the voices of (some) conflict-affected states in certain contexts, but people speak of a '*voice*' precisely because the group is also credited with having created space for that voice to be uttered in different international fora, even if to a limited extent and with frequent setbacks.

There are undoubtedly many limitations to what the g7+ did achieve or can achieve still, as a group and as a collective of individuals. But if, as in the verses above, 'to be alone is to be powerless', *the feat of finding company cannot be discarded as part of a search for alternatives*. Again, the means are relevant—creating bonds and finding commonalities—not only because otherwise, these professionals might simply give up on their work, but mostly because the work they do keeps certain policies afloat, and their absence might mean worse lives for people in these countries. Seeking and cherishing company with passion and solidarity is not for everyone everywhere, but there is a lot be said for what it can achieve.

Togetherness Is a Value and a Practice: Harnessing Commonalities in Order to Move Forward

'One needs three magic words: persistence, perseverance and dedication,' says Helder. 'Doing that kind of work, of course I ask myself all the time "Why am I doing this? Is it for the good of all or for personal glory?" You have to make sure. I keep in touch with the focal points; I try to bring that sense of togetherness'.[12] Of course this is not easily done. Helder has shared examples before of how difficult it can be to keep up with focal points, the national representatives for the routine work the g7+ requires, and with what is going on in each other's countries. In a

---

11   Interview with Herman Kakule Mukululuki, 10 June 2019.
12   Interview with Helder da Costa, 14 April 2020.

famous case, he mentions how '[i]n a euphoric party after the g7+ Busan meeting, Guinea-Bissau's Minister of Economy, Planning and Regional Integration, Helena Nosoline Embaló, graciously offered on behalf of her country to host the g7+ ministerial meeting in 2012'. He continues: 'In New York earlier in the year, we became concerned for her safety during unrest in her country, but were relieved to find that she was well, but had been detained and was unable to leave her country'.[13] There were other cases he mentioned back in 2012, when the group was facing tough growing pains: 'One of our "focal points" from Somalia recently avoided a suicide bombing that injured others who were with him. At each event, our Afghan friends overcome many challenges to be with us. And yet each time they turn up with determination, enthusiasm and a smile. I am indeed very proud of our g7+ family'.[14]

It is not surprising, then, that being together might itself have a different weight and dynamic when it comes to g7+ meetings.

'Coming from a conflict-affected country, having seen war, starvation, you know people want to live in peace', Helder says. Of course, that accords with the g7+'s stated purpose of seeking peace in their countries. It also might indicate how much people in the group tend to value the positive moments of joy, safety and tranquillity and why that is something they see as natural, even if takes some time to assimilate for a newcomer. For Naheed, attending a g7+ meeting for the first time, the informality was surprising: 'Even though the meeting itself was a formal setting, the context was so informal; that's not usual. I had experience with these meetings, aid conferences, discussing pledges, conditionalities, negotiating. That experience is usually rigorous, involves many hours' sitting'. Naheed had been meeting donors and discussing aid for years, but said the atmosphere in these meetings is different. True, anyone coming into the restaurant where the welcome dinner was held on the first night would not have guessed those on the dance floor were ministers and high-ranking professionals. And yet, the hours sitting in the meetings were still long, decisions were made, documents were signed, parallel bilateral meetings were held, a

---

13   Helder Da Costa (2012). 'g7+ and the New Deal: Country-Led and Country-Owned Initiatives: A Perspective from Timor-Leste'. *Journal of Peacebuilding & Development*, 7(2), p. 101.

14   Ibid.

couple of donor representatives said a few words; that is, everything else seems to me to have been the same as in other aid conferences, in terms of the formality of the setting. The difference was that, because people are comfortable with each other (something we could see in the movements on the dance floor), there is perhaps more warmth in the meeting as well, and vice-versa. Sure, Helder, Habib, and the rest of the Secretariat looked stressed, as is characteristic of organisers and hosts, but the *togetherness* was clearly cherished.

Here we might thank Himadeep Muppidi for remembering Chinua Achebe's beautiful words: 'A man who calls his kinsmen to feast does not do so to save them from starving. They all have food in their own homes. When we gather together in the moonlit village ground, it is not because of the moon. Every man can see it in his own compound. We come together because it is good for kinsmen to do so'.[15] In what kind of world would that 'good' not account for much?

Helder talks about his village in Timor-Leste, Loirubi, Venilale, as something that always provides him with inner peace:

> I go there every time I'm in Timor. I cross the river, I look at the mountains and that gives me inner peace. We always [make] a fire there, bake something together. Once, after one of the g7+ meetings in Dili, I brought the representatives of CAR, Somalia, South Sudan, Solomon Islands and DRC to visit the village. I also brought Habib before. They are always impressed. I learned that from my parents, to value my surroundings. They also taught me simplicity, passion, wisdom. I learned from the way they helped people. I think if I didn't have that kind of experience, I would have fallen in[to] many traps when I went to study abroad in Indonesia, New Zealand and Australia. People take their surroundings for granted.

Certain practices have the power to recharge our energy and keep us focused on our values; being together is one of them, in many ways and in many cases. By coming together with others, a group can create their own surroundings. Contemplation, togetherness, and a certain disposition seem to do wonders to one's passion.

---

15   Achebe Chinua, ([1959] 1994). 'Things Fall Apart', as cited in Muppidi, Himadeep (2016). 'The Elements of Bandung', in Phạm & Shilliam (eds). *Meanings of Bandung: Postcolonial Orders and Decolonial Visions*. London and New York: Rowman & Littlefield, p. 32.

The time spent in these meetings need not *only* be functional; there is no reason why joy should not feature in them too.[16] I believe that it does not often make much of an appearance because joy simply does not grow out of thin air: commonalities, motivations, cultural codes, expectations, values—affinities, in general, need to exist. And here I speak of joy because I believe joy and trust can be crucial elements of solidarity. They can also feed passion and generate momentum. In turn, only with passion for *something* can people insist on trying to create alternative ways of thinking (even if limited) when reality pushes back. But passion needs to be nurtured.

Family Ties

Because of the many turns the history of Afghanistan took, there have been many waves of displacement. In between 1980 and 1990; around 6.2 million people left for Pakistan and Iran. 'Having arrived in their areas of resettlement, the majority settled in kin-related groups, either in clusters of nuclear families living in separate housing, or in extended family households'.

(Hatch Dupree, Nancy (2004). 'The Family During Crisis in Afghanistan'. *Journal of Comparative Family Studies*, 35(2), Turbulent Times and Family Life in the Contemporary Middle East, 311–31.)

Solidarity and the joy of being together are also, of course, profoundly cultural and closely related to how families and communities are set up. Modes of being together tend to be absorbed in childhood. Habib speaks of the joint family system with which he is accustomed: 'Everyone provides for everyone. There are 35 people who can rely on me and on whom I can rely to take care of my family. It's like an extension of a social security system. It's tradition'. One can imagine the mark this leaves on one's attitude towards others and one's commitment to collective projects. 'The moment I stop believing in the nobility of the work I do, I will stop working. We invest so much energy, we don't even feel the time. I'm ambitious... People tease me because I daydream about the g7+ helping [to solve] conflict in member countries. [I don't mean to be] overconfident but I feel I can contribute where I am. But believing, working with passion... is not fun, not easy anywhere, because you put your heart in it'.[17]

---

16   Ibid.
17   Interview with Habib Mayar, 23 March 2020.

The way Habib explains how difficult it can be to work with passion is by telling one of his favourite stories: 'Once I was going back to Dili from Afghanistan and the security lady who was checking my suitcase saw the bag with the g7+ pins. She asked what they were. I explained I worked for peace. She asked, "Where is peace here?" There had been an attack in Kabul with 11 or 12 civilians killed', he explains; clearly this was an episode that marked him. 'Such encounters linger on in my mind every time I am at work or in a meeting talking about peace and development', he says and continues: 'I might be naïve about the politics of peace and my colleagues say I take my work too seriously. But we all know how serious the need for peace is for those people who witness sufferings by war and conflict. I sacrificed a lot for the work we do. I know my belief is shared by many others in the g7+'.[18]

His fellow citizen, Naheed, also speaks a lot about what she learned from her family. She recounts how her mother used to teach her about solidarity: 'My mom always says, "When you do things for yourself it's very limiting; do [them] for others and your returns will be bigger"'. We saw how steep her learning curve was when coming back to Afghanistan; the passion and commitment that was infused in her by family and tradition means that she feels compelled to work and do good for her country: 'I lost a lot of my youth. I was very much an adult at 25. Today I take life more easily than at that time. You become very serious when you are handling serious things like all that work. People in that generation in other countries were not like that, so when I was abroad studying, sometimes I felt like I didn't belong so much'.[19]

Yes, it can be lonely to work with passion. That is why one needs solidarity; it is not only that the work itself is tough and that any efforts made will necessarily be collective, but that believing in the work is also difficult. Being together, then, is a way of suffusing work with joy so that one is able to keep moving forward. Nevertheless, being together will not do anything for anyone unless there is enough willingness and trust for people to feel comfortable, and a project cannot create this willingness and trust out of nowhere—it must be practised in everyday life and work, and it is connected to shared values and common backgrounds. That is why these qualities should be harnessed as the asset they can be.

---

18   Ibid.
19   Interview with Naheed Sarabi, 03 March 2020.

Living with Frustration but Leaving No-One Behind: Monitoring the SDGs

In the concept note for the event organized at the UN in 2012 (which saw Helder, Habib and Siafa practicing their skills as 'accidental diplomats'), the g7+ warned: 'Despite recognising the vital importance of the development priorities of the MDGs, not one g7+ country anticipates reaching any of the MDGs by 2015. The g7+ proposes that in order to reach the goals articulated in the Millennium Declaration, first there must be a firm focus on the foundational framework of peacebuilding and statebuilding'.[20] This had been on the table for the g7+ member countries since the beginning of conversations back in 2008. It struck their representatives that the goals being projected, although important, didn't take into account the reality of conflict in those countries and, therefore, were quite blind to the obstacles they faced.[21] 'These goals were not priorities that fitted the situation of many countries affected by conflict, and yet we have been measured against these standards and we were so often shown to be failing. There was no strong representation from countries in a fragile situation in the negotiation of the MDGs framework to ensure the priorities were not using a one-size-fits-all approach'.[22]

It seemed obvious and, still, was yet to be spelled out: '[Donors] said, "Ok, the children are not being educated. The children are stunted. The infant mortality is high, etc." We said, "How can the children be educated if we have instability? There is no security, so which parent is going to allow the children to go to school? Which farmer is going to grow vegetables?"'.[23] Retrospectively, again, it seems obvious, but as

---

20   g7+ (2012). *High-Level Side Event: The New Deal: g7+ Perspectives and Experiences - Concept Note.*

21   See 2019 Independent Review of the g7+ for a discussion on the inclusion of SDG 16.

22   g7+ (2016). *Strength in fragility: "We are writing our own history"*– The emergence of the g7+ group from our own perspective, p. 3.

23   Min. Pires, as cited in Wyeth, Vanessa, de Carvalho, Gustavo, Woldeselassie, Zerihun A., Mechoulan, Delphine, Boutellis, Arthur, Whineray, David, Moreira de Silva, Jorge, Rosand, Eric & Mahmoud, Youssef (2012). 'Interview with Emilia Pires, Chair of the g7+ Group of Fragile States'. *International Peace Institute Global Observatory.* https://theglobalobservatory.org/2012/04/interview-with-emilia-pires-minister-of-finance-for-timor-leste-and-chair-of-the-g7-group-of-fragile-states/.

we saw in the earlier stories, speaking about peace was a complicated matter in the New York bubble. So g7+ leaders explained many, many times: 'We could not achieve the MDGs unless we first achieved peace in our own countries'.[24]

As we saw in the New York debacle around the inclusion of SDG 16—the goal for peace—g7+'s demands were meant to achieve a change in narrative by bringing forth g7+ countries' priorities. This would attend to the overall ambition of changing donor behaviour *and* effectively creating the means for change on the ground in conflict-affected countries.

The inclusion of SDG 16 on peace, justice and strong institutions has been reinforced by the 2030 Agenda's principle of leaving no one behind (LNOB). The 17 Sustainable Development Goals (SDGs) aim to be integrated and indivisible, which means, for instance, that peace and development cannot be dissociated, and that if some countries in the world are afflicted by conflict and extreme poverty, their plights are global plights. Either the Agenda advances everywhere or the failures are global, because a crucial part of the agenda presupposes cooperation and more equality, including in international dialogues. Let's bear in mind, for example, the specific targets 'broaden and strengthen the participation of developing countries in the institutions of global governance' (SDG 16.8)[25] and '[r]espect each country's policy space and leadership to establish and implement policies for poverty eradication and sustainable development' (SDG 17.15)[26] (See Annex V). These would have the potential to address the g7+'s demands for changes in donor behaviour that date back to the first meetings of IDPS.

Nonetheless, as should perhaps be expected, many will say this is the issue people in the g7+ find more disappointing: 'Sometimes, we feel frustrated; changing donors' behaviour is something that we feel we haven't achieved much', says Habib. Similarly, Mukululuki says the biggest challenge for the g7+ has been to get donors to respect TRUST,

---

24   EP Gusmão, Xanana (2016). *Strength in Fragility*, in g7+, p. 4.

25   UN General Assembly (2015). Resolution 70/1. Transforming our world: the 2030 Agenda for Sustainable Development, p. 25. Target 16.8 of the SDGs reads: 'broaden and strengthen the participation of developing countries in the institutions of global governance'.

26   Ibid., p. 27. Target 17.15 of the SDGs reads: 'respect each country's policy space and leadership to establish and implement policies for poverty eradication and sustainable development'.

Leaving No-One Behind (LNOB)

'By emphasizing that the SDGs are "integrated and indivisible", the 2030 Agenda discourages a "pick-and-choose" attitude: just as there can be no peace without development and vice-versa, there is no top performance that should be able to ignore poor outcomes in gender equality or access to clean water, for instance. A discussion paper by UNDP suggests five criteria to help identify who is or can be left behind: a) discrimination; b) geography; c) governance; d) socio-economic status; and e) shocks and fragility'.

The dilemma for the g7+ is 'that of choosing to present themselves as experts in fragility and helping the world in this key aspect of the LNOB agenda, or to precisely advocate against possible stereotypes or stigmas and point out the hypocrisies of a world full of fragility everywhere.'

(Rocha de Siqueira, I. (2019). Op. cit., pp. 81–81.)

---

one of the New Deal's pillars, which involves transparency of aid, risk sharing, use and strengthening of country systems, a strengthening of capacity, and timely, predictable aid. 'Development partners remain largely off-track in delivering on the TRUST principles. While there are some islands of good practice, there have not yet been tremendous changes in donor behaviour. But we must remember this is a long-term endeavour. We are talking about changing narratives and mind-sets that have been in place within the development industry for decades. Changing these will require time, and it will also require greater political commitment on the part of donors'.[27]

Let us see an example of what the expectations driven by these principles would look like. In a study produced by the g7+ foundation comparing experiences of public finance management (PFM) between Timor-Leste and Afghanistan in order to promote peer learning, the conclusion is a pledge for a change in donor behaviour, one that is much in line with the principles of TRUST:

> This focus [of donors] on minimizing fiduciary risk drives the project-oriented and fragmented approach to development that has been a feature of [aid in] fragile states. Projects focus on "safeguarding" donor funds and "end-of-program outcomes" rather than progress towards national goals like self-reliance and the continuous improvement of the

---

27   g7+, *Strength in Fragility*, p. 56.

institutions of the state. There is also the misapprehension that there is a trade-off between the two; that, in order to achieve better development outcomes, donors have to increase their fiduciary risk. The evidence does not support this. In fact, the opposite is more common. By increasing focus on development risk, including by using national systems and building self-reliance, donors are actually in a position to ask for higher levels of accountability and to achieve lower fiduciary risk. Leaving aside donor priorities, governments themselves tend to increase the level of transparency and accountability when budgets increase, as was demonstrated in Timor-Leste during the period of expansion following the increase in oil and gas revenues.[28]

Afghanistan's experience in managing donors' interest and commitment, of course, is a long and complex one—and it is now coming to a halt, because of the Taliban's takeover. Afghan Minister of Economy, Mustafa Mastoor, offered a mixed diagnosis before the takeover: 'In terms of aid and how we manage it, it has changed significantly, but it's not perfect, of course. We are aware of how politically-driven aid is, and because of that, in a certain way, Afghanistan has been privileged, receiving more support than other countries. But for a while the volume of aid has been less relevant than *how* aid is practiced. In that sense, we must say in-budget support is higher than for other countries, but aid hasn't changed much'.[29] The lack of more substantial changes is intimately related to the use of conditionalities that have a history of doing precisely the opposite of what the g7+ stands for: 'We do have a lot of funding, but also a lot of conditionalities. We should highlight this as a group. Sometimes, in Afghanistan, it's like a Christmas tree of conditionalities that we have to implement', says Naheed.[30]

Much of these difficulties boil down to the need to strengthen institutions and build capacity, which the g7+ sees as both a means and an end in itself. The group argues that when aid sidesteps a country's systems, it does not just miss an opportunity of contributing to those ends, but it also might weaken them further. When former Minister of Finance from South Sudan, H. E. Kosti Manibe, proclaimed 'nothing

---

28   g7+ foundation & Institute for State Effectiveness. *State building in conflict-affected & fragile states: A comparative study*, p. 7.
29   Interview with Muhammad Mustafa Mastoor, 17 June 2019.
30   Interview with Naheed Sarabi, 03 March 2020.

about us without us', the idea of putting countries' ownership at the centre of any development cooperation was crucial.[31]

NOTHING ABOUT US WITHOUT US

Addressing these issues requires g7+'s representatives to deal with frustrations about their own challenges at home, which, if clearly painful to address, are nevertheless not ignored. Habib, having pointed out the disappointment at the slow pace of change in donor behaviour, has come forward to publicly suggest solutions to the risk he acknowledges exists in using country systems: 'The g7+ fully recognises the presence of risk perceived by development partners while channelling aid through the treasury of the beneficiary government. g7+ governments are not turning a blind eye to this fact. Thus, it is helpful to jointly sketch a plan of action that assesses the risk and proposes a mitigating strategy. It is this kind of strategic thinking around the use of country systems that is currently still lacking'.[32]

---

31   Quote in g7+ (2016). *Strength in fragility: "We are writing our own history"*–The emergence of the g7+ group from our own perspective.

32   Mayar, Habib Ur Rehman (2014). 'The Journey Towards Resilience Continues: g7+ Priorities to Confront Ebola, Implement the New Deal and Influence the Post-2015 Agenda'. *Journal of Peacebuilding & Development*, 9(3), p. 124.

Indeed, there has historically been a heated debate over aid efficiency that looks precisely into the kinds of corruption such flows might elicit.[33] On the other hand, more critical voices point to the lack of similar interest, within the field of international cooperation, in fencing off corrupt practices on the part of large multinationals everywhere.[34]

Here, a quick detour may be useful.

It is undeniable that there is an enormous challenge posed to international aid and cooperation by inefficient or corrupt institutions. Concern has been followed by research that has historically highlighted two sets of problems: the need to better understand how aid itself can impact corruption levels and have negative effects over governance; and the need to address the dilemma of how to deal with unstable political situations and controversial leaderships, when many of the resources might never reach those in need.[35] In Afghanistan itself, according to a 2021 report to the United Nations Congress, $143 billion was spent on reconstruction since 2002, of which $93 billion was directed to Afghan police and armed forces, and around $50 billion to government and civil society programs.[36] This is a formidable amount of money that has no equal in any other conflict-affected country. Yet, although some positive results have been achieved, it is an understatement to suggest that a lot more should have been possible.

What criticisms like those posed by the g7+ may achieve is the possibility of complicating these matters further, not dismissing them. Undoubtedly, in order for the citizens in these countries to have better lives, corruption and institutional inefficiency need to be addressed, and the g7+'s discourse aligns with that. Nevertheless, drawing attention to the ambiguities and contradictions of an unequal international system can add value to this discussion without minimising the gravity of those problems. For instance, researchers and advisors for the US government

---

33   For recent data, see Andersen, Jørgen Juel, Johannesen, Niels & Rijkers, Bob (2020). 'Elite Capture of Foreign Aid Evidence from Offshore Bank Accounts'. *CEBI Working Paper 07/20.*

34   See Mohran, Theodore H. (2006). *How Multinational Investors Evade Developed Country Laws.* Center for Global Development, Working Paper Number 79.

35   Jenkins, Matthew, Kukutschka, Roberto Martínez B. & Zúñiga, Nieves (2020). *Anti-Corruption In Fragile Settings: A Review Of The Evidence.* Bonn and Eschborn: Deutsche Gesellschaft für Internationale Zusammenarbeit (GIZ) GmbH.

36   United States (2021). *2021 Quarterly Report to Congress.* https://www.sigar.mil/pdf/quarterlyreports/2021-01-30qr-section2-funding.pdf, p. 25.

have long put pressure on the country to strengthen its stance on corruption when it comes to aid allocation. In fact, the US 2019 Global Fragility Act, only recently finally further detailed, is supposed to be a response to these demands, a reaction against corruption scandals of the kind that came to the fore with several reviews of the US actions in Afghanistan, which showed how the reconstruction led by American diplomacy, defence and development personnel were doomed to weaken governance and create incentives for corruption: 'Money, technical assistance, and diplomatic attention do not address, and can even exacerbate, the problems of government illegitimacy, corruption, and collusion with violent groups that make these states unstable'.[37] However, while attention has been rightly drawn to the inaction of donor countries in including measures that can counter incentives to corruption provided by their interventions in conflict-affected countries, there are a number of questions that remain unasked. A recent study has shown, for example, that donor fragmentation itself can be an important factor. Especially under high volumes of aid, donor fragmentation can lead to 'a degradation of ownership, accountability, and responsibility over development outcomes and processes', which, in turn, can facilitate 'an ongoing culture of corruption within state institutions, thereby nullifying aid's otherwise beneficial impact on institutional quality, and the indirect public opinion dividends that ensue (including those related to conflict)'. Another question has been to what extent, in certain contexts, the failures of aid to address, weaken or at least circumvent corruption have not been so much failures, but 'a policy choice', considering the interests of private contractors, for instance.[38] Putting new facts center stage might not be possible if other actors, like the g7+, do not ask how interventions also heavily depend on *how* money is disbursed by donors. There is great value in keeping automatic thinking at bay.

37   United States (2021). *2020 United States Strategy to Prevent Conflict and Promote Stability; Kleinfield, R. (2021). Picking Global Fragility Act Countries: Carnegie Endowment for International Peace.* https://carnegieendowment.org/2021/05/26/picking-global-fragility-act-countries-pub-84610.

38   Landers, Clemence & Aboneaaj, Rakan (2021). *Giving up the "Statebuilding" Ghost: Lessons from Afghanistan for Foreign Assistance in Fragile States.* https://www.cgdev.org/blog/giving-statebuilding-ghost-lessons-afghanistan-foreign-assistance-fragile-states.

Going back to LNOB and the 2030 Agenda, there is something to be said about the discrepancy between the paces at which different groups are expected to move. While many point to the slow rhythm of donors, after the approval of SDGs the call to monitor the implementation of the goals put a lot of pressure on national statistical systems and planning offices, especially in conflict-affected countries. These were required to move fast, although support was also promised. But we should note that things are complex: it is clear that the g7+ representatives find all this reporting extremely important; however, moving forward with it amid the social, economic, and political challenges that member countries face has proved incredibly difficult.

> While the road to achieving the SDGs in g7+ member countries is beset with obstacles, effectively monitoring progress is itself a challenging endeavour. This challenge is all the greater due to the large number of goals (17) and indicators (23[1])[39] in the 2030 Agenda—larger even than in the MDGs. In addition, there is frequently no available baseline data for many of these indicators in g7+ countries. Indeed, for the so-called "tier 3" SDG indicators, the establishment and testing of the standards/methodology is yet to be finalised at the international level.[40] In addition to these universal challenges, the g7+ member countries have reported on their own especially significant constraints. These include a lack of funding, insufficient human resources and technical capacity, lack of coordination between government institutions, insufficient IT capability and, for some of these countries, insecurity and the effects of ongoing conflict. These are problems that have long affected the ability of these countries to undertake national censuses and surveys, but which become more apparent in the context of such an extensive set of indicators.[41]

These are considerable obstacles not only to implementing, but also to monitoring progress in the SDGs in the g7+ countries; for this reason, the group decided to select and prioritise reporting on 20 targets chosen in a 2016 technical meeting (See Annex VI). Goals 12 to 15, which cover consumption and the environment-related goals, are not among them, and any member countries that wish to report on more SDG 16

---

39   Number adjusted to current list of indicators. See: https://unstats.un.org/sdgs/indicators/indicators-list/.

40   See UN Stats (2020). *SDG Indicators: Metadata repository.* https://unstats.un.org/sdgs/metadata/.

41   g7+ (2018). *SDG Report 2018* (draft), p. 3.

indicators beyond those selected are encouraged to do so. In addition, new indicators were added, including one on internally displaced persons (IDPs).[42] The first report was drafted in 2018 but not widely circulated, and no other reports were produced. There was mention of creating an online platform for joint reporting and dissemination, but this has not been implemented so far.

This is a case where it seems passion and motivation come from many directions. There are good intentions behind the decision to see these goals monitored and, most importantly, *implemented* in g7+ countries. However, the reality can be frustrating and the work overwhelming. When we take into account how incredibly complex the review of the global indicators framework for the SDGs has been, the fact that the g7+ member countries struggle with monitoring the implementation of the SDGs comes as no surprise. As of 2020, five years after the approval of the 2030 Agenda, the revision of SDG indicators at the UN was still in progress and 35 indicators out of 231 were still under Tier III—that is, they were indicators for which there are no methodologies for collection and no data; meanwhile 98 were under Tier II, for which there are methodologies but no established routine of data collection.[43] In March 2021, refinements were proposed, and only as of February 2022, finally, are there no Tier III indicators left: 'The updated tier classification table contains 136 Tier I indicators, 91 Tier II indicators and 4 indicators that have multiple tiers (different components of the indicator are classified into different tiers'.[44]

Still, it is estimated around 'US$5.1 billion for the period until 2030 is needed in extra donor funding' to finance SDG monitoring data. 'This equates to some US$340 million per year'.[45] Although some might say this is only a small percentage of Official Development Assistance (ODA), it is a considerable amount of money, and this expenditure may

---

42   See Rocha de Siqueira, I. (2019). Op. cit.
43   See: United Nations (2020). *Compilation of 2020 Comprehensive Review Proposals Received.*   https://unstats.un.org/sdgs/files/2020%20Comprehensive%20 Review%20Proposals_web.pdf.
44   UN Stats (2022). *Tier Classification for Global SDG Indicators.* https://unstats.un.org/ sdgs/files/Tier%20Classification%20of%20SDG%20Indicators_4%20Feb%202022_ web.pdf.
45   See: Jütting, Johannes & Badiee, Shaida (2016). *Financing SDG data needs: What does it cost?* Global Partnership for Sustainable Development Data. http://www. data4sdgs.org/news/financing-sdg-data-needs-what-does-it-cost.

not be such a high priority now, especially after the crisis that COVID-19 is causing around the globe.

This is how Habib reacts to the estimate of how much will be needed to monitor the SDGs:

> While recognizing the need of expertise, technical know-how and international institutions with experts in statistics, it is more important to empower the countries themselves and their national statistical offices and planning departments to be able to undertake the task of monitoring the SDGs. This would have a dual impact: one, it would help building national capacity in conflict-affected countries in general and further strengthen accountability; and two, it would allow for more in-country dialogues on progress across SDGs. While I am not sure what would be included if we talk about 340 million dollar/year to assist in monitoring, I am sure that at least the conflict-affected countries will need a tiny portion of that money to build their national system and mechanisms for statistics. Remember we have countries in g7+ where census is based on mere estimates instead of head counts and where the last physical census was conducted a few decades ago. Moreover, the g7+ practice of joint monitoring the SDGs was and still is expected to show by example that countries can and need to be given the ownership to lead the exercise; and to identify the capacity gap in national statistics.

He concludes by pointing at how the g7+ plans to monitor its priority indicators in terms of the UN 2030 Agenda (see Annex VI). His point, it seems to me, is that *all the money in the world can still leave much undone*. The issue, as many have said before, is how this money is spent.[46]

Putting Solidarity into Practice: Conflict Mediation in the Central African Republic

It is not straightforward to be in solidarity with one another and to work together if one is addressing complex issues, such development and conflict. Even if one wants to do so, the difficult question is usually 'how?'.

In 2014, the Central African Republic (CAR) was going through conflict between diverse armed groups. Bienvenu Hervé Kovoungbo had been the g7+ focal point for CAR since 2011. He speaks with much pride about this work and his country membership:

---

46 See, for instance, Ramalingam (2013).

I started working in the Ministry of Economy, Planning and Cooperation and, soon after, I supported the monitoring of the implementation of the Paris Agreement on Principles for Engagement with Fragile States and Situations, so my supervisors decided to allocate me to deal with all issues related with fragility. I had participated of the IDPS and g7+ meetings in Kinshasa and later, in Monrovia. The first g7+ focal point was very supportive and contributed to my promotion; I am very grateful. Today, I am Director of International Cooperation and I am also the focal point and the chief of the Secretariat of National Coordination that monitors the implementation of the 2030 Agenda. As such, I am in charge of the technical coordination of a team formed by 150 people and of interacting with many other institutions. I am also the focal point for the Global Partnership Cooperation on Effective Development, for South-South and Triangular Cooperation and the Istanbul Declaration and Programme of Action for the Least Developed Countries.[47]

Honestly, this list is impressive. I reproduce it in full because it is important to understand how Bienvenu came to be where he is and why he credits the g7+ with so much of the work he accomplished.

At the end of 2013, CAR was going through severe conflict. French troops intervened in December 2013, followed two months later by a European Union military operation. In the meantime, in October 2013, Bienvenu attended a g7+ meeting in Dili. After listening to the motivational words of Prime Minister Xanana Gusmão, he asked for his support for a possible reconciliation process in CAR: 'I was so impressed with how Timor-Leste had contributed with Guinea-Bissau that I decided to tell him how things were in my country. When I asked whether he would [agree] to come and talk to the armed groups, his response was "yes". I went back to my country and convinced the council of ministers to send a formal invitation to the government of Timor-Leste', Bienvenu recalls with obvious pride.[48]

The situation was very difficult in 2014. In June, Bienvenu attended the IDPS meeting in Freetown that was organised by Abie; however, when the meeting finished, he could not immediately go back home and was held up in Cameroon while his family fled their home due to the violence erupting in Bangui.

---

47   Interview with Bienvenu Hervé Kovoungbo, 24 April 2020.
48   Ibid.

Later, in September 2014, the UN took over and expanded the then-existing peacekeeping mission in CAR.

The same year, PM Xanana Gusmão visited CAR, following the invitation arranged by Bienvenu.

> I elaborated the terms of reference and contacted the leaders of the armed groups. I had authorisation to do so, but it was at my own risk, because the security situation was such that it was very risky to contact the armed groups. No one knew I was doing that, not my wife, not my children. It was too risky. I had hope, I had the power over the destiny of my country. My wife wouldn't accept that. When Xanana Gusmão arrived, I went alone to talk to him about meeting with the groups. They couldn't come to him because they couldn't come to the centre or they would risk getting arrested. He came to them, but when they saw he was white, they said they wouldn't speak to him, because "the white people are the ones behind the coup, the manipulation, the guns", but then Xanana said he was not white, he was Timorese, so he was "like them", he said. He mentioned he had gone through difficult situations too. I was so relieved. I took risks, because all phones can be tapped and anyone who contacts the armed groups can be prosecuted. But I wanted to do that for peace in my country. The government knew I was doing so, but of course it was the ministers who knew, not all judges, not all the policemen... And because I was talking to them, people could think I was their friend.

He still sounds anxious about this.[49] Much academic literature on postcolonial relations stresses the importance of rethinking difference in light of common cultural and historical experiences of exploitation: 'the concept of Black was mobilized as part of a set of constitutive principles and ideas to promote collective action', the idea being to 'generate solidarity' by resorting to 'Black as a political colour'.[50]

> Because of that conversation, we convinced the leaders of the armed groups to go to the Reconciliation Forum, later in 2015. Before the Bangui Forum, the government held a dialogue in Brazzaville, Congo. We transported the leaders of the armed groups there. But some groups which were held up in CAR said they wouldn't support the process and

---

49   Ibid.
50   Brah, Avtar (2006). 'Diferença, diversidade, diferenciação'. *Cadernos pagu*, 26, 329–76, pp. 334, 336. My translation. Original publication: 'Difference, Diversity, Differentiation', in Brah, Avtar (1996). *Cartographies of Diaspora: Contesting Identities*. London and New York: Routledge, ch. 5, pp. 95–127.

wouldn't go to the Forum. The leaders had accepted but some groups wouldn't go, so we needed to talk to them. I coordinated for Xanana to go talk to them. He did so as a former war time leader, and he convinced them; they finally [agreed] to go to the Forum. I will never forget that. The president of the Forum invited him then to stay a few days more in CAR and to participate in a parliamentary session, where he had permission to [make] a speech. Everyone heard it everywhere. This was Xanana's first visit, and he managed to get the leaders of armed groups to agree to attend the Reconciliation Forum, to be held in May 2015.

Bienvenu remembers all the details without any difficulty.[51]

The Bangui National Forum opened on 4 May 2015. The overall objective of the forum was to issue a set of recommendations on peace and security, justice and reconciliation, and socio-economic development. The forum was attended by 600 to 700 participants from around CAR, including high-level representatives of the transitional government, which was under H. E. President Catherine Samba-Panza, besides national political parties, non-state armed groups (Séléka and Anti-Balaka), the private sector, civil society, traditional chiefs, and religious groups.[52]

The g7+ was represented by its Secretariat in response to the invitation of the President of the Interim Government of CAR to the g7+'s Eminent Person, Xanana Gusmão. During the closing ceremony of the Bangui Forum, the g7+ Secretariat read the speech prepared by him. The message is said to have been warmly received and to have 'generated a lot of traction with the audience': 'They all chanted our motto "Goodbye Conflict, Welcome Development" at the end of the speech'.[53]

Helder also wrote at the time: 'On the 11th of May, the g7+ Secretariat was honored to be part of the closing ceremony of the Bangui National Forum for National Reconciliation in [the] Central African Republic. The event served as a heartening reminder of the critical importance of engagement and dialogue for promoting peace and development. We were struck by the passion expressed by participants from all parties'.[54]

---

51   Ibid.
52   Excerpt from g7+ Newsletter, March–May 2015, p. 1.
53   Ibid.
54   Ibid., p. 4.

Conflict in CAR

The Central African Republic (CAR) has had two different experiences with United Nations peacekeeping forces. From 25 September 2007 till 31 December 2010, the United Nations Mission in the Central African Republic and Chad (MINURCAT) was established in eastern Chad and north-eastern CAR to support the efforts concerning the 230,000 refugees from Darfur, Sudan. It had up to 5,200 military personnel and 300 police officers on the ground.

The United Nations Multidimensional Integrated Stabilization Mission in the Central African Republic (MINUSCA) started in 10 April 2014 to protect CAR civilians after the Séléka militia rebellion in 2013 and subsequent formation of the Anti-Balaka militia who confronted them. The conflict resulted in 320,000 refugees fleeing to neighbouring countries and more than 600,000 people internally displaced.

MINUSCA transformed a 6,000 African Union-led peacekeeping force into the UN force that nowadays reaches 13,252 total personnel, mostly composed of African troops. MINUSCA was granted unprecedented capabilities of law enforcement, temporarily taking over the legal system. Nonetheless, the mission faces challenges, with different kinds of abuse still happening, and accusations of sexual violence that led to an entire battalion being sent back home.

(See https://egiuliani.wordpress.com/2014/02/28/central-african-republic/; https://www.bbc.com/news/world-africa-13150044; https://peacekeeping. un.org/en/mission/minusca; GILDER, Alexander (2020). *Human Security and the Stabilization Mandate of MINUSCA. International Peacekeeping*, [S.L.], p. 1–32).

Unfortunately, today, there is again instability in CAR,[55] but as the path to peace is long and full of obstacles, it is important to acknowledge, understand, and reproduce moments when peace had a chance. Again, it is beyond our scope to dive into the details of these events; our focus is on what they generated among the g7+. For those involved, '[t]he Bangui Forum was a major milestone in CAR's transition towards peace and stability. The forum was widely considered a success'.[56] Indeed,

---

55 See Council on Foreign Relations (2022). *Violence in the Central African Republic.* https://www.cfr.org/global-conflict-tracker/conflict/violence-central-african-re public.

56 Excerpt from g7+ Newsletter, March–May 2015, p. 2.

Bienvenu speaks of it as a major milestone in the country's history and in his own, and as a point when he felt the work of the g7+ could be extremely important. He would request the group's aid one more time.

> Later, in April 2016, there was a meeting with people in Washington D.C., where Xanana met my minister. He wanted to come and support the reconciliation process; he asked my minister what the g7+ could contribute with, if they had a priority at this moment. My government mentioned the displaced people in our country. I remember when I saw the camp. I had been in a mission for two weeks. When I came back and saw from the plane the thousands of people displaced in a camp at the airport… Everyone on the plane was crying, *I* was crying. I said to myself "to cry is one thing but I promise in my heart to do everything I can". I played my role; I asked my minister if Xanana could come. The g7+ came to visit the camp in Bangui. It was horrible, families with children, women, all in inhuman conditions…

He tells this story in obvious pain.

There were 28,000 internally displaced people living in the camp. Some had been there for three years since the violence erupted in 2013. The conditions were completely unsanitary; the situation was precarious. French and UN troops kept the area safe (although there are also accusations of abuse)[57] but the camp was still at the airport, so it was risky in many ways, and basic provisions were constantly needed but not always coming through. People depended heavily on humanitarian assistance,[58] yet 'Mpoko [airport] and indeed the Central African Republic never saw a mobilisation of international aid at levels similar to other displaced people or refugee camps in the world'.[59] CAR has always been an aid orphan.

There was some dispute internationally as to the timing of the camp's closure. Some organisations said that it was completely unjustified as families had not received enough support to go back to houses that had been destroyed. The government, in turn, spoke of restoring dignity. And there might have been a strategic measure of public pressure

---

57   See MSF (2017). *Five reasons to care about the closure of Mpoko camp*. https://www.msf.org/central-african-republic-five-reasons-care-about-closure-mpoko-camp.

58   See Baddorf, Zack (2016). *CAR Begins Closing Displaced Persons Camp in Bangui*. https://www.voanews.com/africa/car-begins-closing-displaced-persons-camp-bangui.

59   See MSF (2017). *Five reasons to care about the closure of Mpoko camp*. https://www.msf.org/central-african-republic-five-reasons-care-about-closure-mpoko-camp.

placed on international organisations, as then they would have been more disposed to help provide basic infrastructure for those returning home. Opinions and positions vary:

'The humanitarian organisations didn't want the camps to close down. The reason, for me, was that it was good for trade, finance, their projects, to take pictures... When the g7+ came, they went in the spirit of solidarity and visited the tents. Xanana went in the camp, entered the tents! He cried. Who, what other authorities do that? Then they decided to help and make a donation'.[60] Timor-Leste donated $2 million to help close the camp.[61] 'The fund was channelled directly to CAR's Finance Ministry, using its country system. The Government equally contributed 250 million (CFA francs) to the process', says Bienvenu in a short article written for the g7+ December 2017 Newsletter.[62]

Helche was part of the g7+ team that visited the camp at the Mpoko Airport.

> There were mothers with their babies, they were in such poor conditions. It had rained the night before, so there was a lot of red mud everywhere... We heard so many touching stories from the families at the refugee camp. Some told us that the young girls had no sanitary pads, and I could tell they felt trapped, insecure there. We heard a lot of personal stories. We went from there straight to an all-night meeting. I remember my shoes were covered with that red mud, but we wanted to discuss what we had seen right away. We were thinking "How can we help?". We talked for hours, just to write the report we produced for the UN. We had faced a similar situation back in 1999 in Timor, with the Indonesian military. I knew it was dirty, uncomfortable. As soon as we came back to Dili, the Government of Timor-Leste made the pledge to help people return to their homes. They closed the camp 3 to 4 months after that. I know our support was not that big, but we made it effective.[63]

Bienvenu's words confirm that feeling: 'The place was closed with that help in a consensual manner between the people and the government. People would agree, on a voluntary basis, after receiving some money

---

60 Interview with Bienvenu Hervé Kovoungbo, 24 April 2020.
61 g7+ (n.d.). *7 things to know about Fragile-to-Fragile (F2F) Cooperation*, p. 3.
62 g7+ (2017). Newsletter.
63 Interview with Helche Silvester, 05 March 2020.

to help them return home or find a new home. I will never forget what the g7+ did'.[64]

'Xanana met everyone in the country. He still managed to meet with all leaders of armed groups to congratulate them on the reconciliation. I am very close [to him] still and he has high esteem for me. He really influenced me so much. They call me Xanana Gusmão here!', Bienvenu says laughing.

CAR is still facing many obstacles to peace and development, but the value of solidarity has kept people like Bienvenu confident enough that he works to keep cooperation with others going. 'We live with frustration in our DNA. But we need to be aware and make sure this doesn't control our behaviour. That's my philosophy. Without cooperation, nothing would happen. It's always a matter of improving that cooperation'.[65]

And he also has reasons to *distrust* cooperation.

At this point in the conversation, he excuses himself and starts telling another story. First, he apologises twice for telling me this, but he says he thinks I will understand, being a woman. 'It was 13 January 2016. There was a cease-fire going on in Bangui. I was at home with my wife, and at 1am she went into labour. There was no transport, because of the curfew. We walked on foot until we found MINUSCA troops. I explained I was a civil servant. I said, "You are here to protect civilians, please help my wife, she is in labour". They said that to take my wife [in] their car, my wife who was about to die in pain, they would need to call their bosses in New York and get authorisation. There you have, *cooperation!*', he says with loud outrage. 'I asked my wife, and we decided to go to a small clinic, where they gave her some medicine and someone managed to get a car—I thanked him—to take her to the hospital. In 30 minutes, she gave birth. If she had to walk that much, she would have had to give birth on the road and she might have died! We need to *humanize that cooperation. We have a form of cooperation that sticks to procedures that ignore[s] the dignity of human life, that [doesn't] respect that dignity of life'*, he concludes.[66]

We must remember that the person telling me that story and saying those powerful words is the focal point in CAR for every major

64 . Interview with Bienvenu Hervé Kovoungbo, 24 April 2020.
65   Ibid.
66   Ibid.

cooperation agreement and partnership there is right now in the country. He does believe in international solidarity and cooperation, but the difference might be that he is truly *passionate* about it. He cannot conceive of solidarity and cooperation not being synonymous with each other. He does not see cooperation as a technical, straight-jacketed version of solidarity, or at least he does not believe it should be.

A major contribution the g7+ could make might be to find ways for solidarity and cooperation to exist together, and for the latter to be more humanized.

Challenges to Passion and Solidarity: Seeking Flexibility in the Face of an Obsession with Templates

One of the challenges that the g7+ was created to face is the bureaucratic, managerialist mentality that is pervasive in the development field, and that makes donor behaviour so difficult to change. Most people in the group identify this as their greatest frustration; after all, 'measurability should not be confused with development significance' and 'development programs that are most precisely and easily measured are the least transformational, and those programs that are most transformational are the least measurable'.[67] It is not only a matter of changing the narrative around fragility, but of making this change work in order to affect other changes on the ground as well. The advocacy practised by the g7+ aims to address these issues by promoting different means of engagement, diverse frameworks, and principles. However, these will always be of limited success in a realm where people consume new frameworks like they change clothes.

Around the middle of 2018, Habib wrote in disappointment:

> [A]fter the launch of the New Deal, there was a lot of energy around it... But as time [has] passed by, we see progress only on the technical aspect of the New Deal as is found by its first Monitoring Report in 2014 (IDPS, 2014). In other words, it seems to be falling out of *fashion*, whereas it has a pioneering role in the international system and policies related to conflict and fragility. I am afraid that this might become a global norm of endorsing a new framework and agreeing on principles without attempting to realize the potential of what we have committed to. Thus, the IDPS is in need of consolidating its potential and [to] be utilized for political dialogue, rather than purely technical discussion among the g7+, donors, and civil society.[68]

In a way, it is almost as if 'experts' consider it 'unprofessional' to stick to one's plan, to be passionate about it and want to see it through to its end. Of course, seeing something through cannot mean an absence of adaptation and flexibility; frameworks are always found lacking when faced with reality. But instead of creating things anew, there is value in commitment, especially when it is clear that technical solutions are limited, often wasteful ('experts' cost high fees, as seen in the first budget presented to Guinea-Bissau for their elections),[69] and can only go so far without passion and solidarity. In fact, it is passion that often lays the ground for flexibility, precisely because it keeps things human—and flexibility is key in conflict-affected countries and in complex situations in general.

The g7+ faces other challenges as well; and some of the most considerable challenges are internal. The passion of those individuals

---

67   Natsios, Andrew (2010). *The Clash of the Counter-bureaucracy and Development*. Center for Global Development, p. 3.

68   Mayar, Habib Ur Rehman (2018). 'Sustaining peace and shared prosperity: The question of fragile states'. *Global Social Policy*, pp. 222–27.

69   See also: Peake, Gordon (2013). *Beloved Land: Stories, struggles, and secrets from Timor-Leste*. London: Scribe Publications.

portrayed in these stories, their solidarity, and joy in being together, have so far been generated by only a few people. This problem is well acknowledged by the group; most of the focal points, apart from Antonio, Abie, and Bienvenu, change frequently. We have seen with the three of them and a few others what the amazing gains might be of having people stick around for a longer period of time, but, of course, this is a huge challenge when governments change often. An additional challenge is the underlying financial asymmetry: among member countries, Timor-Leste pays most of the bills related to the g7+, although contributions from other member countries were approved in 2019 and are in the process of being ratified by governments. And usually only a few of the member countries are particularly active internationally, voicing the g7+'s various agendas. Finally, the old challenge of involving Finance Ministers only crops up every now and then; whenever one needs active professional diplomatic engagement, for instance, or larger buy-ins nationally for implementing g7+ mechanisms, such as Fragility Assessments, and the monitoring of priority SDGs. The g7+ has been seeking to expand its range of involvement to other ministries, to chiefs of government, and parliaments.[70] Two initiatives, one on Access to Justice, which might bring the g7+ to the closer attention of Ministers of Justice, and one on the potential creation of a g7+ Inter-Parliamentary Assembly, can be of great benefit in that sense.[71]

Last, but not least, *passion cannot compensate for preparedness, and personal relationships have their limits.* Institutionally, although the close ties of solidarity played an undoubtedly crucial part in what the g7+ has achieved, they are vulnerable to changes in government and the exhaustion of the people who are engaged in the organisation. Moreover, people often cannot implement changes in their ministries and governments by themselves, no matter how invested they are, unless other people are strategically aware and engaged.

That said, the fact that joy, passion and solidarity cannot do everything all by themselves does not mean they are ineffective. As these stories show, there is much to be harnessed there and when facing considerable obstacles, ranging from war to intense frustration, then joy, passion, and solidarity are often the only remedies that can keep people moving forward. They

---

70   See Rocha de Siqueira, I. (2019). Op. cit.

71   g7+ March 2020 Newsletter.

are assets in that sense—not secondary, not dispensable, and not exotic additions.

How to Work with Passion: On the Value of Doing Things Together

1. *Togetherness* needs to be seen as a value and a practice.

2. Learn to live with frustration but leave no one behind.

3. Put solidarity in practice (truly).

5. How to Decide Where your Pride Fits

The 'Fragile States' Label and the Need for a Unified Front

Havia, em Macácar, um crocodilo que se lembrou, certa manhã,
de dar um longo passeio. [...] No céu nem uma nuvem.
Um ar de suave frescura afagava a terra. [...]
Quando estava nestas sérias e aflitas considerações e bons propósitos,
apareceu um rapaz. [...] Recebeu-o sobre o dorso a primeira vez
que ele apareceu na praia e fez-se de longa viagem, sobre as ondas,
a caminho das terras onde nasce o Sol. [...] O crocodilo andou, andou, andou.
Exausto, parou, por fim, sob um céu de turquês, e — oh! prodígio —
transformou-se em terra e terra para todo o sempre ficou —
terra que foi crescendo, terra que se foi alongando e alteando,
sobre o mar imenso, sem perder, por completo, a configuração do crocodilo.
O rapaz foi o seu primeiro habitante e passou a chamar-lhe Timor, isto é, Oriente.[1]

---

1   There was, in Macácar, a crocodile that remembered, one morning,/to take a long walk. [...] Not even a cloud in the sky./An air of soft freshness stroked the earth. [...]/As the crocodile found itself in these serious and distresseing considerations and filled with good purposes,/a boy appeared. The crocodile received him on his back the first time/that he appeared on the beach and a long journey was made, over the waves,/on the way to the land where the sun rises. [...]/ The crocodile walked, walked, walked. Exhausted, he finally stopped under a turquoise sky, and—oh! prodigy—/turned into land and land forever remained—/land that kept growing, land that was stretching and rising,/over the immense sea, without completely losing the crocodile configuration./The boy was its first inhabitant and started to call it Timor, that is, East. See Pascoal, Ezequiel Enes (1967). 'A Alma de

     https://doi.org/10.11647/OBP.0311.05

That poem is one of many versions of a legend about how Timor-Leste was formed. In this version, the crocodile becomes the earth and turns into a country, each scale changing into a mountain, but he never loses his original form and never forgets he was a crocodile. In other versions, perhaps more pedagogic and child-oriented, the crocodile and the boy are both said to be dreamers who have ventured far away. The crocodile had been hungry in his small and dirty swamp and the boy helped him, so both could travel to see more and reach new places.[2] Today, crocodiles are considered sacred by some Timorese people, even if they do attack people from time to time, especially fishermen. As a matter of fact, crocodiles are called 'abo', influenced by the Portuguese word for grandfather, 'avô'. I suppose if your country is half of an island, has been colonized twice in its history, and only recently had the chance to to govern itself, that legend carries a powerful message about pride and tradition; it suggests the possibility of looking ahead and searching the horizon without losing sight of one's origins. Not to mention the fact that being likened to a crocodile with powerful teeth does not do a small nation any harm.

Not all nations in the g7+ are small nations, however; some are big, like the DRC. Not all are islands; some are landlocked, like CAR. Not all have natural mineral resources; the Timorese have oil, the African countries have many minerals, Papua New Guinea has gold and copper, but the Solomon Islands and Haiti count mostly on their agriculture.[3] Therefore, not all are vulnerable to the same risks and threats, human or otherwise. The woes of the g7+ countries are many and varied. Nevertheless, they have many things in common: all g7+ countries have been either colonized or occupied; all have seen conflict or instability; all have difficulties generating more income. All in all, being called 'fragile' might be as reasonable as it has been controversial.

Timor vista na sua fantasia: Lendas, fábulas e Contos', as cited in Paulino, Vicente (2017). 'As lendas de Timor e a literatura oral timorense'. *Anuário Antropológico*, 42(2), Brazil: UnB, p. 168.

2   See: O crocodilo que se fez Timor. http://www3.dsi.uminho.pt/academiamilitar/1999/historia/lenda.htm.

3   Martins, N., Leigh, C., Stewart, J. & Andersson, D. (2014). *Natural Resources in g7+ Countries*. g7+ Secretariat, p. 59. https://g7plus.org/attach-pdf/Natural%20Resource%20in%20g7%20countires.pdf.

'We didn't decide to call ourselves "fragile"; we knew we were "fragile"... But we say we're easy. They can call themselves anything they like. Some say they are less resilient or more vulnerable. Others say "fragile". We don't have an issue. We don't go [on] about all these names...'.[4] This was former Timorese Finance Minister Emilia Pires's statement, back in 2013, that the label did not mean much to her. Indeed, considering how big the g7+'s ambitions were and how assertively they were pressuring for the group to be formed, their representatives did not come across as meek.

Yet the message was confusing: 'It was a branding nightmare', Peter Lloyd, the war correspondent turned communication advisor, says. 'It was a challenging brand', Missy Stephens, another former advisor, agrees. Having coordinated strategic communication for a while, Peter would know: 'It was hard to sell.'[5] For certain member countries, the word created resistance: 'Burundi is not a fragile country, that's not the value we see in being in the g7+', says Cyriaque Miburo, focal point for the African country. But at the same time, he suggests: 'If ministers could understand that there is also no shame in fragility itself, we could move forward more'.[6] Although most focal points indicate this is not a major problem, the issue is known to have prevented the engagement of other countries in the g7+.[7] What happens nowadays, in practice, is that the language is adapted to each context, and 'fragile *situations*' or 'conflict-affected states' have been used more often. Officially, the g7+ stated in 2013: 'A state of fragility can be understood as a period of time during nationhood when sustainable socio-economic development requires greater emphasis on complementary peacebuilding and statebuilding activities such as building inclusive political settlements, security, justice, jobs, good management of resources, and accountable and fair service delivery'.[8] For Habib, the point is simple: 'We have our own definition of the label. Countries which need more care, more support. We make an analogy with a glass of champagne: if you don't handle with care, it can break'.[9]

---

4   Interview with Emilia Pires (2013). Cited in Rocha de Siqueira, I. (2017). Op. cit., p. 175.
5   Interview with Peter Lloyd, 30 March 2020.
6   Interview with Cyriaque Miburo, 19 June 2019.
7   Ethiopia and Nepal.
8   g7+ (2013). *Note on the Fragility Spectrum*. Kinshasa: g7+, p. 1.
9   Interview with Habib (2013). Cited in Rocha de Siqueira, I. (2017). Op. cit., p. 175.

Fragile States — Terminology and Politics

In 1993, the then US Ambassador to the United Nations, Madeleine Albright, stated, in a speech to justify aid and intervention in Somalia:

The decision we must make is whether to pull up stakes and allow Somalia to fall back into the abyss or to stay the course and help lift the country and its people from the category of a failed state into that of an emerging democracy. For Somalia's sake, and ours, we must persevere.

It was the 'ours' that denoted the image 'failed states' were acquiring at the time; their problems were slowly becoming 'global' problems. In 1994, this tone acquired apocalyptic notes when an American journalist, Robert D. Kaplan, wrote what was considered an extremely compelling article, *The Coming Anarchy*. The piece depicted a horrendous near future of human misery and chaos in what he called 'collapsing states', previously part of the 'Third World' and mostly represented by African countries...

It was in this context that the US Central Intelligence Agency (CIA) sponsored a State Failure Task Force, composed of academics from different American universities, tasked with designing empirical research on the 'correlates of state failure' from the mid-1950s onwards... the objective of the Task Force was to measure causes of instability in the post-Cold-War period through data-driven research...

Slowly, terminology moved on to speaking of a continuum and, not least for diplomatic reasons, 'fragility' became more used.

'...the post-9/11 war on terror was a milestone in the international approach to 'state fragility'. The 2002 US National Security Strategy's statement, 'America is now threatened less by conquering states than we are by failing ones' has been repeated ad eternum in policy reports and academic papers. The strategy presented by the document was to become known as the '3Ds': defence, diplomacy and development. It presented development as one key pillar of US foreign policy to the extent it could work against potential security threats: 'Poverty does not make poor people into terrorists and murderers. Yet poverty, weak institutions, and corruption can make weak states vulnerable to terrorist networks and drug cartels within their borders'. Similar moves happened in Europe in regards state fragility.'

Much criticism is based on the colonial tone mobilised by much of the discourses that culminated in 'state fragility'. Indeed, authors (especially American) commonly advocated for new kinds of trusteeships and more intrusive forms of intervention. However, this tone was increasingly abandoned as global politics came to slowly revisit its colonial roots.

(Excerpts from Rocha de Siqueira, I. (2019). Op.cit., pp. 9–12. See also: Albright, Madeleine (10 August 1993). 'Yes, there is a reason to be in Somalia'. http://www.nytimes.com/1993/08/10/opinion/yes-there-is-a-reason-to-be-in-somalia.html; Kaplan, Robert D. (2002). *The Coming Anarchy: Shattering the Dreams of the Post Cold War*. Reprint edition. New York: Random House USA Paperbacks; Political Instability Task Force. 'Political Instability Task Force. Internal Wars and Failures of Governance, 1955-Most Recent Year'; Crocker, Chester (2003). 'Engaging Failing States. Hitting the right targets'. *Foreign Affairs*, 82(5); Matthews, Robert (2006). 'The 9/11 factor and failed states - food for thought notes'. In *Peacebuilding and Failed States*. Some Theoretical Notes. 256. Lisbon: Oficina do CES; Patrick, Stewart (2011). *Weak Links: Fragile States, Global Threats and International Security*. New York: Oxford University Press; USAID (2005). 'Fragile States Strategy'. United States Agency for International Development, p. v.)

I turn to what may sound like a minor academic or diplomatic discussion because I believe it is emblematic of what g7+ people go through when they need to negotiate their own pride on a daily basis, at an individual and collective level. Let us look at the case of Timor-Leste, since we started this chapter with its most famous legend.

After the UN Transitional Administration in East Timor (UNTAET), in 2002, the country was the 'new kid on the block'. The World Bank senior officer I mentioned before, and who later left the Bank, said that 'donors were eager to show... "this time we will get it right"'. She adds: 'I actually heard someone say "This country will go straight from Third World to First World"'.[10] With that spirit everywhere, Timor-Leste was flooded with donor missions and 'experts'. However, a Timorese NGO, La'o Hamutuk, estimated that 90% of all Official Development Assistance (ODA) 'never reached the country, being mostly spent on salaries, overseas procurement, imported supplies, and overseas costs'.[11] At the same time, much weight was put on capacity-building, yet a close observer at the time said, 'Being such an expensive business, you'd think that there would be clear definitions of the most critical objective of all. Not so. I never got an entirely convincing answer from anyone as to what "capacity-building" meant'.[12] How did donors know, then,

---

10   Cited in Rocha de Siqueira, I. (2017). Op. cit., p. 76.
11   Peake, Gordon (2013). *Beloved Land: Stories, struggles, and secrets from Timor-Leste* [Kindle edition]. London: Scribe Publications, position 2746.
12   Ibid.

that they were in fact doing their work? Observer Gordon Peake, who spent some time participating in these dynamics (a former such 'expert' himself), tells us what it was like to be working to 'rebuild' Timor soon after the UN concluded its mission:

> None of what I've written so far would be particularly new to the Dili lunch set, or indeed to anyone who works in a peacekeeping mission or aid organisation. Much of the chat among foreigners in coffee shops is gallows talk about how whatever program they are working on is not achieving its stated aims. "The Timorese just don't seem that interested," they say, engaging in the verbal equivalent of a long shake of the head. Useless colleagues are a standby topic when there is a gap in the conversation; verbally flaying the efforts of others accompanies most lunchtime tête-à-têtes. Their laments are little different from those of the Portuguese in Dili more than one hundred years previously. But then a curious thing happens once the plates and coffee cups are cleared away: the flayers return to their cubicles, and devise reports of success and progress for their respective headquarters, irrespective of whether or not what is reported accords with what is happening.[13]

Well, when the g7+ was founded, the aim was to turn that narrative around, to create a platform to evaluate donors' efforts, debate the various limitations in the international agendas, and show the incongruences, not to say hypocrisies, of the development industry. The problem is one might not make many allies going down that path, so hard choices need to be made.

Proud to Start With: Raising the Ownership Flag

The chief operating officer at the g7+ Secretariat in Dili, Felix Piedade, recalls exactly what it was like growing up with the waves of international 'experts' coming to his country: 'International organisations were coming in to help. I remember realizing "If we Timorese don't prepare, we won't be able to run the country." I saw the UN people; they were young and had higher education. I felt I needed to do that'.[14]

Felix is the oldest of seven siblings. He tells us that he was such a naughty child, his father decided to send him to a religious boarding school, three hours away from Dili, where they lived. 'They drove me

---

13   Ibid., position 2776.
14   Interview with Félix Piedade, 19 March 2020.

there. On the first night, I almost ran away', he says chuckling. 'After a few months, I had many friends and started to like it. The lesson for me is that everything needs a period of adjusting; nothing is easy'. He was in the boarding school for three years; there he learned Portuguese and some English. Felix says the experience helped prepare him to go abroad for college. He got one of nine scholarships offered to Timorese students in his province to go to Indonesia and left in 1995. He remembers it fondly as a very exciting experience, seeing a new place, leaving his country for the first time: 'It changed my life, because it was a semi-military school, so we had to wear uniform and there was a lot of discipline. It truly changed my personality, like the feeling of respect for older people became even stronger. When I came back, my dad was so proud. He said I had been the naughtiest child and now I was the example', Felix reminisces. He then left again in 2001 to do his master's degree in Australia. Felix says the hardest part was learning English, 'but' he had nine months to do so (he says this as if that is a long period of time).

A few years after completing his master's degree, he was working at the Ministry of Finance as a National Research Officer. Felix worked to identify the country's priorities and monitor the implementation of the Millennium Development Goals in Timor-Leste. Later, Felix led the first g7+ Fragility Assessment conducted by Timor-Leste in 2010/2011 (see Annex III).

> There were many challenges involved. I remember one was when people asked, "One more assessment?", as many different assessments had been done in the past. I didn't know how to respond well to this at first. It was also difficult because people expected the problems they mentioned would be addressed. But we couldn't follow up after. I was trying to see how the [g7+'s] PSGs could align to the MDGs. It was also extremely difficult to get enough people for the assessment. I was supposed to find one person to head each working group related to each PSG but it was so difficult to recruit. What we did was we found people we knew to read things through. We also approached the UNDP and civil society— they are strong in justice. And of course, there was also the difficulty in accommodating all the views. But overall, my biggest frustration was when we were doing the workshops [for the Fragility Assessment] and people asked what the benefit was in participating in the g7+. People would say things like "We are suffering in our country and why [do] we need to give money to other countries?", then they would ask whether I agreed or not. It was always the hardest for me to answer.

He is still slightly exasperated.[15]

After this, Felix felt he needed more experience: 'I came back in 2003 after my master's and was working and teaching but I still felt it was not enough'.[16] But it was only in 2014 that he left to do his PhD in Australia, accompanied by his wife and two children. Felix and his family lived in Australia until 2018 and returned to Timor-Leste when his studies were finished. Today, besides working in the g7+ Secretariat, he teaches postgraduate students. Felix still sees many tough challenges ahead for Timor-Leste, but when he speaks of the g7+, these somehow take the form of a *mission*: 'What I am the proudest about is that we are a small country but with a big mission'.[17] Listening to Felix, it seems to me the fact that g7+ people have set themselves an ambitious target is more of a motivating factor than something that causes bitter paralysis, as so often happens when reality does not match one's dreams. Moreover, stories like Felix's tells us not only what people dream for themselves and their countries, but about how people like to be seen and appreciated.

It is telling to observe that, in an industry that can value bureaucracy and poise so much, little attention is paid to how people in conflict-affected countries must feel about not being seen in all their pride: 'I remember years ago IDPS wanted to make a video, but we decided to do one ourselves about the PSGs. The g7+ didn't want people dying, crying, begging... All those countries have hope too and people are doing innovative things. We made our own video'. This instance, which Missy recalls, is symbolic of how often the industry mistakes the need for assistance with an absence of pride—probably to the same extent that crises are not as seriously evaluated for their external causes as for their internal ones.

There are so many other stories full of pride.

Bienvenu's father was a teacher of French and English in secondary schools in CAR:

> Every two or three years we moved to another region of the country, where he was reallocated to teach in another school. We were five siblings. We were middle class, but now I know, when I remember, how much more well-off we were than other people. Every summer, we would go to our hometown to visit our family. That's how we kept in

---

15   Ibid.
16   Ibid.
17   Ibid.

touch with our traditions. We hunted; we went fishing. But there was no running water, no electricity, no doctors, no TV, no public library. Many people left school early because they didn't see the point. That's why I wanted to work in the public administration; I wanted to do my part to offer opportunities of development to my people.[18]

The reason I tell this story, specifically, is because of how much pride is instilled in Bienvenu's memories as he tells them. When we ask him whether there are any specific stories from his childhood that he remembers inspiring him to do the work he does now, he immediately tells us of his ancestors, starting with a powerful idea: 'When you know where you come from, you are able to stick to your path. That's why my father always reminds me that I am the great-grandson of a king. This was King Bangassou, of the Nzakara tribe, in the Southeast of CAR. He resisted colonisation. According to my father, I have the blood of a king. The king guards his people and he works for their peace, fulfilment, and wellbeing all the time, uninterruptedly. That story transformed my life and is at the core of my daily commitment to work'.[19] If we remember his engagement with the Bangui Reconciliation Forum, this is an important thread in Bienvenu's history. He also tells us of how his father has gathered many regional stories and written about the different traditions he has been in touch with after all his travelling in the country, but Bienvenu regrets the fact that his father could never get the support to publish what, by his account, would be the first such compilation. My own view is that, when searching for transcriptions of oral stories from many of the g7+ and other countries, we find articles in English authored by scholars from the United States, the United Kingdom, and other former colonial powers. We do also find digital repositories with those oral accounts in their original versions, but the problem is that not many people outside of the capital cities, and outside of the middle and upper classes, would probably have access to these. And if knowing one's origins is crucial to sticking to a certain path of commitment to one's people future, then these things matter more than a single account can tell.

There is no limit to what these stories can uncover. Naheed tells us of how her mother was the first female governor in the whole of Afghanistan's history and territory. In the last elections held in

---

18   Interview with Bienvenu Hervé Kovoungbo, 24 April 2020.
19   Ibid.

Afghanistan, in 2020, Naheed, who has now had to leave her country, proudly published a picture of her and her mother holding their tinted fingers up after voting. Dr. Habiba Sarabi, Naheed's mother, has her own Wikipedia entry. It reads 'Dr. Habiba Sarabi (Dari: حبیبه سرابی) (born 1956) is a hematologist, politician, and reformer of the post-Taliban reconstruction of Afghanistan. In 2005, she was appointed as Governor of Bamyan Province by President Hamid Karzai, which made her the first Afghan woman to become a governor of any province in the country. She previously served as Afghanistan's Minister of Women's Affairs. Sarabi has been instrumental in promoting women's rights and representation and environment issues'.[20] One can imagine what kind of legacy that constitutes to a young woman starting her career in public administration, and it is inevitable to wonder at the power that telling such stories has in fostering hope even amid great adversity.

These are, in fact, two common characteristics among many of the people involved in the g7+: a deep respect for family, especially their parents, and their family background acting as a constant incentive for them to keep investing in education and hard work.

'I always remember a passage of the Bible from something my father used to say: "Train up a child the way they should go"', Siafa says with tenderness, when he recalls how his mother was respected by him and his siblings as the head of the family and how she took care of everyone when his father passed away in Liberia. 'When we left Liberia and moved to the US, my mother's country of citizenship, I never used to see ourselves as refugees. I didn't like the word, I guess. I remember being bullied about my accent at school. So, you learn to adapt; I quickly lost my accent. But at home we did use it. Also, I guess you always have that guilt feeling when you survive, but there were so many challenges, we didn't talk about the war; it was probably there, in the background, we just didn't talk about it. My mother would go back to Liberia to take care of business; we stayed with my eldest sister and she always cooked Liberian food', Siafa tells us. Another case of a dear sibling who marked someone's trajectory.

---

20 See: 'Habiba Sarābi' (2020). *Wikipedia*. https://en.wikipedia.org/wiki/Habiba_Sar%C4%81bi.

Siafa continues: 'I took my family, my wife and two children to Liberia in 2006. I wanted to show them. We went to the beach because I wanted to show the beautiful side of things too, like in what we use to call "the normal times". But the country wasn't set up for kids then... If you had the choice, you wouldn't want to raise children there at that time'. We know what Siafa did then: He left his family for two years in the US and went back to Liberia with a fellowship, because he wanted to work for the Liberian government and do some public service in the country.

'Certain things stay from when you were a child. Like, we used to fight all the time about who would sit where in the car. One day my father allocated a seat to everyone and that was it. We sat like that' forever, still do'.[21]

If certain things do stick, if they are responsible for the pride that we see in these stories, what do they become? How are they negotiated when it comes to the difficult decisions necessary in policymaking and advocacy? How does one accommodate pride for one's origins with the need to speak softly to people who sometimes might not be interested in that pride, or see it only as an accessory?

TRAIN UP A CHILD THE WAY THEY SHOULD GO

21   Interview with Siafa Hage, 10 March 2020.

How to Decide Where your Pride Belongs: Shame and the World of International Experts

Of course, not all types of pride are equally likely to produce collective gains. 'We leave dear ones aside all the time. We travel all the time; I have been to more than 80 countries. Why am I doing this?'. As the reader might remember, that is when Helder questioned himself in one of our conversations: 'Is it for the good of all or my personal glory?'. One has to acknowledge his bravery in even posing those questions aloud; it is an indication of his constant internal dialogue.

'I believe I'm doing this work for the sake of others who don't have the chance to do this. It's not just reading from a note, a piece of paper that has been prepared; it comes from experience, anecdotes, you know. You put the pride aside when you feel you portrayed a consensus that exists on the ground; people want peace. I always think "Who am I representing here?" It needs to be portrayed with passion'.[22] What Helder is referring to here is that sometimes the pride that anchors him, and makes him believe in the work he is doing, needs to be put aside to achieve something collectively: 'Doing this work, you have to maintain people's interest, their engagement. But governments change all the time. Sometimes, of course, I get frustrated. I think again and again, "Why am I doing this? I'm talking to these people and they don't respond…" Usually, what frustrates me is really the lack of response, the lack of commitment. But then you have to understand this situation is different from when you're working in the office. You can't give up, you have to keep coming back. That's my background, I always keep going', Helder explains.

In the first few years, it seemed that many conversations were taking place, and there were some good intentions at an individual level, but not much dialogue was actually happening:

> [O]ne of the challenges we have faced throughout the existence of the g7+ is that during our regular meetings, it is g7+ ministers who are sent to advocate for countries affected by conflict and fragility, but middle- and senior-level technocrats are sent from the donor side. This is not to discount the quality and commitment of the donor representatives

---

22   Interview with Helder da Costa, 14 April 2020.

we work with but they are ultimately not the decision-makers who are needed to make the changes we are seeking and their frequency of turnover means that we are often dealing with new staff who must familiarise themselves with relevant people and processes. The problem is compounded by the fact that ministers from donor countries are rarely able or willing to travel to our countries—making it difficult for them to comprehend the realities of our situations and to meet us on a level playing field. If donors are to meet their commitments under the New Deal, they will need greater political support at the highest levels.[23]

If we take into account that those who have lived it know their own reality best, then not listening to them directly and not visiting the place that one's government is supposed to be supporting does sound like a doomed approach.

'At the beginning, especially the first four or five years, people used to undermine us', Helder says. And here, doing justice to all the g7+ people's diplomatic skills, I will quote an external advisor instead on what exactly that *undermining* sometimes meant: 'Honestly, it was astonishing how the organisations didn't understand the g7+. They didn't know how *not* to push. They would, for instance, have meetings about indicators without even deciding on priorities first. Sometimes, we would be convened in a place for meetings, and some g7+ representatives needed to take breaks to pray, but donors would want to keep going on with the meetings; it was clear they were impatient', Missy says, still annoyed by it today. There are other examples she gives that can be interpreted as negligence; yet, they still say a lot about how much one needs to adapt and negotiate with one's own pride in order to be in a room with people whose support one needs: 'Imagine flying to a European capital for a meeting, being in and out of a room all day, more than a day, and then they would bring food in for the g7+ representatives: sandwiches on a tray; some of them ham sandwiches. Muslims can't eat ham or anything that was in touch with it! We would need to go out and pay for a meal. Next day, with everyone in the meeting, including donors, lunch was a fancy buffet. Such a big difference!', Missy adds. Such cases tell us that European and American teams can be overly comfortable working in their own cultural context, and that thinking ahead about how to

---

23   g7+ (2016). *Strength in fragility: "We are writing our own history"* — The emergence of the g7+ group from our own perspective, p. 56.

welcome other people into their meetings does not come naturally. In the case of the ham sandwiches, it was another person close to the g7+ but not 'one of them' who ended up writing a cathartic email about the absurdity of the situation. This also goes to show how much one *cannot* say in certain situations, or perhaps how much one would prefer not to say when there are more crucial and urgent issues on the table.

Even among colleagues at the g7+, it is clear that negotiating with one's pride can be tricky. The stories that historically are told and the images they conjure can be difficult to let go, even when one knows better because of certain commonalities. There is much to be said about this, again regarding international meetings. Habib shares some of his experience helping organize one of the g7+ ministerial meetings, which took place in Afghanistan in 2016. This story has another tone to it after the Taliban takeover.

> International meetings have usually taken place in developed countries, where it is logistically convenient. But the g7+ has conducted most of meetings in member countries despite logistic and practical challenges. During the third ministerial meeting in 2014, the Government of Afghanistan announced that it would host the fourth Ministerial meeting in Kabul. The announcement came at a time when Afghanistan had just concluded its presidential election, which resulted in a peaceful transfer of power, through democratic means, for the first time in decades, as Dr. Ashraf Gahani was elected president. I remember during the IDPS meeting that took place right after the third ministerial meeting [the ministers and representatives travelled from Lomé to Freetown for this] how stressful the situation in Afghanistan was. The result of the elections was being contested and that finally ended in a power-sharing agreement after weeks of negotiations. The year of 2014 was a stressful year because it was during this time when the security transition from NATO and ISAF to the Afghan national security forces was taking place.

This is when, during our conversation, Habib starts sharing the concerns and anxieties he personally felt at the time.

> During the IDPS meeting, a representative from a donor country commented that Afghanistan might become the next Iraq. As an Afghan national and representative, I lambasted [them] by saying that Afghanistan had just concluded [an] election and there was a consensus that there would not be a power vacuum. I hoped that the international community had [learned] its lessons from 1992, when it abandoned Afghanistan altogether. After the meeting was concluded and just as I

walked into the lobby of the hotel, my eyes fell on the TV where the newscaster was talking about the controversial results of the elections in Afghanistan. I stood there staring at the TV and the negative vibe I felt in the meeting room with the comments from the representative was echoed on the TV as well. With a deep sigh I walked into the room thinking and praying the situation would be stable in Afghanistan for our next meeting.

In between that meeting and the g7+ event, from 2014 to 2016, the Afghan ministries of Finance and Foreign Affairs worked together with the g7+ Secretariat. For the first time, one of the group's high-level meetings would be hosted inside a government building, where the Ministry of Foreign Affairs was located. 'Known for our hospitality, I was confident about the Government of Afghanistan's preparation for the meeting in terms of protocol and other logistics. The meeting venue was prepared elegantly. What concerned me, though, was the security threats. The year of 2016 was not very peaceful. The Government of Afghanistan had to provide security during the meeting without the help of the international security forces stationed in Kabul', Habib explains somewhat tense still. The he goes on to describe exactly how security was provided, since he ended up directly involved: 'I was in Kabul well in advance of the meeting to personally observe all the preparation. My phone never stopped ringing as I was a contact person for everything, ranging from protocol and security to substance like briefings, speaking notes and communiqués. Colleagues from the ministries of Finance and Foreign Affairs worked tirelessly to ensure success. The part of the city surrounding the Ministry of Foreign Affairs was cordoned off and security personnel were stationed on the road from Kabul International Airport to the Ministry of Foreign Affairs. Each of the guests was received with high protocol and tight security'.

Remembering how much work went into these preparations, Habib shares his frustration with the fears that some of his colleagues revealed:

> For many of the participants of the g7+, it would be their first time visiting Afghanistan and that was without having any clue what it looks like other than the images they had [seen] on [the] media. There were participants who admitted that they were advised not to go to Afghanistan for this meeting due to the perceived threats. Well before the meeting, I already got some impressions from our focal points and other guests. The former Deputy-Minister of Indonesia called Helder saying that he had kids and

[a] wife, giving the impression his life would be under risk if he travelled to Afghanistan. He had been invited by the Eminent Person of the g7+ to attend the meeting and share the experiences of reconciliation with Timor-Leste. Helder had told him that I was in Kabul to make sure that there was enough preparation and security. I think he had also called the Indonesian embassy in Kabul, which had also assured him of the preparation by the Government of Afghanistan.

That all clearly saddened him at the time, but he also seems to consider the reasons people had for concern.

'People were scared because they would always hear the news of suicide attacks that are difficult to contain even if there is tight security. In addition, the Government chose Kabul Serena Hotel to host the guests. Kabul Serena had been attacked twice in the past. So the moment one would google the name Kabul Serena, those images from the attack would pop up. There were several representatives and officials who would contact us asking how safe Kabul Serena was. Of course the hotel was well protected then', he says, a little exasperated. 'Recognizing the security threats, yet being confident, I would still feel very disappointed [about] how the perception of insecurity was affecting the image of our country. Having travelled to countries like Somalia where I was not that nervous at all... maybe I am used to such [an] environment... I could understand how a foreigner would think about going to a country like Afghanistan. But what I couldn't understand was their mistrust [of] the Government's capacity, which contains and deals with daily incidents of insurgency at a large scale and had taken the responsibility to host this meeting and provide [the] protection needed'. At this point it became clear to me, at least, that the issue was not whether people had reasons to worry about the situation in Afghanistan itself, but whether they were showing an inclination to trust government officials who were assuring them of their safety (and working hard to guarantee it).

'We had many high-profile people attending, figures who meant a lot to their own countries, like Xanana Gusmão. I couldn't dare to imagine any bad incident happening. This would be a matter of sovereign shame for Afghans'. That is why he talks with obvious pride about how it felt to observe people's reactions when they arrived: 'As the guests started arriving and as they observed the city and the preparations, many of them told me that they were surprised. They would say that it was not the city they knew from the news'.

The story has a happy ending: 'The meeting was concluded successfully without any mishap. It was very well-prepared, and everyone left with appreciation for the Government and the g7+. I felt so relieved. The weeks before the meeting and the days when the meeting took place were extremely stressful for me and the rest of the team. But as I bid the last guests goodbye and as the driver drove me back from the airport, I looked ahead to the road grateful that the prediction by that colleague at IDPS meeting in 2014 had proven false. I felt emotional, yet very happy', Habib concludes.

Despite these stories, there are also many moments that are full of pride. Missy tells us of how it was when she met then Minister Emilia Pires: 'When I was first hired to support the Timorese government, I was told to go to Minister Pires. I sat there and I started to say "You need to…" She very calmly said "Be quiet, you know nothing. Just listen." It took her four months to ask me for some advice. And you know what? I never *ever* started speaking to people like that again: "You need to…", "You should…" Never'.[24] Missy was a seasoned international advisor by then, not a young unexperienced professional who ought not react badly to being asked to be quiet. It seems that she chose to understand why she was asked not to speak. For other people, perhaps with reason, such attitudes might come across as rude or unfriendly, but perhaps sometimes that is how it must be. Or perhaps it is only human to react like this.

In the negotiations about pride, sometimes recognition comes unexpectedly. Although the first years were difficult, Helder is happy to remember how once the work of the g7+ was acknowledged in the Vatican. He recounts that event with emotion. Let us bear in mind that he was named after Dom Helder Câmara, a Brazilian Catholic Archbishop: 'My father had read his biography, so I was named after him. I grew up having him as an idol, in addition to Nelson Mandela. I admired their wisdom, their passion, but also their simplicity and the way they helped people, how they held themselves in public'.[25] The visit to the Vatican happened because of the g7+'s work to close the camp of IDPs in CAR. Helder briefed the Secretary for Relations with States within the Holy See's Secretariat of State, Mr Paul Gallagher. 'The Prime Minister

---

24   Interview with Missy Stephens, 12 March 2020.
25   Interview with Helder da Costa, 14 April 2020.

Xanana Gusmão had been in CAR in March 2015. And the Pope had visited as well, in October 2015. So, after the g7+ visited and after it provided help to close the camp, we were invited to the Vatican to tell of the cooperation on Bangui, in July 2016. I was so proud. The Prime-Minister of Timor-Leste, Dr Rui Maria de Araújo, had asked me earlier on to brief the Vatican officials on the work of the g7+ in CAR. I keep the picture of the meeting in the office. It reminds me of what we can achieve even with little'.[26]

The risk, as it happens, is that stories of travelling and being introduced to authorities like that can feed into the belief that all professionals in the field, including those in the g7+, are only interested in self-promotion, travel and *per diems*. I think it is about time that these beliefs are addressed in this case. Perhaps a good point of departure is the numbers I mentioned many pages earlier: '15,000 donor missions in 54 recipient countries per year'—and in some countries this has amounted to 'over 20 official visits per week'.[27] Looking at these figures, one can safely say there is definitely too much travel in the development industry. Nevertheless, perhaps one should initiate scrutiny by asking oneself whose journeys or what types of travel are outrageous, and I suppose the answers depend on many factors, all of which should be carefully considered as generalizations, which are, by design, not accurate, and therefore hardly ever fair.

'I still remember leaving Afghanistan and my family behind and not knowing the place I was going to', Habib tells us about when he took the job at the g7+ Secretariat in Dili. 'Getting visas with an Afghan passport is not easy, which only increased my anxiety. *I never had a travel insurance in my life.* And travelling across continents with an Afghan passport is a huge challenge...' He is reluctant to go on at this point. He says he does not often tell these stories—'What's the point?'—but I insist that this sounds important. If we take into account the general impression that travelling in this field often seems to take center stage instead of the work itself, I wanted to ask: What is travelling like for people in the g7+? So, Habib goes on:

---

26   Ibid.
27   Ramalingam, Ben (2013). *Aid on the edge of chaos: Rethinking international cooperation in a complex world.* Oxford: Oxford University Press, p. 3.

> I am singled out for interrogation so many times... I think I have been
> through this 14 or 15 times. I had one situation when I was disembarked
> from a plane. A lady came, I was already [in] my seat, and she asked for
> my boarding pass. Then she came back and asked for my passport. At
> this point, they announced over the sound system that the plane would
> take off. And then, she came back again and asked me to get my bag
> and follow her. And you know *nothing* of what's going on. Everyone was
> looking, some people even had their phones up recording, thinking "they
> got a wanted person". I didn't say anything. I stepped outside; there were
> ten people waiting in the jet bridge. And I could see a police car outside,
> on the tarmac. I didn't know who these people waiting were. "I need
> to check your documents", one of them said. The plane was waiting.
> "Either he goes with you or with us", the security personnel said. I was
> worried they would interrogate me, because these things take forever.[28]

At this point, I was surprised: Habib was not worried about the
interrogation itself—I suppose he has indeed been through it many
times—but he was concerned it would take too long, which would mean
missing his flight and potentially his connection. The story continues:
'The pilot wanted to close the door. The guy with the passport was
shouting. Then the plane just left. And... five minutes later, the guy
with my passport said, "You can go now". I finally said, "Go where?"'.[29]
That is the first time he sounds angry while telling the story, and he was
probably angry then too. 'People looked embarrassed. I said, "No, no.
I need to go and I need to make it in time for my connection flight." A
person from the airline company then said, "We will take care of you"'.
He ended up flying later on, but who knows what the people who
recorded him getting off the plane did with those videos? And the mere
act of being filmed caused enough distress. 'Apparently, it was again my
middle name. This happened before. Someone else has the same middle
name', Habib explains. Honestly, *I* was angry listening to all this, but
Habib seemed just fine at the end—not with the situation itself, but he
seemed reasonably calm when talking about it. 'I don't tell such stories,
usually. We Afghans are embarrassed by those things'.[30]

After a while, Minister Emilia Pires intervened directly and managed
to get Habib a temporary Timorese service passport, which makes those

---

28   Interview with Habib Mayar, 23 March 2020.
29   Ibid.
30   Ibid.

trips easier, perhaps, but he does not have Timorese citizenship. He is still an Afghan citizen, and the work for the g7+ still does not include travel insurance.

In addition, travelling, for Habib at least, does not mean sightseeing, although it could do. (Why should travelling for work not involve some cultural exchanges, too, and some joy in visiting the places one is supposed to be representing or with whose representatives one has been negotiating and learning? Perhaps there should not be an issue with sightseeing, but with the amount and quality of work actually done. These things get confused.)

> Even before joining the g7+, I had visited more than 20 countries. For us [Afghans], it's not fun at all. I don't have insurance', Habib repeats. 'And look, I'm going to Somalia, CAR... I always step up and go. I remember I was on a mission to Somalia with Emilia and the OECD-DAC chair once. The travel was facilitated by the UN mission there and hence we had to conduct our meetings at Mogadishu airport where the Prime Minister and his Ministers had to come and meet us. We (the g7+ delegation) were not comfortable with such arrangement as we had to be respectful of the Somali authorities. But we couldn't do much as that was the only option for us. During the meeting, Minister Emilia, who was the chair of the g7+, asked the Prime Minister if I and Nik could visit the Ministry of Planning [g7+ focal Ministry] and the Prime Minister agreed. We told the peacekeeping authorities that we were ready to visit the ministry at our own risk. But UN restrictions didn't allow this.

He then adds: 'My interest is just the work, to have some impact'.

It is understandable, but also definitely ironic that someone who is travelling to Somalia without travel insurance and willing to walk around on his own is stopped from doing so by UN protective measures. He goes on, talking about a different trip: 'When I went to Nicaragua for a meeting, for instance, I travelled for two nights and two days and didn't stay beyond the time of the meeting'.[31]

What is interesting is that there are as many forms of pride as there are kinds of people, which, of course, is a banal point to make. Yet how would one really know without asking?

---

31   Ibid.

I am constantly travelling for the secretariat

People often ask me what that's like

Going from one place to another all the time

Excuse me, sir, can I please see your boarding pass and passport?

I'm sorry, but you'll have to deboard and come with me

14th time...

Yeah, I have been to many places and seen many things...

I'm afraid your flight has taken off. We apologize for the inconvenience

Somali Diaspora

'Canada was a preferred destination for Somali refugees in the late 1980s through 1995, as it had generous asylum and family reunification policies, as well as expansive resettlement and welfare programs. By the early 1990s, Toronto possessed one of the largest populations of resettled Somali refugees in the world for that time, estimated at 25,000...The 2006 Canadian census list[ed] the total number of Somalis in Canada today at 37,785...but is widely believed to understate the total number, which a more recent federal study estimated at 150,000...A more realistic estimate is probably in the range of 70,000–100,000.'

As we speak of migration numbers, Somalia is also well known for the role remittances play as a lifeline for many people: 'In 2016, remittances to Somalia were estimated to amount to USD 1.4bn per year and comprised the largest single category of external financial support that entered the country (equivalent to 23 per cent of Somalia's GDP). Overseas Development Assistance (ODA), for 2016, was £1.3bn.'

(See: Hammond, Laura et al (2011). 'Cash and Compassion. The Role of the Somali Diaspora in Relief, Development and Peace-Building'. United Nations Development Program (UNDP), p. 35; Majid, Nissar, Khalif Abdirahman and Shamsa Hassan (2018). 'Remittances and Vulnerability in Somalia'. Rift Valley Institute Briefing Paper, p. 1.)

Since we have mentioned Somalia, it is a good time to introduce someone new to our story. Hodan Osman was the g7+ focal point for Somalia for a while. She was born in Dubai as her family was fleeing to Canada from Somalia, to escape the conflicts and instability in the country. She sees herself as Somali, though.

Hodan grew up in Toronto. When I ask what led her to become the focal point in Somalia, a country she had only visited a few times (and never the capital) she says 'You know, I had always wanted to do something meaningful, but the reasoning I grew up with was "A migrant doesn't volunteer in NGOs". The idea was to prove yourself [worthy] and do what people do in that country where you are now, which was to make money. My parents didn't go to school. They wanted me to be successful, have money and a good life. But when I had the opportunity and found my way to Somalia, I was thinking "How often do we get to be part of the reform? How often do we get to do things as a first?"'.[32]

It seems this is a potent feeling for some people who become involved with state-building. As Naheed said about her return to Afghanistan, one sees the change so much more when every change counts so much in people's lives. I suppose the impacts are really felt when so many things are so necessary simultaneously. There is good reason to be proud if one is brave enough to face the challenge, and the frustrations that unavoidably accompany it. 'To do something meaningful', after all, is so many people's desire, but how many feel they have achieved that?

The Micro and Macro Challenges to Pride: Geopolitical Negotiations and National Priorities

Now, because we are talking about pride, I want to change tack again and move onto a story that made the headlines in many newspapers at the time. It concerns the negotiations around a refugee camp that Australia wanted to establish outside of its borders.

When we start talking, Peter recalls how it was that he first came to be involved with Timor-Leste, and then with the g7+. As a good storyteller, he starts with controversy and soon has us on the edge of our seats: 'I remember it was 2010, 11am on a weekday and I heard the Prime Minister Julia Gillard talking about creating a processing center for refugees in Timor-Leste. I was surprised. I immediately called Missy, because she was the contact point for Timor in Sydney. I said '"Why has Timor-Leste agreed to this?". She said it was the first she was hearing about it. Australia hadn't talked to the government of Timor'.[33]

In fact, the Australian Prime Minister had apparently briefly discussed the proposal with then-Timorese President José Ramos Horta, but she not taken it to the government of Prime Minister Xanana Gusmão.[34]

In any case, in an interview with an Australian TV programme, President Ramos Horta, the g7+ Special Envoy for Peace since 2019, said he had been tasked by the Prime Minister with holding conversations

---

32   Interview with Hodan Osman, 24 April 2020.
33   Interview with Peter Lloyd, 30 March 2020.
34   See Everingham, Sara (2010). *Growing opposition to 'Timor Solution'*. Reliefweb., https://reliefweb.int/report/timor-leste/growing-opposition-timor-solution.

with the Australian government. He was adamant, saying Timor-Leste would only consider moving ahead with the processing centre on humanitarian grounds, that they could agree to do it only on the basis of sympathy towards 'desperate and destitute refugees': 'We are prepared to listen to the details of the proposal', he said, meaning these had not been put to the Timorese government prior to the announcement. 'We have to look at this in a formal tête-à-tête discussion... We have not even received a letter or [had] a meeting with the ambassador or anyone from Canberra'.[35]

President Ramos Horta goes on in the TV interview to give examples of what would be required in terms of infrastructure and says that this is, for him, a matter of strong conviction about wanting to help people in need. 'It's not a favour, not to Australia, to New Zealand or to Indonesia, the countries that are mostly affected by the boat people and asylum seekers. It's to help people in need'.[36] At this point, the journalist mentions that the previous night, Prime Minister Gillard had said 'she wouldn't rule out the possibility of shifting the thousands of asylum seekers, most of whom or many of whom are already classified as refugees, from Indonesia, where they are stuck in a kind of limbo, where the only way out for them is to go to people smugglers, to East Timor'; then he asks 'Would you be prepared to accept those refugees from Indonesia?'.[37] This is how President Ramos Horta replies:

> Well, if there are displaced persons, refugees in Indonesia who are bona fide refugees, refugees who have no criminal records, who are eligible, on legal and humanitarian grounds, to be transferred to countries like Australia, New Zealand or elsewhere, then that's where they should go and not moving [them] from one facility to another, because Timor-Leste would be a temporary facility... Then I don't understand the point... We are talking about possible *new* arrivals, destitute people, people who flee violence... who are in high seas, who are in danger of drowning... Well, this is what *I'm* talking about, not to be [the] recipient of IDPs... who are already safe in another country.[38]

Asked whether Timor-Leste would try to link these negotiations with any other of the country's interests, such as an onshore processing

---

35 See ABC News Australia (2010). *Ramos-Horta speaks to Lateline* [Video]. YouTube. https://www.youtube.com/watch?v=_lwqU3paaeA.
36 Ibid.
37 Ibid.
38 Ibid.

facility for gas, President Ramos Horta answers immediately: 'No, this is out of the question. Neither I, nor the Prime Minister or anyone in this country would *debase* ourselves by linking something that is purely humanitarian, out of our deepest convictions as human beings, with something like a pipeline. No, we will not bargain with Australia, we will not bargain with anyone.... This is not in my culture, not in my convictions'.[39] At the end of the interview, he concludes by saying, 'We think of our own background, how only a few years ago, Australia hosted us when we fled violence, how Portugal and other countries gave us asylum, gave us shelter, gave us food, gave us jobs. Today we are in a slightly better situation and we should open our shores, our doors to those who flee persecution or extreme poverty'.[40]

I relate so much of this story here because it says so much about how the micro practices I have been describing link up to the very macro politics of how other nations tend to deal with fragile and conflict-affected countries. On all levels, we are talking about pride—as well as other things, of course. One needs only to hear the emphasis President Ramos Horta puts on the word '*debase*'. By the way, the conclusion of this process—which started without a real dialogue—was that Timor-Leste refused to host the centre. But Papua New Guinea (PNG), another g7+ country, did. Manus Island, in PNG, became a very disputed issue, and in terms of jobs and funding, few of the promised advantages of the implementation of the refugee processing centre have become a reality.[41]

One element which is very much valued in g7+ discourse is state sovereignty, which means each member country will count on the support of everyone else to make its own decisions. Yet, perhaps a unified voice can help negotiate political and economic incentives and come up with a unified front against possible infringements on that very sovereignty. This is very sensitive territory.

For this reason, let us take a detour to cover some background history.

---

39   Ibid.
40   Ibid.
41   See *Manus Island*. https://www.theguardian.com/australia-news/manus-island; Liljas, Per (2018). *One of Australia's notorious refugee camps has become an economic crutch for Papua New Guinea island*. The Washington Post. https://www.washingtonpost.com/world/asia_pacific/one-of-australias-notorious-refugee-camps-has-become-an-economic-crutch-for-papua-new-guinea-island/2018/05/08/25e78634-433d-11e8-8569-26fda6b404c7_story.html.

Eminent Person Xanana Gusmão was the first elected president of Timor-Leste after independence, occupying the position between 2002 and 2007. After that, he was Prime Minister from 2007 to 2015, while Ramos Horta was president. He had been a militant since the 1970s, fighting against the Indonesian occupation as part of the Revolutionary Front for an Independent Timor-Leste (FRETILIN, in Portuguese) since Indonesia invaded Timor after Portugal left. EP Xanana Gusmão soon became heavily involved in organising and leading the resistance, but later moved on to negotiate an important ceasefire, which made possible the creation of a nationally organised clandestine network. He gained international prominence in the 1990s by denouncing the violence in the country. As a result, in 1993 he was arrested and received a life sentence in Indonesia. He was released in 1999 but is known to have carried on with the coordination of resistance from the prison, and used to receive famous dignitaries there, like Nelson Mandela.[42]

During the past two decades, as EP Xanana Gusmão and Ramos Horta have been heads of government either as Prime Minister or President, Timor-Leste has faced an international battle with Australia about oil and gas.[43] 'Timor-Leste is the second most oil-dependent nation in the world, and reserves are running down. 'Which is what makes the sea boundary dispute between Australia and Timor-Leste so critical', says Kim McGrath, a 'friend of Timor', and long-time researcher on the subject.[44] Australia has advanced claims on oil and gas resources on Timor-Leste's side of the median line in the Timor Sea. That interest, she found, goes back to Indonesian plans to invade Timor-Leste in the 1970s. In the episode recounted above, on the issue of refugees, there was, therefore, a background to the conversations being held. EP Xanana Gusmão tells us: 'There is no politics without interest; just see our history with Australia. So much about the oil field. And if we think that we have a refugee agency in Timor-Leste. For what? To get resources. There are no refugees in Timor. There is no one here, in the agency, either, so when we have refugees, where are they? No one wants to come; they think it's

---

42   See Government of Timor-Leste (2014). *Biography: Prime Minister and Minister of Defense and Security of the Democratic Republic of Timor-Leste.* http://timor-leste.gov. tl/?p=3&lang=en.

43   McGrath, Kim (2017). *Crossing the Line: Australia's Secret History in the Timor Sea.* Carlton: Black Inc. Redback.

44   Ibid., Introduction.

dangerous. For me, it's like when we consider peacekeeping in CAR. What peace have they achieved, really? People have interests, they are interested in making more money'.[45] What I take from his words and the stories above is that leaders on the ground are best positioned to know how much and when to cede to international pressure.

The fact is that, on the theme of refugees and IDPs policies alone, the g7+ has many interests. Even before the current crises, in 2019, two of its member countries, Afghanistan and South Sudan, were among the major sources of refugees worldwide, with 2.7 and 2.3 million, respectively.[46] In addition, four out of the top ten countries with the largest population of IDPs in the world are members of the g7+ (in order from the largest): DRC, Yemen, South Sudan and Afghanistan, with numbers varying from almost 1.8 million to more than 2.2 million.[47] And yet, '[m]any of the global policy agendas regrettably lack specific goals and indicators on internal displacement'.[48] In fact, among the SDG priority targets selected by the g7+, the group established new indicators, one of them being on IDPs—even though there are no methodologies for collection so far, because, problematically, 'no SDG targets or indicators [are] specifically related to internal displacement'.[49] With a rise in right-wing movements around the world and the impacts of the COVID-19 pandemic, these concerns are bound to be a source of disappointment for the g7+.

On the other hand, g7+ representatives consider that some changes have been achieved in that area within Multilateral Development Banks, especially the World Bank, whose recently published *Fragility, Conflict and Violence Strategy*[50] has a Window for Host Communities and Refugees (WHR) as one of its four pillars.[51] This is where another story

---

45   Interview with EP Xanana Gusmão.

46   See UNHCR (n.d.). *Figures at a glance.* https://www.unhcr.org/figures-at-a-glance.html.

47   OECD (2018). *States of Fragility*, p. 109. The discussion on IDPs is an excerpt from Rocha de Siqueira, I. (2019). Op. cit., p. 86, box 2.

48   See Walicki, Nadine (2017). *Tackling internal displacement through the SDGs.* UNA-UK. https://www.sustainablegoals.org.uk/tackling-internal-displacement-sdgs/.

49   See IISD (2018). *To Leave No One Behind, Brief Calls for Considering IDPs in SDG Implementation.* http://sdg.iisd.org/news/to-leave-no-one-behind-brief-calls-for-considering-idps-in-sdg-implementation/.

50   World Bank Group (2020). *World Bank Group Strategy for Fragility, Conflict, and Violence 2020–2025.*

51   See International Development Association (n.d.). *Window for Host Communities and Refugees.* https://ida.worldbank.org/replenishments/ida19-replenishment/

about pride in micro to macro politics features prominently in the g7+'s trajectory.

IDA Resources

The International Development Association is one of the five arms of the World Bank. Its resources are dedicated to the countries that have no access to standard loans. Every three years, the IDA Replenishments decide on the criteria and formulae for allocation and revise procedures.

(See: https://ida.worldbank.org/about/what-is-ida)

For a while, in fact, the g7+'s strategy with the World Bank has been considered one of its key advocacy successes. By actively engaging in consultations and meetings, some say the g7+ managed to contribute to positive changes in the way the Bank allocates resources to fragile states. 'I would not attribute it exactly to the g7+, because the conditions were there, people had been thinking about how these countries were different for a while, but the g7+ definitely did the best they could with the resources and capacity they had. They did a good job of keeping attention [on] this topic [fragility, conflict and violence]', a former World Bank officer said at the time of the g7+ 2019 Independent Review.[52] One of the ways this contribution and its timing can perhaps be analysed is through IDA17 (2013), entitled 'IDA's Support to Fragile and Conflict-Affected States', when fragile states were largely incorporated into the World Bank's International Development Association (IDA) replenishment exercise. The group proudly comments: 'In 2013, the g7+ achieved observer status at the International Development Association's (IDA) 17th replenishment round meetings and helped secure an agreement for a new IDA allocation formula and a new Turnaround Facility'.[53]

Explaining the technicalities of what has changed within the World Bank's engagement with fragile states, we can sum up by saying that

---

windows-host-communities-refugees.
52 Interview with Gary Milante, 18 June 2019. See parts of this discussion in Rocha de Siqueira, I. (2019). Op. cit., pp. 49–50.
53 g7+ (2016). *Strength in fragility: "We are writing our own history"* — The emergence of the g7+ group from our own perspective, p. 43.

'IDA17 increased financing to FCS by about one-third, introduced Risk and Resilience Assessments (RRAs), introduced the Turnaround Regime (TAR) to help accelerate transitions out of fragility, and advanced... knowledge of what works and what does not', in the Bank's own words. Moreover, after that, '[u]nder IDA18 [the following replenishment exercise], changes to the resource allocation framework doubled core IDA support to FCS to US$14.4 billion. The Risk Mitigation Regime (RMR) was introduced to pilot approaches to prevention and risk mitigation, and the Refugee Sub-Window (RSW) was introduced to support host countries to respond to forced displacement'.[54] But more than the technicalities themselves, what was at stake was getting a seat at the table. The g7+ Secretariat published in a document: 'Since April 2012, the g7+ has obtained an agreement from the World Bank President to hold two meetings every year with g7+ Ministers on the sidelines of the World Bank Spring and Annual Meetings. These opportunities provide our countries with a chance to voice their concerns directly to the senior management of the Bank and ensure that it is aware of the challenges we are facing', the text says.[55] Indeed, in 2019, one such meeting took place to discuss the new World Bank FCV strategy, before public consultations started in May. If nothing else, a seat at the table is a step towards fighting decades of a *'poverty of influence'*, something that resonates with the history of many initiatives from postcolonial countries.[56]

Earlier in this book I mentioned that one of the main concerns of the g7+ has always been to prevent new crises that can put any recent achievements at risk, in addition to guaranteeing predictability in international engagement. Well, IDA19 and the World Bank's FCV Strategy have recently established prevention as a key pillar for the Bank's engagement on the ground. This has also included an investment in more staff in fragile states: the Bank states it is seeking to 'strengthen rewards and incentives, such as the introduction of Hazard and Fragility

---

54   See World Bank Group (2019). *IDA19—Special Theme: Fragility, Conflict & Violence*. International Development Association. New York: World Bank, p. 2.

55   g7+ (2016). *Strength in fragility: "We are writing our own history"* — The emergence of the g7+ group from our own perspective, p. 43.

56   This is a notion mobilized by the 1990 South Commission in the key document, 'The Challenge to the South. The Report of the South Commission', a milestone in developing countries' struggles to change the game.

Pay for local staff' and that it 'will continue to focus on strengthening the employment value proposition for staff through the FCV Strategy's section on "Personnel" which will recommend measures in key areas such as deployment processes, staff preparedness, enhanced learning offerings, ongoing support including health and safety, next assignment planning, staff rewards, and career development'.[57] The 20th replenishment exercise (IDA20) began a year earlier than scheduled due to the emergency situation posed by the pandemic, and has dedicated $93 billion 'to help low-income countries respond to the COVID-19 crisis and build a greener, more resilient, and inclusive future'. Although of course *how* is always the main question—and the one that the g7+ has historically emphasized—it seems that conflict-affected countries never left the Bank's radar, and indeed became a significant category.

Of course, knowing that someone requires that many incentives to work in your country cannot be easy on anyone's pride. But as long as the job is done and done well, it can bring benefits. These changes are allegedly still under way, however, and one should bear in mind that in the 2019 g7+ Ministerial Meeting held in Lisbon, many ministers and focal points commented on the fact that many of the Bank's employees are inaccessible and that they make decisions without consultation.[58]

As a matter of fact, a representative of the World Bank on FCV—who is also a former representative of the g7+—gave a presentation of the new World Bank FCV Strategy in the 2019 g7+ Ministerial Meeting. In summary, Amara Konneh, from Liberia, offered a few important pieces of advice if g7+ countries were to take the opportunities offered by IDA19 and the FCV Strategy (then under elaboration). He emphasised that the World Bank cannot invest directly in peace and security, so these issues must be covered by countries' national budgets, allowing the Bank to direct its funds to other areas—like infrastructure, a major demand of the g7+. He also advised the g7+ governments to engage with World Bank employees on the ground; for example, to organise joint workshops where employees can tell government officials how to 'move from the conceptual to the implementation level on the ground'.[59] He said that this was how ministries could move 'upstream'

---

57   World Bank (2019). *IDA 19 — Special Theme: Fragility, Conflict & Violence*, p. 5.
58   These comments are based on my own notes of the meeting, which are anonymised.
59   Ibid.

and get access to what the new financing windows were offering. The g7+ member countries responded to all that with much scepticism. I was quite surprised to notice that the tone was slightly tougher with a former insider than it had been with the American who presented the most recent strategy that had been cooked up by the United States to 'prevent extremism'. As Konneh finished, g7+ ministers and focal points mentioned many problems and talked about why engaging with the World Bank was difficult. There were references to the fact that 'many conditionalities made any use of the instruments impossible', that 'often, task team leaders are not in the country, but elsewhere, and that trying to engage with them is usually a waste', that 'resources are big but impacts are little', that 'the rhythm of disbursement doesn't usually match the discourse' and so on.[60] The list was long.

What (Then) of Pride?

The issues that trigger the most push-back in these meetings are hard to pin down, as there is so much variation depending on who is engaged. But it seems that it is often the perception that there is no one listening that punctures people's pride. To be in a position of less power and having to fit into a broader political agenda can be accommodated; being asked to fill in matrices, worry over formulae, planning ahead according to specific headings and priorities, and then finding that all these investments of time and resources are not acknowledged, or do not pay off as expected, seems to create more dissatisfaction than other kinds of disappointment. Now that we know more of what drives some people in the g7+ to do their work, and what they base their beliefs on, there is some sense in that. Now that we have also seen how much pride they take in their family stories, in their upbringing, in the hopes and sacrifices they invest in order to pursue quality education and opportunities, it is perhaps clearer how much is at stake in each micro and macro negotiation. Of course, these negotiations are, more often than not, extremely unequal, vested with powerful interests, and involving high stakes. These are not easy paths; one needs diplomatic skills and passion, but also the ability to envisage where one's pride lies.

---

60   Ibid.

In situations such as those we just depicted, this is a matter of strategy and also a sense of duty, a responsibility towards collective goals and towards one's own personal stories.

How to Decide Where your Pride Lies: Working to Get the Job Done

1. Be proud to start with.

2. But decide what your priorities are and where your pride lies if you are to get the job done.

---

6. How to Act Responsibly

On the Sense of Duty

Em que língua escrever
As declarações de amor?
Em que língua cantar
As histórias que ouvi contar
Em que língua escrever
Contando os feitos das mulheres?
E dos homens do meu chão?
Como falar dos velhos
das passadas e cantigas?
Falarei em crioulo?
Falarei em crioulo?
Mas que sinais deixar
Aos netos deste século?
Deixarei um recado num pergaminho
Nesta língua lusa que mal entendo.[1]
by Odete Semedo

All countries worry about keeping their best brains, but some need to worry more than others. Among fragile and conflict-affected states, this is a major concern. Crises tend to encourage people to leave and once they are settled abroad, it is not so easy or common to return.

---

1   In what language to write/Declarations of love?/In which language to sing/The stories I heard tell/In what language to write/Counting women's achievements?/ And the men on my floor?/How to talk about old people/of the strides and songs?/Will I speak in Creole?/Will I speak in Creole?/But what signs to leave/ The grandchildren of this century?/I'll leave a message on a parchment/In this Portuguese language that I barely understand. See Augel (2007). 153, in Dutra, Robson, p. 72 (translation from Portuguese by the poet).

   https://doi.org/10.11647/OBP.0311.06

In addition, incentives to go abroad to study might lead young people seeking job opportunities wherever they get their degrees. Of course, there is the important and well-known fact that diasporas are responsible for an immense volume of resources returning to the countries as well, as seen in the case of Somalia. In 2018, OECD's *States of Fragility* said that 'remittances to fragility-affected countries already eclipse[d] official development aid and foreign direct investment', and tend to grow 'faster and more steadily'. Moreover, the report suggested that 'diasporas that send the remittances also have good knowledge of local contexts and how to support development'.[2] In 2018, remittances were 45% of external financial flows to 'fragile contexts', against 28% of ODA and 22% of foreign direct investments (FDI).[3] With the pandemic, remittances showed resilience and fell only by 1.7% in 2020, rising again by 7.3% in 2021, according to World Bank projections.[4] Nevertheless, as the g7+ has said since its first declaration, development and peace are not just about the volume of economic resources a country has available (although, of course, that is important as well). Having skilled people to design, implement, and monitor national development plans, for instance, is crucial.

We might remember Felix's story, for instance, about how difficult it was to get professionals to head the working groups for each PSG in Timor-Leste's Fragility Assessment, or the fact that Abie also requested support from UNDP to help conduct the Fragility Assessment in Sierra Leone. As we have seen, g7+ countries have many assets, but their people will be the first to say that there is also much that is lacking, especially in countries that have faced recurring crises. How does one foster a sense of duty in public service when sometimes the material conditions cannot be met? How do civil servants in g7+ countries negotiate their own sense of responsibility for their people and countries when they might also take advantage of the opportunities they may have if they stay abroad? And what can the fact that some skilled professionals choose to do that service say about the group's potential? What can we learn from these experiences?

---

2   OECD (2018). *Development Co-operation Report 2018: Joining forces to leave no one behind*. Paris: OECD Publishing, p. 41.

3   Ibid., p. 170.

4   World Bank (2022). *Remittance Flows Register Robust 7.3 Percent Growth in 2021*. https://www.worldbank.org/en/news/press-release/2021/11/17/remittance-flows-register-robust-7-3-percent-growth-in-2021.

When Felix was finishing his PhD in Australia in 2018, he says it was difficult to convince his kids to go back to Timor-Leste: 'My son was 14 years old and my daughter 11. When we came back, in the first week they complained a lot, questioned a lot. Their mindset was so different; it's like a reverse cultural shock. It was hard for them to adapt back. In two weeks, we went to see the schools. They didn't want to go to the public school. My daughter kept asking me about the bathrooms, because she had heard some schools had bathroom outside. We had to put them in an international school', he explains.

It is perhaps easy for some to judge that statement. But then, Felix's family went back to their country. This is also not to say that going back is what anyone *should* do, necessarily. (It is bad enough that xenophobia is on the rise with recent waves of conservatism in many parts of the world; we do not need to reinforce that message.) It is more productive, instead, to understand *what* such decisions entail. The reasoning behind the stories is rich and, again, says much about the assets the g7+ can harness among the individual and collective experiences of its members.

> One year after we came back to Timor-Leste, we decided to renovate the house. One day, when we left to the office, one of our windows was closed only temporarily with zinc so it didn't close properly and someone broke in. My daughter was so upset. She said, "Dad, it's not safe here, it's not good". I think the governments everywhere need to question whether they are doing enough and to have in mind the children. They should ask themselves "Why don't children want to be in this country? How can we change their mindset?" The answer to that is key. We need them to want to stay. When the house was robbed, I told my children "You see, imagine this house is Timor-Leste. We are the owners. Imagine if you left the house unprotected. Someone would come in, rob and destroy.

We don't know what effect that had on Felix's children, but he is emphatic: 'If not us, who else?'.[5]

The motivations vary but the common thread of responsibility and duty is present in many of the stories we heard. *This certainly cannot be extrapolated to apply to everyone. Instead, we want to explore what differences such motivations can make for agendas like those of the g7+, and how these motivations might be nurtured somehow.* And, as I just mentioned, for anyone living in a country that has seen its share of crises—not necessarily

---

5   Interview with Félix Piedade, 19 March 2020.

a g7+ member country—it is not difficult to relate to the feeling that, whilst there is nothing wrong with wanting to live elsewhere, the fact that some people (including foreigners, of course) decide to work in difficult contexts is a vital part of any potential path forward for these countries. As such, it needs to be understood.

Hodan, for instance, is a different case entirely, but she was also moved by some sense of responsibility that perhaps she did not need to elaborate on at the time. However, looking back, she reasons: 'It's not about being patriotic or nationalistic. I wanted to work in Africa, I wanted to work on economic development, and I thought I would be much more effective in Somalia being a Somali. I very much believe in doing reforms from the inside, being able to do that is a lot of what drove me. You're able to do things as a first in conditions like these too'.[6] One might argue this sounds like many outsiders' discourses: people who stay for two weeks, take pictures and write down 'expert with experience in the Horn of Africa' on their CV, for instance.[7] But Hodan took a different approach. The beginning was probably somewhat similar: she went to school in Canada and went on to study business. She worked for eight years in commercial banking, then decided to do her master's degree in the United States, where she took a step towards what she calls 'doing something more meaningful' and studied Human Rights. After that, she did an internship in Denmark with the UN for a year. It was with a UN mission that she finally went to Mogadishu. She had been to Somaliland before, visiting family, but never to the capital. 'I have eight siblings; we are a very tight-knit family. My parents left Somalia as refugees in 1989 to Toronto. My parents didn't go to school. When I talked about going to Somalia, they were absolutely against it, also because they are from the North and I was going to the South. I went there in 2013 against my family's advice', Hodan explains.[8]

Her arrival was eventful, as was her first year there: 'I remember the flight from Nairobi to Mogadishu had a lot of turbulence. I was just so scared already because I didn't know anyone, I was going to a place

---

6   Interview with Hodan Osman, 24 April 2020.
7   See Win, Everjoice (2004). '"If It Doesn't Fit on the Blue Square It's Out!" An Open Letter to My Donor Friend', in Groves, L. & Hinton, R. (eds). *Inclusive Aid Changing Power and Relationships in International Development*. London and Sterling, VA: Earthscan.
8   Interview with Hodan Osman, 24 April 2020.

people said was dangerous, then we had the problem with the plane... And everyone was so calm! We disembarked back in Nairobi. That was such a bad start! And then we went again. And now I know that's not common at all; I don't know why everyone was so calm'. Having said that, Hodan goes on: 'But arriving is always such a good energy, because it always feel like you'll land on the water. That's something I never got tired of. The airport wasn't really built by then, it was these kinds of prefab things that we went through. We got taken to the compounds in these armed vehicles... you know, war imagery right away. It's interesting that then you are there, in the middle of a war zone, talking about structural reforms in meetings'.[9]

Hodan continues: 'A few months after I arrived I was with the government', to which I ask, 'why?'. She says: 'It was very hard to get anything done. To be fair, I think you need to be part of the machinery. And with the UN, there was so much security, the protocols... I was part of UNOPs [UN Office for Project Services], and they worked directly with UNSOM [UN Assistance Mission in Somalia]. If I wanted to go to a meeting, I needed to get security clearance, I was travelling with two casspirs—not even armed vehicles, casspirs! Besides, there were twelve soldiers and one security person who had to be my close protection, just to go to a meeting outside. I then realized "I just can't see what I'm contributing". It was also not my area of expertise'.

She had taken a position with a security mission just to go to Somalia. 'A guy who today is the UN Ambassador for Somalia, he is the one who eventually said, "You have this banking experience, come to the government and work with us". He set up a meeting, and I remember having to sneak out of the compound to go to this meeting at the Central Bank. We used to work in this other building that was adjacent to the compound. The hotel was across that building. I asked the person to meet me in that hotel. I arranged with security to go to that adjacent building, and once we were there, I told the security "Hey, you didn't see me" and I just walked out'.[10]

That is how Hodan recalls her first months in Somalia. Being someone with a background in business, she was soon working for the Central Bank. 'Somalia was used to the diaspora, so it was not a problem

---

9   Ibid.
10   Ibid.

The Symbolism of Casspirs

An explanation provided in the context of an art project is poignant:

'Casspir is an anagram of the acronyms SAP (South African Police) and CSIR (Council for Scientific and Industrial Research). Designed in South Africa in the late 1970s and brought into service in the early 80s, the Casspir was used extensively by the Apartheid-era South African Police, as well as by the South African Defence Force. Bulletproof and mine-resistant, the Casspir was very much a military vehicle, yet it was used extensively in urban, township areas in South Africa against civilian populations. By the mid-1980s, the Casspir was the ubiquitous heavy hand of apartheid oppression in the townships of South Africa, its mere presence a form of terror.

Anyone who has spent time in South Africa in the 1980s shares some history with the Casspir: it is as familiar as the smell of tear gas and burning tyres, as heavy-handed as P.W. Botha and his cadre of generals. Nothing said "police intimidation" like the smell of diesel fuel and the roar of the 165 horsepower engine. Nothing was as potent as seeing one of these ironclad beasts flying through narrow township streets at 90 km/hr.'

'Post-apartheid, Casspirs were decommissioned in South Africa, their hulls left to rust, a relic of the past better forgotten. Except for the ones that were sold to the United States during the Iraq war years and, later, to local police forces. In the age of Ferguson and Black Lives Matter, the Casspir has returned; a poltergeist from the past which continues to haunt us. The issue of over-militarized police departments, who have purchased war equipment like one would buy LPs at a tag sale, has come to the forefront of the American debate on police tactics and aggression.'

(The Casspir Project, https://wri-irg.org/en/story/2017/casspir-project)

---

not having been born there. But I had a problem with the language. And there were two women at the Central Bank, the other one was the cleaning lady. This was out of more or less 100 people'. At this point, when I ask whether this presented problems for her, she says: 'There was, generally, a deficit of trust and I understood that. I didn't have problems for being a woman so much as because people simply didn't trust so easily. You have to show your competence'.[11]

---

11   Ibid.

Hodan ended up staying for five years, one at the Central Bank, three and a half as an advisor at the Ministry of Finance, and later, working on designing IMF's Staff-Monitored Program (SMP) in Somalia.[12] She has a very curious take on that experience: while most people seeking a more equal dynamic in international cooperation would be undoubtedly critical of the IMF, Hodan says the IMF helped to legitimise Somalia as a financially solid country, so donors could come in. 'We negotiated the benchmarks and agreed on what we should do. That gave us some political clout with the Parliament too'. The SMPs are programs designed by country authorities that informally count on IMF staff for monitoring. Having someone with such a mixed background as Hodan's can certainly be productive for a group like the g7+. The diversity is, in any case, a plus, especially considering the weight such organisations as the IMF have in development cooperation. Not coincidentally, she became the focal point of the g7+ for Somalia around two years after arriving in the country, and her arrival in Somalia marked, for her, her entry in the development sector. 'It was the right timing when I went. The first recognised government had just come into place, so it was the rebuilding of a nation. I mean, how many times do you get to be part of that?'.[13]

As soon as she became the focal point, Hodan worked on the elaboration of the g7+ Compact, part of the New Deal. 'The compact fell under the Minister of Planning, but I led on the partnership agreement and the Compact negotiations with donors, which was information that would need to go into the Compact. There was a lot of rhetoric, which as such, didn't always translate [on] the ground, but having said that, I think the rhetoric is a good first step. At the end of the day, you're really signing on to this bunch of words, and if you think about it, what's going to happen if you don't follow these words—and what do these words mean anyway...? And yet we do commit to this process, we negotiate every word...'.[14] This was the Mutual Accountability Framework, which was to be the backbone of new donor commitments, a part of the New Deal.

---

12   See Federal Government of Somalia's website information on SMP at https://mof. gov.so/smp.

13   Ibid.

14   Ibid.

'It's all an interesting pretence in a way, but maybe it's a necessary pretence. You go back and forth on language... At the end you have those beautiful words, but you know this is not guiding anything because all of those programs have been cooked up five years in advance, because that is the pipeline you need for all of these programs to come through', Hodan says. But she makes an important point about that: 'I think so much depends on personality. I came to realise the people on the ground have a lot of power'.[15] To my mind, that reinforces the importance of looking at the stories of people from and in these countries, what motivates them and how they engage with others, especially in difficult contexts.

Listening to Abie about going back to her country after a short trip abroad adds to this sentiment. Abie tells us of when she went to the United States for a meeting: 'It was during the war in Sierra Leone. I remember I was there and people kept saying "There is a war and you're going back?" But my answer was "I came with a ticket paid for by my government and I'm going back"'.[16] Abie's only regret is that she and her husband didn't go to do another degree in Malaysia when they had the chance: 'I had some family issues and couldn't leave. I also thought we would have another chance, but it ended up never happening'. However, that seems minor when she speaks proudly of her three children, one already at university. 'When I look behind, I feel fulfilled'. That is not a minor achievement, nor the fact that, regardless of events, she keeps working on challenging subjects. Her new challenge is clear: 'Getting our own indicators right and monitoring the priority SDGs won't be easy',[17] she says right at the end of our conversation.

Naheed also surprised me with the way she ended our talk: 'I hate symbolic representation. I want to bring value as deputy chair of the g7+. We're trying to find out how Afghanistan can play a better role. Aid Management is the counterpart now, not me, but I receive reports. I hope to be more active after the elections and maybe help negotiate some international principles'. This willingness was in itself positive, especially with everything that must have been on the radar at the time in Afghanistan, with the agreement between the United States and

---

15   Ibid.
16   Interview with Abie Elizabeth Kamara, 19 March 2020.
17   Ibid.

the Taliban for the withdrawal of American troops and the political
instability that followed the elections held in February 2020.[18]

Withdrawal of American Troops from Afghanistan

'The war cost $2 trillion and took the lives of more than 3,500 American
and coalition troops and tens of thousands of Afghans since the U.S.
invasion in aftermath of the Sept. 11 attacks, which were plotted by Al
Qaeda leaders under the protection of the Taliban.

The withdrawal of American troops — about 12,000 are still in
Afghanistan — [was] dependent on the Taliban's fulfilment of major
commitments that have been obstacles for years, including its severance
of ties with international terrorist groups such as Al Qaeda.

The agreement also hinge[d] on more difficult negotiations... between
the Taliban and the Afghan government over the country's future.
Officials hope those talks will produce a power-sharing arrangement
and lasting cease-fire, but both ideas have been anathema to the Taliban
in the past.'

(Mashal, Mujib (29 February 2020). 'Taliban and U.S. Strike Deal to
Withdraw American Troops from Afghanistan'. *The New York Times*.)

Indeed, at the end, the withdrawal of US troops has been widely and
heavily criticised for how it was conducted: 'the withdrawal culminated
in a frantic effort to evacuate tens of thousands of U.S. citizens, allies,
and at-risk Afghans following the Afghan government's unexpected
rapid collapse.'

(Gramer, Robbie; Mackinnon, Amy and Detsch, Jack (2021). 'State
Department Launches Review of Afghan Withdrawal'. *Foreign Policy*,
https://foreignpolicy.com/2021/12/10/state-department-review-
afghan-withdrawal)

How do we avoid these crucial potentialities going unnoticed and
unharnessed? How do we even begin to think about all these varied
senses of responsibility as assets? To do that in a strategic way, instead
of individually, is even more of a challenge.

---

18   The complete withdrawal was planned to take 14 months and started in February
      2020.

As with any big and diverse group with ambitious aims, there are divergences in terms of what people think the g7+'s priorities should be. However, these divergencies are more related to strategies than goals; that is, as the g7+ 2019 Review also showed, most differences have to do with what people feel should be the *means* to achieve the group's ends rather than the ends themselves.

For Siafa, for instance, the future of the group necessarily requires investing in those social bonds.

> That kind of trust helps implementation a lot. But of course, the trick is that who is in these positions changes all the time. I do think, though, that social connections are key, investing in getting to know each other. This has to come from the leadership. It doesn't necessarily means meeting in person; in my experience, sometimes even just calling people instead of writing an email counts a lot. Small things, like taking note of people's birthday, to actually take the time to think of people. I don't know how this can be done in the g7+, I really don't know, but I think there is something in that.[19]

It does not work for everyone, nor does it achieve anything by itself. But investing in people, motivating their passion, their feeling of belonging, their trust, solidarity and sense of duty *towards a collective*, these cannot perhaps be the ends, but seem to be powerful means. Again, it is not that they accomplish ambitious goals like changing global narratives by themselves, but rather that it seems no changes can happen without them at all, not in terms of the macro politics we are talking about. Here, I am humbly asking a question that has been asked before: '*How then are we to read the*[*se*]*... stories... without reducing them to romance narratives of "overcoming, vindication, salvation and redemption" or forms of tragedy that focus on the contingent, the ambiguous and the paradoxical?'*.[20] How can we avoid reading too much into individual stories and yet see in them the profound common narratives they offer?

I will not pretend to answer anything about strategies myself. I turn here to *some* of the strategies that were proposed and agreed in the 2019

---

19   Interview with Siafa Hage, 10 March 2020.

20   Scott (2004). '11' as cited in Opondo, Sam Okoth (2016). 'Entanglements and Fragments "By the Sea"', in Phạm & Shilliam (eds). *Meanings of Bandung: Postcolonial Orders and Decolonial Visions*. London and New York: Rowman & Littlefield, pp. 43–44.

g7+ Ministerial Meeting, so we can get a sense of the things for which people think they are responsible, now and in the future.

Advocating for Context and Country Leadership on Peace and Development

'At the root of conflict and fragility lie injustice, human rights violations, inequality, exclusion, poverty, poor management of natural resources and the absence of inclusive political settlements and capable institutions. Supporting transitions out of fragility requires political and not just technical responses. It is crucial for these processes to be grounded in indigenous contexts. They must be locally driven, locally owned and locally led'.21 Ownership and contextuality have been at the core of the g7+'s discourse and advocacy. If we recall from earlier in this book the understanding that 'those who survived are the experts', it makes absolute sense that any attempt to address complex local issues would require recognition of the value of what people on the ground know and feel about these. However, as a strategic priority, it has been hard for the g7+ to advocate for changes in that sense, as there is the usual accompanying demand for new frameworks, methodologies, and other technical instruments. One does not get far with speeches alone; technical tools are the infrastructure of any possible changes in how development and peace are practised in international cooperation, and at the beginning, the g7+ proposed their own: 'The donors were following what? There was no leadership from the fragile states themselves, and you need that. Because they [donors] want to align their objectives with something and they couldn't. Align to what? There was no framework. It was all done by donors, so it was their understanding. They didn't understand our problems, they didn't understand our challenges, so we had to start something. They want to help, but if I, in a fragile state, don't tell them, they will do something else, because nobody else told them how to do it'. That is how former Minister Emilia Pires explains what led the g7+ to think of the Fragility Assessments and the Fragility Spectrum,

---

21 IDPS (2016). *Stockholm Declaration on Addressing Fragility and Building Peace in a Changing World.* https://www.government.se/contentassets/8c2491b60d494dd8a2 c1046b9336ee52/stockholm-declaration-on-addressing-fragility-and-building-peace-in-a-changing-world.pdf, p. 2.

when, at the same time, many critical voices in the development field, especially from civil society, were wary of new frameworks.[22]

We only have to recall the questions that disturbed Abie and Felix when they went around their countries conducting the assessments: 'Another assessment?', and the accompanying expectations that the priorities listed would be promptly addressed by the government, something they could not promise, not least because local problems often have external causes.

Ownership, leadership, and contextuality have been central for the g7+'s advocacy because all the g7+ member countries have long had relationships with a variety of donors or partners, and the lack of regard for local knowledge has often led to disastrous responses to complex problems. It is both a matter of how issues are addressed, which has led to discussions on aid effectiveness, and of how professionals deal with each other, which cuts deep into historical, social and economic factors. Academics, activists, and politicians have their own way of addressing both of these matters. As the g7+ representatives and focal points are people responsible for economy and planning, perhaps they have another method. If the international community wants frameworks, it seems they thought, 'fine, we will produce them', but the emphasis was on the *'we'*: 'It is about doing the assessment *ourselves*, measuring ourselves, and focusing on our priorities, our structures, our national systems. Sometimes donors want to do something now but it will not be sustainable after they leave, it's too much. We prefer what is sustainable. We are always being measured, ranked... We need to do it [the measurement] ourselves', Habib explains.[23]

The *'doing it ourselves'* has been a strategic priority; it is about ownership, leadership and contextuality. Rather than a means to achieve these ends, it is a crucial part of the advocacy of the group. It is related to making sure capacity is really being built, guaranteeing long-term conditions for development and peace, honouring the idea that survivors know best, respecting people's pride in their history and knowledge, showing solidarity in practice, and offering opportunities for accountability that are key to strengthening institutions in the

---

22   Interview with former Minister Emília Pires, 2013. Cited in Rocha de Siqueira, I. (2017). Op. cit., p. 135.
23   Interview with Habib Ur Rehman Mayar. Cited in ibid.

long run. *The focus is less on offering the most beautiful, perfectly technical instrument for measurement than on making sure that the act of measurement, including deciding what to measure, is a locally-driven process.* Of course, this is incredibly challenging and not automatically inclusive. It is also a process frequently disturbed by changes in power and instability, and frustration can rise with the difficulty of advancing much in that front.

Antonio, having been a focal point for Guinea-Bissau for 10 years, told us of how frustrating it can be to try to conduct a national assessment while the government is changing all the time: 'We were one of the first to initiate the Fragility Assessment, right after Busan; we could have been one of the pilot studies for the implementation of the New Deal, but the internal crises got us delayed. The process was then started in 2014, but we didn't manage to do the Fragility Assessment until 2016/2017. It took us about three years to finish a process that should have lasted around three months. And soon we were going through a period of instability again'. He then explains: 'We managed to complete the matrix [of the Fragility Spectrum], which we included in the National Development Plan ["Terra Ranka", 2015–2020] but only to the technical level. We decided we couldn't wait any longer. The government then acknowledged the work done but didn't participate initially. The Council of Ministers never approved. The government was supposed to move to elaborate the Compact, but this is still in the drawer'.[24]

Mr Moses Mabior, Director of Aid Coordination in the Ministry of Finance of South Sudan, recounts similar experiences: 'We initiated the first Fragility Assessment in 2012. At the time, in the meetings, we concluded we were not at the level of Crisis; we had surpassed that. We had signed the peace agreement years before, in 2005, so we concluded our stage was Rebuild and Reform in the Fragility Spectrum. But unfortunately, in 2013, we went back to Crisis. We did another assessment in 2017, when we went again into Crisis. Now we plan to conduct a new one in 2021, so it can be part of the revitalizing agreement, and we plan to finally have a compact. We tried to have a compact in 2011, right after

24   Interview with Antonio Co, 11 June 2019. For information on the monitoring of the New Deal implementation and the pilot-countries, see International Dialogue on Peacebuilding and Statebuilding (2011). *New Deal Implementation- Country Level Progress.* https://www.pbsbdialogue.org/en/new-deal/implementation-progress/

independence, but Crisis had erupted'.[25] It is telling how many times Mr. Mabior uses the word 'crisis' in such a brief part of our conversation. And striking how many turns the recent history of South Sudan took (see annexes for Fragility Assessments and Spectrum).

He continues citing another important government document: 'In 2018, we elaborated our first Development Strategy, now we want to work on a revised one. But the situation has changed; there aren't many partners around now'. At the same time, Mabior is optimistic about the future: 'The future of South Sudan is bright. We have abundant natural resources and land. Land is key; land is everything. What we need to do is to put our heads together, think of how to do proper exploitation of the resources we have. We need proper management, because resources can finish. Oil can finish, it's not going to last forever'. His conclusion is humbling: 'We need to understand no one is an island. We need to look around, look back at history. Our challenges have been faced by others before too. People also forget they had problems once. We will start off from where everybody left, meaning we have to learn with others' experiences. That's what we're trying to do now'. By 'we', I understand Mr Mabior means South Sudanese; by 'people', I guess he means donors, because he finishes by saying 'We need to join hands, but South Sudan needs to be in the driving seat'.[26]

The Fragility Assessments and the Fragility Spectrum were elaborated by the g7+ as their own instruments to understand and establish priorities in their countries, but they achieved limited implementation as member countries faced all kinds of obstacles. We first heard Antonio's stories a few pages earlier: he has been a civil servant for decades and one of the first focal points of the g7+; nevertheless, the challenges have been considerable. When Antonio speaks with pride of how he studied and worked with Planning his whole life and now lives in a planned neighbourhood, one can imagine there is some frustration with not seeing the Fragility Assessment through. Not that he shows much—again, he is such a calm storyteller. But we can imagine what taking on new responsibilities might entail when your work is already challenging and results unfortunately depend little on your own sense of duty. Similarly, Mr Mabior went to do his master's degree in the

---

25   Interview with Moses Mabior.
26   Ibid.

United States in the 1980s, after having graduated from the University of Khartoum. He went back to South Sudan in 1986 to 'join the struggle for liberation', he says. After the 2005 peace agreement, he decided he would 'contribute more by joining the Ministry of Finance, leaving others to do the military work'.[27] After having listed all the turns his work with the g7+ and aid management in general have taken, when asked about the challenges ahead for South Sudan, he says, like a prayer: 'Let it be the last agreement [the one of 2018]'. 'Our leadership has declared nobody is going back to war. The agreement is supposed to last three years and there will be elections. A lot will depend on the last months before that'.[28]

Let us see, then, in more detail, what these assessments were to represent in terms of the strategic priorities of the g7+, so we can understand slightly better what they involved for the people engaged.

Making Sure Assessments Do Not Become Ends in Themselves

In 2013, a technical note on the Fragility Spectrum said 'There is... a clear need for monitoring frameworks that are more attuned to the realities of fragile contexts and that take account of the stage of fragility a country is in. Fragile states themselves are best positioned to develop such frameworks, familiar as they are with both their strengths and weaknesses. The fragility spectrum was thus proposed as a tool to enable countries themselves to analyse and describe the unique nature of their fragility according to a number of 'stages' across each Peacebuilding and Statebuilding Goal'.[29] The Fragility Assessments were planned to involve an inclusive local dialogue with different constituencies who would define fragility in their own terms, goals and targets, and decide on the best contextual indicators. The 2013 document went on: 'A key concern of the g7+ is the measurement and categorisation of fragile states according to donor monitoring frameworks, which try to assess the nature of their situations with a standard yardstick. Furthermore, difficulties around data collection in fragile states mean donors often rely on out-of-date statistics'.[30]

---

27   Ibid.
28   Ibid.
29   g7+ (2013). *Note on the Fragility Spectrum*. Kinshasa, g7+, p. 3.
30   Ibid., p. 2.

South Sudan

South Sudan obtained independence from Sudan on 9 July 2011 following a 2005 agreement that ended Africa's longest-running civil war. However, civil war broke out in 2013 'when the president fell out with his then vice president, leading to a conflict that has displaced some 4 million people...'

'South Sudan has significant natural resources including gold, silver, iron ore, copper, diamonds and timber, all of which remain virtually untapped. The most significant resource and primary driver of the economy is, however, oil. South Sudan is the most oil-dependent country in the world. Even prior to the outbreak of violent conflict in December 2013 the country faced significant challenges in managing its oil resources and maximizing returns while enabling stability and promoting development. ... In July 2011 South Sudan seceded from Sudan following a decades-long civil war. Roughly 75% of the petroleum resources of the former Sudan are today located in South Sudan, whereas the pipelines and infrastructure needed to evacuate the oil passes through Sudanese territory. Continued disagreement after independence about the transit fees for transporting South Sudan's oil through Sudan, led South Sudan to completely shut down its oil production in January 2012. Production resumed in April 2013 but has yet to reach pre-shutdown volumes, partly due to threats from Sudan to shut down the pipelines.'

A power-sharing agreement was signed between the two sides in August 2018 after five years of renewed civil war.

(g7+ Natural Resources Maganement, p. 71; see also: https://www.bbc.com/news/world-africa-14069082)

The idea was to provide contextual and country-led measurements of the reality on the ground in g7+ countries, allowing for peer-learning based on common experiences, but also making room for country-specific conditions and local leadership on priorities. This is how the first g7+ chair, former minister Emilia Pires remembers the idea behind the assessments:

When we came together [in 2008, Accra], we found out we had so many similarities... Shouldn't we maybe share our experiences: "How did you solve this problem...? This is how I did..." So we wouldn't feel we are alone. And then it just developed through... We should have a voice and a position on this, because this is a policy that affects all of us. We needed to know we were not alone...At the beginning, it was very hard. It felt like we were backwards, or there was something wrong with us... But we said "no, there is nothing wrong with us. It's the situation we ended up in, we are all human beings, should all be respected and look at each other as normal human beings, and you happened to be born in a country that was not correct [sic], so now that you are there, you want to fix it, let's give hands to each other". So we tried that... and slowly we managed not to feel this complex of inferiority, guilt, whatever... It is like... "Hey, I am here to fix it, nobody is forcing me, I want to do it myself, and I want to do it because no one else is doing for me, so I have to do it. If I wait for others, they cannot understand my problems properly...".[31]

Since the development field produces new templates on a daily basis, relying on others to establish priorities, baselines and strategies is not only something that can go against nurturing capacities on the ground, but it can put countries on extremely vulnerable positions, having to be in a constant training process, following the latest procedures and language—and often wasting precious time and personnel on this.

Multiplying Impacts: Responsibilities Go Up and Down

The assessments were hard to implement and replicate on the ground throughout the years, for reasons ranging from crises and conflict to an abundance of international frameworks that already constantly threaten to overwhelm national offices. Perhaps for this reason, the g7+ found a way of continuing to advocate for context *internationally* as part of a broader agenda on peace and ownership. This is because the search for a framework that would—at least, in theory—support local leadership, self-assessment and offer flexibility for the very volatile situations on the ground found some resonance as the UN entered a process of reformulating its own peace architecture, and other organisations also went through transformations in some of theirs.

In 2016, the UN Sustaining Peace twin resolutions (General Assembly Resolution 70/262 and Security Council Resolution 2282) inaugurated the notion of *'sustaining peace'*, so to speak, stating that it 'should be broadly understood as a goal and a process to build a common vision of a society, ensuring that the needs of all segments of the population

---

31 Interview with Min. Emilia Pires 2013. Cited in Rocha de Siqueira, I. (2017). Op. cit., pp. 182–83.

are taken into account'.[32] The documents finally acknowledged the increasing consensus that 'the end of violence should be both an objective and an enabler of development',[33] something the g7+ members had been advocating since before the group had even been formally established. The concept of *sustaining peace* means, at least in theory, that peace is not based on clear sequencing—pre-, during and post-conflict are not perfectly demarcated moments in anyone's societies—implying that a more contextual understanding is needed if peace is to be achieved. The UN has had to adapt accordingly, which involved revising its organisational structure.

The g7+ commissioned a study in 2017 to take the opportunity to showcase the lessons learned by host g7+ nations after decades of UN missions and to analyse how these could perhaps link with the reforms taking place. The document looks at the changes the UN implemented: for the acronym-savvy, the regional desks of DPA (Department of Political Affairs) and DPKO (Department of Peacekeeping Operations) were merged, and PBSO (Peacebuilding Support Office) moved to the new D(P)PA (Department of Political and Peacebuilding Affairs).[34] This is supposed to be an answer to an increasing recognition that 'peacebuilding and peacekeeping are interrelated and peacekeeping mandates... often incorporate aspects of peacebuilding'. 'In other words, the activities of peacemaking, peacekeeping and peacebuilding are no longer seen in a linear manner'.[35]

The implications, again, in theory, could be considerable, with peacebuilding not necessarily only occurring in 'post-conflict' situations but 'also during and even before a situation breaks out into violence',[36] which is precisely what the g7+ has been advocating for. As Naheed said in the 2019 g7+ ministerial meeting, commenting on the peace negotiations with the Taliban, 'peace is not only the absence of bullets'.[37] I believe this is something that all g7+ people very clearly believe for

---

32 UN General Assembly Resolution 70/262, p. 2.

33 United Nations & World Bank (2018). *Pathways for Peace: Inclusive approaches to preventing violent conflict*. Washington, DC: World Bank, p. 1.

34 g7+ (2017). *Host Nation Views on UN Peace and Security Reform Proposals*, p. 1.

35 Lucey, A. (2015). 'Implementing the Peace, Security and Development Nexus in Africa'. *Strategic Analysis*, 39(5), p. 502, as cited in Rocha de Siqueira, I. (2019). Op. cit., p. 25.

36 Ibid.

37 Interview with Naheed Sarabi, 03 March 2020.

themselves and, although others might say it out loud and understand it rationally, it is not a fact that is really felt or experienced outside of conflict-affected states.

Indeed, the g7+'s priorities with the change in international approaches to peace and development go beyond the academic and bureaucratic debates, in that these transformations can have long-term impacts in terms of creating capacity, strengthening institutions, empowering local groups, and articulating responses to conflict with economic concerns in the long run. The g7+ document on host nations' impressions offered several examples after interviewing authorities from member countries. It requested more flexibility and the delegation of authority on the ground, pointing out a general lack of contextualization:

> Practical examples included the inability: (i) of the Special Representative of the Secretary-General (SRSG) in Timor-Leste to provide for the basic needs of Timorese resistance fighters in cantonment areas, and to retain high-performing staff who were assisting the local authorities; (ii) of the SRSG in Liberia to assist government in transporting payments to civil servants in outlying areas; (iii) of the mission in Guinea-Bissau to use locally warehoused street lighting poles for the benefit of safety in the capital city; and (iv) to provide for the transport of delegations from Sierra Leone and Liberia to assist in mediation processes.[38]

The issue is that whatever concept of peace is used internationally, it would need to be translated on the ground in terms of countries' priorities and social dynamics and, for that, country ownership and leadership are crucial. Much can be said about the lack of resources and political will, and the presence of corruption, instability, and other issues, and the g7+ people would be among the first to acknowledge that. What we heard from them was not that local or national leadership is the only way to go, but that it cannot be left aside, nor be made secondary.

In fact, in the g7+ publication, some of the key advantages of the UN reforms on peace architecture are related to their potential impacts for long-term state-building: 'Looking beyond transitions, host nations see other advantages to merging the regional desks [of DPA and DPKO]. One is facilitating a longer-term engagement in capacity-building and strengthening national institutions—a priority for host countries'.[39]

---

38   g7+ (2017). *Host Nation Views on UN Peace and Security Reform Proposals.* p. 1.
39   Ibid., p. 4.

According to this argument, the reforms on peace architecture would mean investing in national institutions and systems. The point of making use of country systems is crucial for accountability, which, in turn, is central for any sense of responsibility on the part of civil servants and other citizens alike. To be able to demonstrate and utilize functioning institutions that can endure crises and instability is fundamental to building up relations of trust among citizens and between society, government institutions, and private investors. That is how peace and development are intrinsically connected.

Felix's thoughts help us make sense of this connection:

> When I finished my education, I wanted so much to develop the Timorese economy in non-oil sectors. I thought this was extremely important for stability and to provide all services to the population. But when I came back, in 2018, I couldn't find a job in the government to do this work. This is always a challenge in Timor. With the g7+, I have been using my knowledge, my experience. For instance, the country is looking to be part of ASEAN [Association of Southeast Asian Nations]. I see Singapore as an example, because it's not about resources, it's about investing in people. Still today, there aren't many options for post-graduate courses in Timor, for instance, so young people go abroad to continue their studies. That's what I did. Today I teach.

This is Felix's experience. He wanted to build opportunities in his country, for people to have jobs and to contribute themselves the same way he believes he is doing; his own family offers a powerful example. At his parents' insistence, all seven siblings studied hard. Three now live in the UK; four stayed in Timor, including himself. Of these, one is working at the Ministry of Finance, one in the Ministry of Petroleum and Mineral Resources, and one stays at home to take care of his mother. If we remember Felix's conversations with his children, there seems to be a constant thread of reflection about how the country can retain people: 'My children were born here and they are tempted to go. How can we then attract foreigners and foreign direct investment? We need to invest in development'.[40] He is talking about long-term investments—in institutions and economic revenues.

Listening to Mr Mabior also again brings to light this issue of how citizenship, leadership, responsibility, and the willingness to do

---

40   Interview with Félix Piedade, 19 March 2020.

something for country and people can perhaps be nurtured, and how important it is that they are. 'I'm a product of the rural community. I was born in the rural area. I went to bush school for two years, then primary school for another two years, and again the same for intermediary school. Finally, University of Khartoum and master's in the US, from 1984 to 1986. But I'm a rural boy', he repeats, then continues: 'Being a rural boy, unfortunately, I didn't go back to the rural area. That's the problem with the education; it's outwards-looking, not inwards. The child goes to school then they don't go back to the rural area, they think it's a place for backwards people, people who don't know anything. I haven't lost my traditions, but my kids are the product of war, in that they grew up outside the country because of war, so *they* have lost those traditions'. Mr Mabior then says something that stayed with me: 'In South Sudan, we have a Ministry for Culture; it takes care of our cultural inheritance. But the culture *is* people; the ministry is another thing. They have a lot to do to catch up. In South Sudan, 85% of the population is still in the rural areas, so these traditions are strong, but in the next stages, if we're being serious, that'll disappear. But, of course, the world is changing. Nobody thinks that we should continue as it was. But something reasonable needs to be there'.[41]

How the local and the global, the village and the international, the traditions and the new can cohabit is a question as old as can be. Yet it needs to be addressed as effectively as possible, if one is to act responsibly, take care of the next generations and plan for the future. How can a country develop without the stamina, innovation, and passion of its young and brilliant minds? How can peace be encouraged and sustained without precisely including these young people, full of energy and in need of hope? The g7+ has struggled with these questions as much as any organisation in the business of politics, and its people have to deal with them while also striving to keep cohesiveness within the group, despite its being such a diverse cohort of countries and people. I will come back to this.

---

41   Interview with Moses Mabior.

Strengthening Within: Finding Cohesion with a Diverse Group

The g7+ has established quite a number of strategic priorities in terms of strengthening the group as a platform for conflict-affected states. One of these is to get more member countries to ratify a financial contribution to the group's work. As of 2020, Sierra Leone and Afghanistan have done so. Until then, Timor-Leste had funded the Secretariat.[42] Apart from the financial aspect, the group wants to diversify leadership initiatives among member countries, by assisting focal points to create awareness of the g7+ in their countries and inspire other ministries and authorities. The bottom line is that the g7+ has faced difficulties getting buy-in from member countries; the group was created by Finance Ministers and never really got traction in other areas. We saw there are many obstacles—people change positions all the time; governments change; there is often instability; and priorities are many. Yet, the more the group expands its agenda and composition, perhaps the more crucial it is to have people who can voice political positions more freely. Two recent initiatives have been meaning to address this challenge of buy-in: the plan to generate cooperation among Justice Ministers on the theme of access to justice, and the possible creation of a g7+ Inter-Parliamentary Union Assembly.[43]

'Many challenges are challenges of provision of basic services. I would say for us the priorities are, for instance, providing access to water, food security, education, health, and electricity to the most vulnerable people. I think we could benefit much from parliamentary diplomacy. We could share experiences among legislators'.[44] That is the view of former Minister Kamitatu of the DRC, who was the president of his parliament in times of transition and has the key experience of having helped get a new constitution approved. As discussed earlier in this book, we might imagine that there are many opportunities to exchange experiences about the challenges of implementing something from scratch. On that question, Kamitatu says 'I am convinced of the value of fragile-to-fragile cooperation. It's also dignifying to exchange these experiences; we get

---

42   See g7+ Annual report 2017–2018, p. 18.
43   g7+ Newsletter March 2020.
44   Interview with Olivier Kamitatu Etsu, 21 April 2020.

strong by sharing them.'[45] If one is comparing one's own experiences with another whom one considers to be a 'brother' or a 'sister', with whom one has something in common, instead of talking about generic lessons and standardized formulae only, then there is indeed potential for something more promising.

During a meeting of the g7+ held in 2019, on the sidelines of the General Assembly of the Inter-Parliamentary Union (IPU) that was held in Belgrade, Serbia, there was a wider agreement to create a g7+ Inter-Parliamentary Assembly: 'Recognizing the increasing role of parliamentary diplomacy and the fundamental role of legislative bodies in peace and stability, the g7+ parliamentary assembly will help in consolidating the g7+ membership. In addition, this will help in sharing the collective perspective and inputs on how democracy evolves in conflict-affected countries'.[46]

The issue of access to justice, in turn, has been an extension of the approval of SDG 16 and central to the g7+'s advocacy. Not only does the potential cooperation among Justice Ministers offer the opportunity to get greater buy-in from member countries, but the very substance of this possible cooperation is central to these countries. Abie's testimony about the first meeting on Justice is positive: 'When we had the Justice Ministers' meeting in Freetown, in 2014, it was key to show how advocacy in that area is relevant for the countries in the g7+. Justice is at the basis of what is going on in our countries and the reforms we want to implement, especially to reach the most vulnerable. It was challenging to get everyone there, get the visas, but it was important'.[47]

In 2019, the g7+ Secretariat and the Rule of Law Collaborative held a meeting during the 16+ Forum Annual Showcase in Dili, Timor-Leste, to follow up from the Declaration and Joint Action Plan adopted at the Ministerial-Level Meeting on Access to Justice, held in the Hague in June 2019. The meeting was attended by Ministers of Justice from Solomon Islands and Timor-Leste, representatives from Sierra Leone and Togo, donor representatives, and civil society organizations. 'Countries with disperse[d] population[s] and limited resources have peculiar challenges in pursuing access to justice for all. Minister of Justice from

---

45   Ibid.
46   g7+ Newsletter, March 2020, p. 3.
47   Interview with Abie Elizabeth Kamara, 19 March 2020.

Solomon Islands, for example, highlighted that there is one high court and three magistrate courts in his country, that has over 900 islands'.[48]

'Given the important role of customary institutions in access to justice in conflict-affected countries, the g7+ is considering [the] sharing of experiences in integrating formal and informal Justice institutions where the two can complement each other'.[49]

The sense of justice for all is fundamental to stability, peace, and development. It affects how the different social groups relate to each other: whether they trust the formal and informal institutions to support demands for justice is a key determinant in avoiding violence and political struggles. 'In an important sense, peace is not just the absence of violence, but the presence of social solidarity',[50] and, in that sense, justice is central for the kinds of trust and accountability that avoid social divisions.

Last but not least of the strengthening strategies, since there was so much said about the way the g7+ acquired UN Observer Status, what is to be done with it is a matter of great responsibility. After all, as Helder said, there will be costs to maintaining a presence in New York; these might be funded by the Secretariat, perhaps with contributions to be offered by member countries, or by a possible partner, but this always has implications, one way or another. The g7+ has been in conversation with the African Union (AU), a key organisation and one that also holds the UN Observer Status. There are now three African countries among non-permanent members in the Security Council (A3). Some assess that the fact that the AU has Observer Status might facilitate engagement with A3 in terms of issuing joint statements to the council, defining joint negotiating positions for outcome documents, and convening joint public press stakeouts: 'The role played by the AU permanent observer mission to the UN is particularly important. It can help coordinate A3 and AU engagements, facilitate regular interactions with diplomats and officials in Addis Ababa, and retain AU and UN institutional memory'.[51] The fact is, as with the diplomatic steps to get SDG 16 and the UN Observer

---

48   g7+ Newsletter, March 2020, p. 2.
49   Ibid.
50   Murithi, T. (2006). 'African approaches to building peace and social solidarity'. *African Journal on Conflict Resolution*, 6(2), 9–34, p. 10.
51   See De Carvalho, Gustavo & Daniel Forti (2020). *What will it take for the A3 to shape debates, break geo-political deadlocks, and guide collective action?* Institute for Security

Status approved, increasing the presence in New York can bring many benefits to the g7+. It is, however, also a matter of great responsibility to make sure this brings real changes on the ground in member countries. EP Xanana Gusmão is adamant about what purpose the UN Observer Status should serve: 'We need a frank, honest dialogue. That's what we want with the UN Observer Status. [The] UN's resources are not [the] UN's. We need to defend this idea and correct this fact somewhat. As the UN Secretary General said, *"We don't want more reports, we want results."* We need an open debate and leadership. To act, it's necessary [to have] a general view of the country and the leaders know their countries. This is our mission, not just sitting and listening there at the UN'.[52]

The risk of adopting business-as-usual practices is always present when one plays the game, especially with major organizations such as the UN.

Engendering Interest and Responsibility in the Next Generations

In the study that comments on host nations' views on peacekeeping missions, the g7+ member countries commented on the many challenges to the integration of peace and development, of short- and long-term commitments. The representative of Afghanistan, for instance, 'noted that a large number of the threats facing the country are regional and external', and that '[t]he previous peace and security architecture did not facilitate addressing these...'.[53] But the issue of external forces—be they geopolitical interests, or climate change, which is something still incipient in the g7+ agenda—is always extremely hard to put on the table: 'Who funds the wars in our countries know that inside our people are divided', a representative said in the 2019 g7+ Ministerial Meeting.[54] As some in the g7+ worry over issues of responsibility for the difficult changes the group wants to implement, the matter of external forces is always present, but is diplomatically difficult to press or to open for

Studies. https://issafrica.org/iss-today/africa-can-become-more-influential-in-the-un-security-council.

52   Interview with EP Xananda Gusmão.
53   g7+ (n.d.). *Host Nation Views on UN Peace and Security Reform Proposals*, p. 4.
54   Oswaldo Paz, STP, in the 2019 g7+ Ministerial Meeting, my notes.

'frank debates', as EP Xanana Gusmão put it. This is not particular to the g7+'s work or to g7+ countries, but it is perhaps even more critical in these contexts.

And these external forces are not only directly belligerent but can be treacherously indirect. Indeed, it is important to notice that taking context and national priorities into account means considering the roots or *drivers of fragility*, which might vary considerably, including among the g7+'s member countries, and to think not only of present and internal drivers, but of external ones and potential causes of conflict that might lead countries to lose the gains they have already made. One key issue in that sense is the fact that some g7+ countries are facing the dangers of climate change. For the Solomon Islands, for instance, this is an urgent matter: 'We have lost six islands already'.[55] Of course, that increases the stakes for responsibility: how can authorities in fragile and conflict-affected countries *not* address the need for generating interest and responsibility in the next generations? How can a future of solidarity *and* responsibility be harnessed among the young with the help of stories and experiences like those just described?

How to Act Responsibly: On the Sense of Duty.

1. Prioritize key strategic goals.

2. Advocate for context and country leadership on peace and development.

3. Make sure assessments don't become ends in themselves.

4. Multiply impact: remember responsibilities go up and down.

5. Generate interest and responsibility within the next generations.

---

55   g7+ 2019 Ministerial Meetings, my notes.

7. The Way Forward

We are still facing a series of crises caused by the COVID-19 pandemic and this book could not avoid reflecting on this difficult scenario. The health concerns are compounded by the huge economic challenges many countries are already facing or will soon face. The effects of such problems upon fragile and conflict-affected states are bound to bring to the fore many urgent matters simultaneously, while the international resources available may dwindle. In March 2020, the g7+ Secretariat issued a statement of solidarity: 'Countries affected by conflict and fragility are more prone to its adverse impact. It is not only the pandemic that has endangered the lives of people of these countries but the economic and social consequences of measures taken will impact the wellbeing these nations more than others. With the already constrained institutional capacity, these countries need immediate assistance to enable them to curb the pandemic and its impact.'[1]

The Secretariat also says they are 'exploring possible ways to facilitate the sharing of knowledge, expertise and support in public health to help our members curb the spread of the coronavirus'. The statement of solidarity supported the call circulated by the UN Secretary-General Antonio Guterres for a global ceasefire[2] and made a strong claim: 'While the... response of countries around the world has been shutting borders, the exponential propagation of COVID-19 shows that global cooperation is needed to curb the pandemic. No country alone can tackle this crisis and hence we need human solidarity more than ever'.[3]

In 2020, the g7+'s annual report read: 'Border closures badly affected flow of trade and businesses and this further resulted in rising

---

1   g7+. Statement of Solidarity, March 2020.
2   See United Nations (2020). *Secretary-General Calls for Global Ceasefire, Citing War-Ravaged Health Systems, Populations Most Vulnerable to Novel Coronavirus.* https://www.un.org/press/en/2020/sgsm20018.doc.htm.
3   g7+ (2020). Statement of Solidarity, March 2020.

   https://doi.org/10.11647/OBP.0311.07

unemployment and hence extreme poverty. Cash-strapped governments in conflict affected countries struggled to help people and businesses to survive. Vulnerable people such as women continued to suffer the most.'[4]

There is no way forward without cooperation; it was true before the pandemic and it is true now. The g7+ countries were hit hard: 'South Sudan experienced economic downfall due to reduction in oil prices while Timor-Leste lost USD$1.8 billion (60%) in its petroleum fund due to fall in the oil prices globally. Furthermore, Central African Republic and Togo face economic difficulty. Other member countries such as Haiti experienced increase in risk of food insecurity and high inflation.'[5]

Habib co-authored an article on the opportunities that there might be for fragile and conflict-affected states to make progress despite the health crisis, especially as health responses are by nature institutional responses; after all, no sizeable health crisis such as the pandemic can be tackled without the rapid, organised, and coherent response of the appropriate institutions. In that sense, Habib and his co-author, Céline Monnier, wrote about the potential to create room in this crisis for 'building trust in institutions, decreasing inequalities, and fostering social cohesion'.[6] The idea is that people will respond positively to the perceptions of being cared for and having an effective government: 'Governments and donors in conflict-affected countries should identify opportunities to strengthen and build trust in institutions—for instance, by improving the effectiveness and inclusivity of the health system. Beyond the immediate benefits for public health, these measures will also improve public perceptions of the state as a care provider, thereby strengthening the social contract and contributing to the prevention of conflict.'

There is a lot at stake. At this point, inadequate responses might cost lives now and in the future. As many have pointed out, in different countries there has been a beacon of hope to be found in the

---

4   g7+ annual report (2020), p. 3.
5   Ibid.
6   Monnier, Céline & Mayar, Habib (2020). *Making Sure Peace Isn't a Casualty of COVID-19 in Fragile States*. World Politics Review. https://www.worldpoliticsreview.com/articles/28734/making-sure-peace-isn-t-a-casualty-of-covid-19-in-fragile-states?fbclid=IwAR2HZAV3FiZ6tJo75gOJbMSs9Q-1ZiUabjzKmP6O6kyNAkqSVDisVJYdYz8.

communitarian initiatives, with local leaders helping to identify those most in need and making sure aid reaches them; neighbours sharing the little they have; medical staff going far beyond any job description to support their communities; and so on. There is power in all that if countries can identify, work with, and preserve those social bonds while at the same time offering much-needed institutional support. As a well-known African scholar said, '[a]n integral part of the process of achieving positive peace is the need to promote social solidarity'.[7] And Helder himself also once said he sees in the g7+ the same bonds: 'Ours is a bond of solidarity'.[8] Well, as I have tried to do justice to the stories of our characters in this book, I have found that much can be done with these bonds, but I have also found out about just how difficult this work can be.

7   Murithi, T. (2006). 'African approaches to building peace and social solidarity'. *African Journal on Conflict Resolution*, 6(2), p. 13.

8   Da Costa, Helder (2012). 'g7+ and the New Deal: Country-Led and Country-Owned Initiatives: A Perspective from Timor-Leste'. *Journal of Peacebuilding & Development*, 7(2), 96–102, p. 102.

The challenges the people in the g7+ have faced so far are, first and foremost, the challenges of dealing with people and politics. Before being in this group, our characters were already civil servants and professionals who believed in planning and implementing public policy, in the possibility of mobilizing political will for peace and development, and, in many cases, in the viability of engaging international partners in more equal dialogues. Being part of the g7+, these beliefs are challenged by the difficulties of working for a diverse collective and with people who are far apart and have their own incredibly tough obstacles to overcome. Moreover, the already broad individual agendas of these people become perhaps bigger and the stakes become higher as they become part of a group.

The stories in the book have explored how these professionals engage in the difficult search for a voice. As part of that search, we have seen there is a strong need to listen and to develop relations of trust so that conversations can be franker and more effective. Decades of painting rosy pictures at international tables have done fragile and conflict-affected countries little good. On the other hand, we also learned of the ways dialogue can seem to be open but actually be severely constrained by political methods disguised as efficient techniques: annotated agendas and pre-set solutions to negotiations that were never truly held are common traps. Nevertheless, acting in such contexts can be likened to a sprint, whereas winning over important international positions are more like marathons—we saw how dangerous it is to lose stamina too soon.

It must be extremely difficult, when one has seen family and friends go through war, crises, and other difficulties, to have patience, to set one's eyes on the far away horizon while also keeping things afloat right here. Those who survive, we saw, can develop important skills, such as the ability to keep the focus on what is needed. But in order to face some of the obstacles that politics imposes, one also needs to be strategic and to be fair; that is, to look for ways of multiplying opportunities as well. Surviving is good; helping others to survive and strive is even better, or so I have been told.

The thread is passion; that is what permeates all these accounts. That is what makes them valuable. It is also what makes it so difficult to cultivate similar attitudes. Passion has a convoluted genealogy. Who teaches one to keep going? So many factors are important. And, at the same time, passion can lead to naiveté without adequate strategic preparation.

But how does anyone prepare without having the appropriate resources? Some of our characters can be called 'accidental diplomats': They have developed diplomatic skills without attending preparatory courses for diplomats; they negotiate, often well, without the background on mediation. It is also common, however, to negotiate with one's pride in these settings. One does not go into dozens of international political disputes with 'career diplomats' or 'experts' without having one's pride at least slightly singed in the process a few times. Our characters have had to face this experience perhaps more often than others, both because they were willing to, for the sake of the horizon ahead, and because that is the nature of the game, something that one learns (or does not, it seems).

For all that, there is constant learning going on that can be painful, exasperating but also rewarding. All our characters claimed it is their duty to believe in politics, to invest in the education of the next generation, to create the conditions for young people to want to stay in the country or help the country and its people in some way and to create more permanent solutions to the thorny issues of poverty and violence.

Meetings cannot be outcomes; assessments cannot be results; travels cannot become the *modus operandi* for any truthful collective changes; there cannot be no templates to solve the complex issues we have heard about; and with all those lessons, responsibilities travel up to major organisations and down to the local professionals on the ground: one needs to impact narratives, frameworks, and agendas, but also make sure there are changes on the ground. There can be no path forward without the buy-in of young people. Let us say the job starts with one's children, for instance: how does one pass the torch?

The Next Generations

'My father used to write letters, each telling me about how things were going on at home, about how things had changed; there was a lot of advice in there, but no prescriptions. He encouraged me to think of how I could change things; it was always very forward-looking'. Naheed's father's way of teaching his child to seek and prepare for change is quite remarkable. I do not intend to even try to offer prescriptions; I am not meant to be one of the voices in this book and these are not my stories. For the way forward, we can pick up from where the g7+ left off, with much advice, concern, and hope.

'What I want for my children is good education, that they be independent people and very confident. These things can lead you anywhere', says Helder. The two older ones live in New Zealand with their mother; the baby daughter is with him and her future schedule already includes French classes: 'My biggest regret is not learning French. That's when I feel less confident'. At the risk of reading too much into this pleasant bit of conversation, it says a lot that this is the biggest regret belonging to someone who is surrounded daily by the knowledge of overwhelming challenges. Or perhaps he just does not want to be pessimistic or negative at the end of our conversation, which is nonetheless interesting.

The hopes and the dreams people have for their children say much about what they have in common, what they would like to change in their reality, and what they would do to achieve that. At the same time, when asked about this, most people will respond with the simplest answers, because basic things are so important. 'All I want for my children is for them to be good human beings', Habib says. He really does stop there; he is not tempted to complete the sentence with more details.

Helche says she wants her little son to speak English, keep the family bonds strong, and 'just be human'—and, at age two, her baby boy's name was already down on the waiting list of a good school.

When I asked Antonio what he was proudest of after so many years as a public servant, as the reader may recall, he mentioned the fact that he had studied and worked with Planning all his life and now lives in a planned neighbourhood; on a par with that he talked about seeing his children through school. Antonio thinks of the next generations in general too, as we come to the end of our conversation: 'My biggest wish for the g7+ is that it tries to create mechanisms to deal with political instability'. I then ask what he would say to the young Antonio decades ago if he could: 'I would tell him to work more to help the country. We need a new strategy'.[9] He tells us, by the way, that even though he is

---

9   Interview with Antonio Co.

retired, he was still visiting the office to finish handing over some work and to train the new officers. Antonio also mentions with pride the fact that he was among the first people to teach at the first university in the country, Universidade Amílcar Cabral, starting in 2004.

The passion for education and the sense of responsibility to pass the torch is clear in the extent to which some of our storytellers engage in some kind of mentorship. Siafa volunteered as a mentor in the President's Young Professionals Program (PYPP) of Liberia. He had two mentees, who he says have been very successful: 'I learned a lot from them— as much as I was able to teach. It is difficult to mentor. At the time I was working in Liberia, I could *do* but not really teach. Mentorship is important but so difficult. They have both come to occupy important positions. This was six or seven years ago and we still keep in touch', he says, clearly very happy about the experience.[10]

There is so much potential in that idea of passing on key skills, motivating people with passion, infusing pride in working for one's people, and taking responsibility for a collective. These are at the heart of any important societal change.

There are a few paths forward that have been pointed out by our characters. Some suggest the group should invest in mentorship, exchange, and even internship programs, so that the younger generations can have the important experience of developing the skills we have been talking about here, while exposed to the kinds of environment they would realistically face in their professional lives. These would be ways of developing the next cohort of leaders as well, and would perhaps increase the chances of guaranteeing changes on the ground by *trickling down* the opportunities (and I use this expression with irony). The social bonds of solidarity and the passion they help nurture have proved such vital assets to the group and their member countries, and yet they are difficult to recreate artificially. Consequently, they need to be truly understood in their complexity and nurtured as powerful political practices.

What becomes clear after so many pages is that these crucial political practices are also, therefore, profoundly cultural. The enigmatic way to nurture social bonds capable of propelling positive changes will

---

10   Interview with Siafa Hage.

vary from context to context, as the group emphasizes, but it is clear it includes a strong component of valuing one's culture—and that also means cultural *diversity*—and making sure this message is passed on to the next generations. How else can one be proud? How else can young people have hope and seek to work for their people's well-being when there are so many challenges ahead, including the challenge of standing tall when others expect you not to? Many g7+ member countries know well the reality of having huge diasporas with firm roots in their country. People can travel and yet never leave; people can stay and yet their minds roam everywhere. Unfortunately, in a field full of templates and frameworks, people and their culture can be forgotten. This book was a very humble attempt to show their importance in a very specific context where these things are so often undervalued.

Lessons from the People of the g7+:
How to Find a Voice: On Being an Accidental Diplomat
1.　One needs to listen.
2.　Trust is the biggest currency.
3.　Be wary of the annotated agenda.
4.　In the search for a voice, avoid hoarseness.
5.　Have your people in the room.
How to Use your Survival Skills: On Patience and Opportunities
1.　Find something sacred and go beyond survival.
2.　Have patience but be strategic about it.
3.　Seize and multiply opportunities for yourself and others.
4.　Make changes and see things through.
How to Work with Passion: On the Value of Doing Things Together
1.　*Togetherness* needs to be seen as a value and a practice.
2.　Learn to live with frustration but leave no one behind.
3.　Put solidarity in practice (truly).
How to Decide Where your Pride Lies: Working to Get the Job Done
1.　Be proud to start with.
2.　But decide what your priorities are and where your pride lies if you are to get the job done.
How to Act Responsibly: On the Sense of Duty
1.　Prioritize key strategic goals.
2.　Advocate for context and country leadership on peace and development.
3.　Make sure assessments don't become ends in themselves.
4.　Multiply impact: remember responsibilities travel up and down.
5.　Generate interest and responsibility within the next generations.

Bibliography

Acosta, Alberto, & Breda, Tadeu (2018). *O Bem Viver: Uma Oportunidade Para Imaginar Outros Mundos*. Rio de Janeiro: Elefante.

African Union (2013). *Agenda 2063: The Africa We Want*. https://au.int/en/Agenda2063/popular_version

Ahmed, Ali Jimale (2002). *The Somali Oral Tradition and the Role of Storytelling in Somalia*. Minnesota: Minnesota Humanities Center.

Al Jazeera (2022). *Taliban delegation holds talks with EU, US diplomats in Doha*. https://www.aljazeera.com/news/2022/2/16/taliban-meets-with-eu-us-in-bid-to-unlock-funds-for-afghanistan

Amy, Lori (2011). 'Listening for the Elsewhere and the Not-Yet: Academic Labor as a Matter of Ethical Witness', in Inayatulla, Naeem (ed.), *Autobiographical International Relations: I, IR*. Milton Park, Abingdon, Oxon: Routledge. https://doi.org/10.4324/9780203837221

Ashcroft, Vincent, Laing, Andrew & Lochart, Claire (2017). *Statebuilding in Conflict-Affected & Fragile States: A Comparative Study*. g7+ and Institute for States Effectiveness, LSE.

Andersen, Jørgen Juel, Johannesen, Niels, & Rijkers, Bob (2020). 'Elite Capture of Foreign Aid: Evidence from Offshore Bank Accounts'. *CEBI Working Paper 07/20*. https://doi.org/10.2139/ssrn.3551078.

BBC News (2022). *Guinea-Bissau: Many dead after coup attempt, president says*. https://www.bbc.com/news/world-africa-60220701

Beja, Olinda (2015). *À Sombra Do Oká: Poemas*. São Paulo: Escrituras Editora.

Bousquet, F (2022). *Fragile and Conflict-Affected Economies Are Falling Further Behind*. World Economic Forum. https://www.weforum.org/agenda/2022/02/fragile-conflict-economy-states-pandemic-covid19-debt

Center for Global Development (n.d.). *Scott Family Liberia Fellows*. https://www.cgdev.org/topics/scott-family-liberia-fellows

Chancel, L., Piketty, T., Saez, E., Zucman, G. et al. (2022) World Inequality Report 2022, World Inequality Lab, wir2022.wid.world

Chang, Ha-Joon (2002). *Kicking Away the Ladder. Development Strategy in Historical Perspective*. London, UK: Anthem Press.

Constantinou, Costas M., Cornago, Noé, & McConnell, Fiona. Transprofessional Diplomacy. *Brill Research Perspectives in Foreign Policy and Diplomacy*, 1(4). https://doi.org/-10.1163/24056006-12340005

Costa, Helder (2012). 'g7+ and the New Deal: Country-Led and Country-Owned Initiatives: A Perspective from Timor-Leste.' *Journal of Peacebuilding & Development*, 7(2), 96–102. https://doi.org/10.1080/15423166.2012.743819

Costa, Helder & Hage, Siafa (2013). *Putting peace at the core of development*. Development and Peace Foundation.

Crewe, Emma & Harrison, Elizabeth (1998). *Whose Development? An Ethnography of Aid*. London and New York: Zed Books.

Crook, Matt, (2010). *Development: fragile nations speak up to donors*. Inter Press Service. http://www.ipsnews.net/2010/04/development-listen-to-us-fragile-states-tell-donors/

Da Costa Guterres, Francisco (2017). *Reconciliation between Timor-Leste and Indonesia: A Forward Looking Model of Reconciliation*. g7+ Foundation.

De Carvalho, Gustavo, & Forti, Daniel (2020). *Africa Can Become More Influential in the UN Security Council*. Institute for Security Studies: ISS Today. https://issafrica.org/iss-today/africa-can-become-more-influential-in-the-un-security-council

Dunn, Kevin C. (2003). *Imagining the Congo: The International Relations of Identity*. London and Basingstoke: Palgrave Macmillan. https://doi.org/10.1057/9781403979261.

Edelman, Marc, & Haugerud, Angelique (2005). *The Anthropology of Development and Globalization from Classical Political Economy to Contemporary Neoliberalism*. Malden, Mass: Blackwell Pub.

Edwards, Sophie (2019). *In decentralization push, World Bank to relocate hundreds of DC staffers*. Devex. https://www.devex.com/news/in-decentralization-push-world-bank-to-relocate-hundreds-of-dc-staffers-95875

Everingham, Sarah (2010). *Growing Opposition to 'Timor Solution'*. ReliefWeb. https://reliefweb.int/report/timor-leste/growing-opposition-timor-solution

Federal Government of Somalia (n.d.). *Home*. Ministry of Finance—Somalia. https://mof.gov.so/.

G.A. Res. (2016). '70/262. Review of the United Nations peacebuilding architecture'. *A/RES/70/262*. undocs.org/en/A/RES/70/262

Government of Timor-Leste (2014). *Biography: Prime Minister and Minister of Defense and Security of the Democratic Republic of Timor-Leste*. http://timor-leste.gov.tl/?p=3&lang=en.

Guarascio, Francesco (2022). *Poorer nations reject over 100 mln COVID-19 vaccine doses as many near expiry.* Reuters. https://www.reuters.com/business/healthcare-pharmaceuticals/more-than-100-million-covid-19-vaccines-rejected-by-poorer-nations-dec-unicef-2022-01-13

'Habiba Sarābi' (2020). *Wikipedia.* https://en.wikipedia.org/wiki/Habiba_Sar%C4%81bi

Hearn, Sarah (2016). *Independent Review of the New Deal for Engagement in Fragile States for the International Dialogue on Peacebuilding and Statebuilding.* New York: Center on International Cooperation, New York University.

Honório do Couto, Hildo, & Embaló, Filomena (2010). 'Um país da CPLP'. *Literatura, Língua e Cultura na Guiné-Bissau*, 20. Brazil: Thesaurus Editora.

Human Rights Watch (2022). *Afghanistan: Events of 2021.* https://www.hrw.org/world-report/2022/country-chapters/afghanistan

IDPS (2016). *Stockholm Declaration on Addressing Fragility and Building Peace in a Changing World.* https://www.government.se/contentassets/8c2491b60d494dd8a2c1046b9336ee52/stockholm-declaration-on-addressing-fragility-and-building-peace-in-a-changing-world.pdf

IISD (2018). *To Leave No One Behind, Brief Calls for Considering IDPs in SDG Implementation.* http://sdg.iisd.org/news/to-leave-no-one-behind-brief-calls-for-considering-idps-in-sdg-implementation/

International Development Association (n.d.). *Window for Host Communities and Refugees.* https://ida.worldbank.org/replenishments/ida19-replenishment/windows-host-communities-refugees

International Dialogue on Peacebuilding and Statebuilding (2011). *A New Deal for Engagement in Fragile States.* https://www.pbsbdialogue.org/media/filer_public/07/69/07692de0-3557-494e-918e-18df00e9ef73/the_new_deal.pdf

International Dialogue on Peacebuilding and Statebuilding (2011). *A Political Strategy to Secure International Acceptance of the PSGs. Meeting of the Steering Group.* Nairobi: IDPS.

International Dialogue on Peacebuilding and Statebuilding (2014). *New Deal Monitoring Report.* https://www.pbsbdialogue.org/media/filer_public/bd/e3/bde37bb3-abd0-4faa-9a85-c4eaa438a32b/ndmr14.pdf

International Dialogue on Peacebuilding and Statebuilding (2011). *The Monrovia Roadmap on Peacebuilding and Statebuilding.* https://www.icnl.org/wp-content/uploads/Transnational_monrovia.pdf

International Dialogue on Peacebuilding and Statebuilding (2017). *The Use of Country Systems and the New Deal: The State of Play in 2017.*

International Dialogue on Peacebuilding and Statebuilding (n.d.). *Realisation of the SDGs in Countries Affected by Conflict and Fragility: The Role of the New Deal.* Conceptual Note.

International Monetary Fund (IMF) (2022). *COVID-19 Financial Assistance and Debt Service Relief.* https://www.imf.org/en/Topics/imf-and-covid19/COVID-Lending-Tracker#CCRT

Institute for Economics & Peace. (2022) Global Peace Index 2022: Measuring Peace in a Complex World, Sydney, June 2022. http://visionofhumanity.org/resources, p. 4.

Jassey, Katja (2004). 'The Bureaucrat', in Groves, Leslie & Hinton, Rachel (eds), *Inclusive Aid: Changing Power and Relationships in International Development.* London and Sterling, VA: Earthscan, 2004.

Jenkins, Matthew, Kukutschka, Roberto Martínez B. & Zúñiga, Nieves (2020). *Anti-Corruption In Fragile Settings: A Review Of The Evidence.* Bonn and Eschborn: Deutsche Gesellschaft für Internationale Zusammenarbeit (GIZ) GmbH.

Jütting, Johannes & Badiee, Shaida (2016). *Financing SDG data needs: What does it cost?* Global Partnership for Sustainable Development Data. http://www.data4sdgs.org/news/financing-sdg-data-needs-what-does-it-cost

Kadende-Kaiser, Rose M., & Kaiser, Paul J. (1997). 'Modern Folklore, Identity, and Political Change in Burundi'. *African Studies Review*, 40(3), 29–54. https://doi.org/10.2307/524965.

Landers, Clemence & Aboneaaj, Rakan (2021). *Giving up the "Statebuilding" Ghost: Lessons from Afghanistan for Foreign Assistance in Fragile States.* https://www.cgdev.org/blog/giving-statebuilding-ghost-lessons-afghanistan-foreign-assistance-fragile-states

Li, Tania Murray (2010). 'To Make Live or Let Die? Rural Dispossession and the Protection of Surplus Populations'. *Antipode*, 41(1), 66–93. https://doi.org/10.1111/j.1467-8330.2009.00717.x.

Liberia Governance and Economic Management Assistance Program (n.d.). http://www.gemap-liberia.org/

Liljas, Per (2018). *One of Australia's Notorious Refugee Camps Has Become an Economic Crutch for Papua New Guinea Island.* The Washington Post. https://www.washingtonpost.com/world/asia_pacific/one-of-australias-notorious-refugee-camps-has-become-an-economic-crutch-for-papua-new-guinea-island/2018/05/08/25e78634-433d-11e8-8569-26fda6b404c7_story.html

Lucey, A. 'Implementing the Peace, Security and Development Nexus in Africa'. *Strategic Analysis*, 39(5), 500–11. https://doi.org/10.1080/09700161.2015.1069970

Martins, N., Leigh, C., Stewart, J. & Andersson, D. (2014). *Natural Resources in g7+ Countries.* g7+ Secretariat. https://g7plus.org/attach-pdf/Natural%20Resource%20in%20g7%20countires.pdf.Mayar, Habib Ur. Rehman (2014). 'The Journey towards Resilience Continues: G7+Priorities to Confront Ebola, Implement the New Deal and Influence the Post-2015 Agenda'. *Journal of*

Peacebuilding & Development, 9(3), 122–26. https://doi.org/10.1080/1542316 6.2014.985977.

Mayar, Habib Ur Rehman (2018). 'Sustaining peace and shared prosperity: The question of fragile states.' *Global Social Policy*, 18(2), 222–27. https://doi. org/10.1177/1468018118789808.

McConnell, Fiona (2017). 'Liminal geopolitics: The subjectivity and spatiality of diplomacy at the margins'. *Transactions of the Institute of British Geographers*, 42(1), 139–52. https://doi.org/10.1111/tran.12156.

McGrath, Kim (2017). *Crossing the Line: Australia's Secret History in the Timor Sea*. Carlton: Black Inc. Redback.

Monnier, Céline, & Mayar, Habib (2020). 'Making Sure Peace Isn't a Casualty of COVID-19 in Fragile States'. World Politics Review. https://www. worldpoliticsreview.com/articles/28734/making-sure-peace-isn-t-a-casualty-of-covid-19-in-fragile-states?fbclid=IwAR2HZAV3FiZ6tJo75gOJb MSs9Q-1ZiUabjzKmP6O6kyNAkqSVDisVJYdYz8

Moran, Theodore (2006). 'How Multinational Investors Evade Developed Country Laws'. *Center for Global Development Working Paper 79*. https://doi. org/10.2139/ssrn.984044.

Mosse, David, & Lewis, David (2005). *The Aid Effect: Giving and Governing in International Development*. London: Pluto Press. https://doi.org/10.2307/j. ctt18fs3zx.

Mosse, David (2008). *Cultivating Development: An Ethnography of Aid Policy and Practice*. London: Pluto Press. https://doi.org/10.2307/j.ctt18fs4st.

MSF (2015). *An unprecedented year: Médecins Sans Frontières's response to the largest Ebola outbreak*. https://www.doctorswithoutborders.org/latest/ unprecedented-year-msfs-response-largest-ever-ebola-outbreak

MSF (2015). *Pushed to the Limit and Beyond: A year into the largest ever Ebola outbreak*. https://www.msf.org/ebola-pushed-limit-and-beyond.

Murithi, T. (2006). 'African Approaches to Building Peace and Social Solidarity'. *African Journal on Conflict Resolution*, 6(2). https://doi.org/10.4314/ajcr. v6i2.39402

Mwai, Peter (2022). *Are military takeovers on the rise in Africa?* BBC News. https:// www.bbc.com/news/world-africa-46783600

Najam, Adil (2005). 'Why environmental politics looks different from the South', in Dauvergne, P. (ed.), *Handbook of Global Environmental Politics*. Cheltenham, UK, Northampton, MA: Edward Elgar.

Nandy, Ashis (1983). *The Intimate Enemy: Loss and Recovery of Self under Colonialism*. Delhi: Oxford University Press and Bombay Calcutta Madras.

Natsios, Andrew (2010). *The Clash of the Counter-Bureaucracy and Development*. Center for Global Development.

Nay, Olivier (2014). 'International Organisations and the Production of Hegemonic Knowledge: How the World Bank and the OECD helped invent the Fragile State Concept'. *Third World Quarterly*, 35(2), 210–31. https://doi.org/10.1080/01436597.2014.878128.

New Deal (n.d.) *About the New Deal.* https://www.newdeal4peace.org/about-the-new-deal/.

O crocodile que se fez Timor (n.d.). http://www3.dsi.uminho.pt/academia militar/1999/historia/lenda.htm

OECD (2005). *The Paris Declaration on Aid Effectiveness.* https://www.oecd.org/dac/effectiveness/34428351.pdf

OECD (2018). *Development Co-operation Report 2018: Joining forces to leave no one behind.* Paris: OECD Publishing. https://doi.org/10.1787/dcr-2018-en.

OECD (2019). *Development Co-operation Report—A fairer, greener, safer tomorrow.* https://www.oecd.org/dac/development-co-operation-report-20747721.htm

OECD (2020). *States of Fragility.* http://www3.compareyourcountry.org/states-of-fragility/covid/0/

OECD (n.d.). *History.* https://www.oecd.org/about/history/#d.en.194377

OECD (n.d.). *Organisational structure.* http://www.oecd.org/about/structure/

Office of the Special Inspector General for Pandemic Recovery (2021) *Quarterly Report to the United States Congress.* https://www.sigpr.gov/sites/sigpr/files/2021-07/SIGPR-Quarterly-Report-June-2021-Final.pdf

Olatunji, Felix O. & Bature, Anthony I. (2019). 'The Inadequacy of Post-Development Theory to the Discourse of Development and Social Order in the Global South'. *Social Evolution & History*, 18(2), 229–43. https://doi.org/10.30884/seh/2019.02.12.

Paulino, Vicente (2017). 'As lendas de Timor e a literatura oral timorense'. *Anuário Antropológico*, 42(2), 157–79. https://doi.org/10.4000/aa.2175.

Prunier, Gérard (2009). *Africa's World War: Congo, the Rwandan Genocide, and the Making of a Continental Catastrophe.* New York: Oxford University Press.

Peake, Gordon P. (2013). *Beloved Land: Stories, struggles, and secrets from Timor-Leste* [Kindle Edition]. Melbourne: Scribe Publications.

Phạm Quỳnh N., & Shilliam, Robbie (2016). *Meanings of Bandung: Postcolonial Orders and Decolonial Visions.* London and New York: Rowman & Littlefield.

Ramalingam, Ben (2013). *Aid on the edge of chaos: Rethinking international cooperation in a complex world.* Oxford: Oxford University Press.

Republic of Sierra Leone (2012). *Fragility Assessment.* http://g7plus.org/resources/sierra-leone-fragility-assessment

Republic of South Sudan (2012). *Fragility Assessment*. http://g7plus.org/resources/south-sudan-fragility-assessment-report/

Republic of Timor-Leste (2013). *Fragility Assessment*.

Republic of Timor-Leste (2015). *Fragility Assessment*.

Rocha de Siqueira, Isabel (2019) *Independent Review of the g7+*, BRICS Policy Center—International Relations Institute (PUC-Rio).

Rocha de Siqueira, Isabel (2017). *Managing State Fragility: Conflict, Quantification and Power*. London: Taylor & Francis. https://doi.org/10.4324/9781315536613.

Roessler, Philip, & Prendergast (2006). 'Democratic Republic of the Congo' in Durch, William J. (ed.), *Twenty-First-Century Peace Operations*. Washington, DC: United States Institute of Peace and the Henry L. Stimson Center, 229–318.

Schwikowski, Martina (2020). *Coronavirus: How Africa is bracing for pandemic's impact*. DW. https://www.dw.com/en/coronavirus-what-the-world-could-learn-from-africa/a-53259048

Shani, Giorgio (2016). 'Spectres of the 3rd World: Bandung as a Lieu De Mémoire', in Phạm, Quỳnh N. & Shilliam, Robbie (eds), *Meanings of Bandung: Postcolonial Orders and Decolonial Visions*. London and New York: Rowman & Littlefield.

South Commission (1990). *The Challenge to the South: The Report of the South Commission*. Oxford: Oxford University Press.

The Federal Republic of Somalia (2013). *Somalia Compact*.

São Tomé e Príncipe (2019). *Avaliação da Fragilidade*. PNUD.

The Group of 77 at the United Nations (2020). https://www.g77.org/

The Guardian (n.d.) *Manus Island*. https://www.theguardian.com/australia-news/manus-island

The Fund for Peace (n.d.) *Fragile States Index*. https://fragilestatesindex.org/.

Transparency International (n.d.) *Corruption Perceptions Index*. https://www.transparency.org/en/cpi/2021.

UN Careers (n.d.). *Where we are*. https://careers.un.org/lbw/home.aspx?viewtype=VD

UNESCO (2018). *Expert Meeting on "Measuring Intercultural Dialogue: Strengthening data to enhance impact on the ground"*. https://en.unesco.org/events/expert-meeting-measuring-intercultural-dialogue-strengthening-data-enhance-impact-ground

UN General Assembly (2015) Resolution 70/1. Transforming our world: the 2030 Agenda for Sustainable Development.

UN General Assembly (2016) Resolution 70/262. Review of the United Nations peacebuilding architecture.

UNHCR (n.d.). *Figures at a glance.* https://www.unhcr.org/figures-at-a-glance.html

UN Stats (2020). *SDG Indicators: Metadata repository.* https://unstats.un.org/sdgs/metadata/

UN Stats (2022). *SDG Indicators.* https://unstats.un.org/sdgs/indicators/indicators-list/

UN Stats (2022). *Tier Classification for Global SDG Indicators.* https://unstats.un.org/sdgs/files/Tier%20Classification%20of%20SDG%20Indicators_4%20Feb%202022_web.pdf

United Nations (2020). *Compilation of 2020 Comprehensive Review Proposals Received.* https://unstats.un.org/sdgs/files/2020%20Comprehensive%20Review%20Proposals_web.pdfUnited Nations (2020). *How do organizations and non-member states get observer status in the General Assembly?* https://ask.un.org/faq/14519

United Nations (2020). *Progress towards the Sustainable Development Goals: Report of the Secretary-General.*

United Nations (2020). *Secretary-General Calls for Global Ceasefire, Citing War-Ravaged Health Systems, Populations Most Vulnerable to Novel Coronavirus.* https://www.un.org/press/en/2020/sgsm20018.doc.htm

United Nations (2021). *'Time for action' to support most fragile States: Guterres.* https://news.un.org/en/story/2021/10/1102752

United Nations (2022). *Afghanistan: 500,000 Jobs Lost since Taliban Takeover.* UN News. https://news.un.org/en/story/2022/01/1110052.

United Nations (n.d.) *Common African Position on the Post-2015 Development Agenda.* https://sustainabledevelopment.un.org/index.php?page=view&type=400&nr=1329&menu=35

United Nations & World Bank (2018). *Pathways for Peace: Inclusive approaches to preventing violent conflict.* Washington D.C.: World Bank.

United States (2021). *2020 United States Strategy to Prevent Conflict and Promote Stability.* https://www.state.gov/wp-content/uploads/2021/01/2020-US-Strategy-To-Prevent-Conflict-and-Promote-Stability.pdf.

Walicki, Nadine (2017). *Tackling internal displacement through the SDGs.* UNA-UK. https://www.sustainablegoals.org.uk/tackling-internal-displacement-sdgs/

Win, Everjoice (2004). "If It Doesn't Fit on the Blue Square It's Out!' An Open Letter to My Donor Friend'., in Groves, L. & Hinton, R. (eds), *Inclusive Aid Changing Power and Relationships in International Development.* London and Sterling, VA: Earthscan.

World Bank (2019). *IDA19—Special Theme: Fragility, Conflict & Violence.* International Development Association. New York: World Bank.

World Bank (2018). *Poverty and Shared Prosperity: Piecing Together the Poverty Puzzle.* https://www.worldbank.org/en/publication/poverty-and-shared-prosperity-2018

World Bank (2020). *World Bank Group Strategy for Fragility, Conflict, and Violence 2020—2025.* New York: World Bank.

World Bank (2021). *Global Community Steps Up with $93 Billion Support Package to Boost Resilient Recovery in World's Poorest Countries.* https://www.worldbank.org/en/news/press-release/2021/12/15/global-community-steps-up-with-93-billion-support-package-to-boost-resilient-recovery-in-world-s-poorest-countries

World Bank (2022). *Remittance Flows Register Robust 7.3 Percent Growth in 2021.* https://www.worldbank.org/en/news/press-release/2021/11/17/remittance-flows-register-robust-7-3-percent-growth-in-2021.

World Bank (n.d.) *Classification of Fragile and Conflict-Affected Situations.* https://www.worldbank.org/en/topic/fragilityconflictviolence/brief/harmonized-list-of-fragile-situations.

World Health Organization (2020). *Depression.* https://www.who.int/news-room/fact-sheets/detail/depression

World Health Organization (n.d.). *Ebola outbreak 2014–2016.* https://www.who.int/emergencies/situations/ebola-outbreak-2014-2016-West-Africa

Wyeth, Vanessa (2012). 'Knights in Fragile Armor: The Rise of the "g7+"'. *Global Governance: A Review of Multilateralism and International Organizations*, 18(1), 7–12. https://doi.org/10.1163/19426720-01801002.

Wyeth, Vanessa, de Carvalho, Gustavo, Woldeselassie, Zerihun A., Mechoulan, Delphine, Boutellis, Arthur, Whineray, David, Moreira da Silva, Jorge, Rosand, Eric & Mahmoud, Youssef (2012). 'Interview with Emilia Pires, Chair of the g7+ Group of Fragile States'. *International Peace Institute Global Observatory.* https://theglobalobservatory.org/2012/04/interview-with-emilia-pires-minister-of-finance-for-timor-leste-and-chair-of-the-g7-group-of-fragile-states/

Zondi, Siphamandla (2016). 'A Decolonial Turn in Diplomatic Theory: Unmasking Epistemic Injustice'. *Journal for Contemporary History*, 41(1), 18–37. https://doi.org/10.18820/0258-2236/jch.v41i1.2

Videos

ABC News Australia (2010). *Ramos-Horta Speaks to Lateline* [Video]. https://www.youtube.com/watch?v=_lwqU3paaeA.

g7+ Publications

g7+ (2010). *Dili Declaration.* http://g7plus.org/resources/3235/

g7+ (2013). *Note on the Fragility Spectrum.* Kinshasa, g7+.

g7+ (2014a). *The Haiti Declaration.*

g7+ (2014b). *Lomé Communiqué.*

g7+ (2014c). *Pathways toward Resilience. The Journey Continues.*...http://www.g7plus.org/sites/default/files/resources/g7plus-Charter_0.pdf

g7+ (2015). *Annual Report 2014–2015.* http://g7plus.org/resources/g7-annualreport-2014-2015/

g7+ (2016c). *Aid instruments for peace- and state-building: Putting the New Deal into practice.* http://g7plus.org/resources/aid-instrument-for-peace-and-statebuilding-puttingthe-new-deal-into-practices-2016/

g7+ (2016d). *Strength in fragility: "We are writing our own history"—The emergence of the g7+ group from our own perspective.* http://g7plus.org/resources/strength-infragility-we-are-writing-our-own-history/

g7+ (2017). *Host Nation Views on UN Peace and Security Reform Proposals.*

g7+ (2018). *Annual Report 2017–2018.* http://g7plus.org/resources/annual-report-2017-2018/

g7+ (2019). *Annual Report 2019.* https://g7plus.org/belakang/uploads/page/resourceContent-20210201-4156a30026.pdf

g7+ (2020). *Annual Report 2020.* https://g7plus.org/attach-pdf/ANNUAL%20REPORT%202020%20-%20ENGLISH.pdf

g7+ (2020). *Host Nations Views on UN Peace and Security Reform Proposals.* g7+ and Center on International Cooperation (CIC): New York University.

g7+ (n.d.). *g7+ Policy Note on Fragile-to-Fragile Cooperation.* http://g7plus.org/ourwork/peer-learning-and-cooperation/

g7+ (n.d.). *7 Things to Know About Fragile-to-Fragile (F2F) Cooperation.* http://g7plus.org/our-work/peer-learning-and-cooperation/

g7+ (n.d.). *g7+ SDG Report 2018,* partial draft.

g7+ (n.d.). *g7+ Newsletters.* http://g7plus.org/g7-newsletters/

ANNEX I g7+ Statements — A Selection
1. 10 April 2010, Dili, Timor-Leste

Statement of the g7+

We the representatives from Burundi, the Central African Republic, Chad, the Democratic Republic of Congo, Liberia, Nepal, the Solomon Islands, Sierra Leone, South Sudan and Timor-Leste, assembled for the g7+ Country Partners Meeting, gathered to signify the will of fragile states to reduce poverty, deter conflict and provide better conditions for the people of our nations.

We thank the international community for giving us the space to conduct this dialogue, share our experiences and learn from our lessons. This gives us a stronger voice to speak to the international community about our needs and circumstances.

Therefore, we recognize that to assist the development partners in designing their assistance to fragile states, we must take leadership and express a strong, long-term vision. This vision should be reflected in our national plans, which must guide donor intervention in our countries. We should also recognize that this transformation is a long process that takes time and requires flexible approaches that are sensitive to the stages of fragility and political context. The long-term vision will be set out in our development plans, frameworks and strategies. These plans will prioritize the following areas:

1. GOVERNANCE

- Political
- Public administration and decentralization
- Economic, financial

Fragile nations recognize the need for good governance that empowers its people through open and transparent public administration and financial management, political representation and leadership. It is through the principles of good governance that effective and efficient public administration can be achieved. Leadership and effective systems of political empowerment are also essential to ensure development and social inclusion. There is recognition that democracy must be implemented in accordance with local circumstances.

It was agreed that in some fragile nations the needs of good governance require the implementation of a program of decentralization to bring service delivery and representation closer to citizens.

2. ECONOMIC DEVELOPMENT

- Infrastructure development (highlighting roads, telecommunications, transport, energy)
- Natural resource management
- Land issues and agriculture
- Poverty reduction
- Environment and climate change
- Job creation

Statement of the g7+

With widespread poverty experienced by our nations as a root cause of our conflicts, we agree that economic development is central to our stable futures. To achieve economic development, the importance of infrastructure development is a priority. Among infrastructure needs, connectivity through telecommunications, quality roads, water and sanitation, and electricity and energy are basic requirements for our development.

Greater emphasis must be focused on aid effectiveness, which can contribute to these core infrastructure needs that will deliver immediate relief and economic development.

3. HUMAN AND SOCIAL DEVELOPMENT

- Health
- Education
- Human resources, capacity
- Gender equality

Our societies cannot develop without basic conditions that allow our citizens a good quality of life that sustains the human and collective spirit. Education, health, water and sanitation, gender equality and job creation are fundamental to human and social development. Effective programs that protect and strengthen the most vulnerable and reach the most remote and inaccessible areas are critical to both sustainability and stability.

Aid must be distributed fairly across the country to reduce the risk of conflict, and ensure social inclusion and a common national identity that is respected by international partners.

4. SECURITY

- Conflict resolution and prevention
- Reconciliation
- Social Inclusion
- Peacebuilding, dialogue
- Rule of law

There was a shared recognition that without security there can be no development. We acknowledge that we have a responsibility to address and resolve our internal conflicts. Common to the experiences of fragile states is the occurrence of conflict and the existence of latent tensions and disagreement.

We have all dealt with what have often seemed intractable problems and social division. We acknowledged these problems and agreed on the approaches that are necessary to bring peace and security. This includes the need for reconciliation, social inclusion, dialogue, the institution of the rule of law, and for an honest examination of the root causes of conflict and our national mentality.

Statement of the g7+

10 April 2010, Dili, Timor-Leste

There must be recognition that a change of national mentality is a long process that takes time. As we have all experienced conflict, there was agreement that we can learn from our individual and collective experiences and discuss together how we addressed our problems.

Resolution of conflict takes time due to the internal dynamic and complexities of our country circumstances. Security and stability require the integration of all groups in society which should engage in a process of self-examination leading to a common purpose. International partners must integrate their intervention accordingly.

Action must be taken to operationalize these priorities. **There is a strong spirit of solidarity between our countries and a strong desire to continue to work together in the g7+ group of fragile states** to share experiences, challenges, failures and successes, to make a rapid transition to sustainable peace and development, and to bring tangible results for the people of all our nations.

We believe this dialogue between fragile states has provided clarity in our shared challenges in nation building. We recognize our collective responsibility given the urgency of the situation, and given the effect of conflict. We are the furthest away from reaching the MDGs and we recognize we will not achieve them within the current time frame.

In order to work effectively with donors, fragile nations must develop and communicate their own planning, programs, models and strategies of development through strong leadership. The fragile nations acknowledge that each country must take ownership by developing these frameworks to address individual circumstances and within the national context. We recognize that ownership comes with a responsibility to define our needs and be accountable for delivery. We want donors to adhere to this principle and align accordingly.

When considering these circumstances, we agree there are common themes through shared characteristics and challenges amongst fragile states. All must be addressed with action and aid assistance that is effective.

We recognize fragile states are in a transitional stage – in order to further explore the above themes and to discuss our common and collective issues, **it is necessary for the g7+ Country Partner meetings to continue.** It is through this dialogue and institutional grouping that we can discuss our priorities and our approaches, and in doing so, allow for empowered and effective communication with the donor communities.

We believe fragile states are characterized and classified through the lens of the developed rather than through the eyes of the developing; and that in order to make long-lasting change and implement the principles of good engagement; the national context must guide each distinctive path to sustainable development, and donors must first harmonize to this concept and then implement without undue process. Although we all accept international standards, the donor community must be aware of our conditions and needs. That is why we must give ourselves a transitional period to reinforce our capabilities and systems and not have complex and slow procedural requirements and conditions imposed upon us.

Statement of the g7+

Fragile nations, above all states, understand the meaning of urgent action, that a government's responsibility to address the needs of the people is a priority which often requires swift, immediate, and decisive responses to avoid potential or escalating threats to national stability. International partnerships are critical at this time. A two-pronged approach is necessary, requiring flexibility in systems and untying restraints that could prevent aid delivery while establishing medium- to long-term planning.

We realize the need to have a collective voice as member countries in a formal forum, supported and accepted by the international community.

Links

🌐 www.g7plus.org

[f] www.facebook.com/g7plus

[t] g7plus

2. Port-au-Prince

The Haiti Declaration

Port-au-Prince 14 November 2012

We the representatives of the g7+ participating in the Second g7+ Ministerial Retreat in Port-au-Prince, Haiti, are pleased to make this Haiti Declaration.

We confirm that during our meetings in Haiti, delegates have accepted the request of the Union of the Comoros to join our group. We welcome the Union of the Comoros into the g7+ family now numbering 18 nations.

We take this opportunity to unreservedly declare our solidarity as a group and to reaffirm our commitment to the collective efforts of advocacy in the international arena and ongoing peer-to-peer support amongst our member states. Together we recognise that the achievements of the past twelve months since the first Ministerial Retreat held in Juba, South Sudan, are a clear testimony to what we can achieve together with an effective and united voice.

We acknowledge the generosity and hospitality of the Government of the Republic of Haiti and pay tribute to the resilience and courage shown by the Haitian people in the face of adversity. The g7+ stands together in deep friendship with the Republic of Haiti. Each of our member nations are engaged in efforts to achieve the same outcomes; to build resilient States in order to provide better living conditions for the Peoples of our nations.

We recognise the contributions of the Prime Minister of Haiti, His Excellency Laurent Salvador Lamothe and the Prime Minister of Timor-Leste, His Excellency Kay Rala Xanana Gusmão, in this Second Ministerial Retreat and extend our appreciation to the Chair of the g7+ Her Excellency Emilia Pires.

In this Haiti Declaration the g7+ emphasises its' respect for the national sovereignty of it's members and the principle of country-owned and country-led transitions towards resilience and national development.

Whilst the g7+ is committed to promoting mutual transparency and trust in development partner relationships we remain respectfully aligned with other groupings who hold the principled position that aid should not be conditions based, and that developed countries must respect the sovereignty of developing countries, recognising national ownership of priorities, planning, policy and process.

The g7+ welcomes and appreciates emerging South-South cooperation as a compliment to North-South cooperation. We continue to respectfully urge developed countries to honour their ODA commitments.

3. Lomé

Lomé Communique

We, the Ministers and Delegates from the g7+ countries participating in the third g7+ Ministerial Meeting in Lomé, Togo, on the 29th and 30th of May 2014, are pleased to gather in the spirit of solidarity and cooperation that characterises our association.

We applaud the progress made in the implementation of the New Deal in several g7+ countries, and welcome the launch of the New Deal fragility assessments in Guinea-Bissau and Comoros.

We congratulate the people and government of Afghanistan and Guinea-Bissau for conducting successful elections.

At the same time we empathise with the people of the Central African Republic and South Sudan as they experience a period of crisis. We stand in solidarity with the government and people in those countries and commit our collective efforts to restore peace and resilience.

We welcome the Republic of Sao Tome and Principe and the Republic of Yemen as new members of the g7+ family.

We endorse the g7+ Charter and confirm Dili to be the headquarters of the g7+ Secretariat.

We announce H.E. Minister Kaifala Marah of Sierra Leone as the new g7+ Chair and H.E. Deputy Minister Alfred Metellus of Haiti as Deputy Chair.

We appoint the outgoing Chair H.E. Emilia Pires, as the g7+ Special Envoy and the Prime Minister of Timor-Leste, H.E. Kay Rala Xanana Gusmão, as a member of the g7+ Advisory Board.

We reaffirm our commitment to the realization of the New Deal principles and call on our development partners to fulfil their commitment thereto.

We welcome the initiative of "Fragile to Fragile" (F to F) cooperation and encourage peer learning among member countries. We commit to explore ways in which the g7+ can increase awareness of emerging crises and tailor responses accordingly.

We endorse the 2013 Annual Report and the 2014/15 Work Plan.

We strongly support the inclusion of a separate goal on Peaceful Societies and Effective Institutions, in the Post-2015 Development Framework.

We conclude our meetings in Lomé, Togo, with deep appreciation to the Government of Togo for generously hosting this third g7+ Ministerial meeting.

We look forward to the next Ministerial meeting in Afghanistan.

Lomé, Togo.

30th May 2014.

4. Kabul

Kabul Communiqué

We, the Ministers and Delegates from the g7+ countries, met during the 4th g7+ Ministerial Meeting in Kabul, Afghanistan, on the 23rd and 24th of March 2016.

We applaud the progress made by all countries towards the Peacebuilding and Statebuilding Goals. We congratulate the people and governments of the Democratic Republic of Congo (DRC), Guinea, Liberia and Sierra Leone in overcoming the Ebola crisis of 2015. We congratulate the Central African Republic (CAR) and Togo for their successful elections and we look forward to Somalia's upcoming electoral process.

Despite progress, numerous challenges are faced by member countries. We stand in solidarity with the people of Burundi and reaffirm our commitment to see stability re-established. We stand in solidarity with the people of Yemen and support the ongoing peace process. We recognize the signing of a peace agreement in South Sudan and encourage its implementation. Furthermore, we support Afghanistan's call for a result-oriented regional cooperation to ensure the success of the Afghan peace process and we support Timor-Leste's call for recognition of its legitimate rights on border delimitations, under international law.

We reiterate our resolve to reconciliation and peace as cornerstones for resilience and support political dialogue to that end. We commit to mobilizing influential personalities from within the g7+ to help in promoting peacemaking and peacebuilding. We wish to collaborate with the United Nations and other actors on conflict prevention in our countries. We believe that Civil Society is an important actor in restoring trust between states and citizens and in promoting peace and reconciliation. We call upon Civil Society to constructively engage with the government and other national actors in helping reach inclusive political settlements.

As we remain convinced that sound economic foundations with a specific focus on job creation, women's and youth empowerment and private sector development are essential to sustain peace and resilience, we call upon development partners to help g7+ countries in strengthening these foundations. This requires more investment in infrastructure and skills development as critical enablers for economic growth. We call upon multi-laterals and in particular the World Bank Group to enhance their support to private sector development in g7+ countries, through country specific reforms and effective implementation of existing policies.

In line with the New Deal principles, development aid needs to unleash the economic potential of our countries and promote self-reliance. Development aid must be allocated by the recipient countries and spent through county systems. This will ensure country ownership of development. We acknowledge the findings and recommendations of the Independent Review, re-commit to the implementation of the New Deal and reaffirm partnership with the International Dialogue on Peacebuilding and Statebuilding.

We welcome the launch of the 2030 Agenda and commit to contextual implementation of the Sustainable Development Goals (SDGs) in our member countries. In particular, we commit to prioritize and jointly report on progress against the agreed list of SDG indicators through the portal established in the g7+ Secretariat and using the New Deal principles to achieve the SDGs. We will continue sharing experiences through "Fragile-to-Fragile" cooperation in peacebuilding and statebuilding under the spirit of volunteerism and solidarity.

We strongly urge the United Nations, in particular UNDP, to mobilize support to the g7+ and to host a high level session on the SDGs in New York.

We endorse the 2014-15 Annual Report and the 2016-17 Work Plan and entrust the g7+ Secretariat to facilitate its implementation.

We conclude our meetings in Kabul, Afghanistan, with deep appreciation of Government of Islamic Republic of Afghanistan for generously hosting this 4th g7+ Ministerial meeting.

We look forward to the next Ministerial meeting in 2017.

5. Lisbon

5th g7+ Ministerial Meeting, 26-27 June 2019

Lisbon Communiqué

We, the Ministers and Delegates from the g7+ countries, met during the 5th g7+ Ministerial Meeting in Lisbon, Portugal on 26-27 June 2019.

We express our sincere appreciation and gratitude to the Government and People of the Democratic Republic of Timor-Leste for its continuous support to the g7+. We are also grateful for the support of our Development Partners,and in particular for the financial support to the g7+ Secretariat from Sweden and the pledge from Finland.

We are encouraged that the g7+ has become an increasingly influential constituency on the global stage and we reaffirm our resolve to continue playing an active role at the global level.

While recognizing that conflicts are still ongoing in some of our member countries, we are encouraged by the Peace processes that are underway in member countries such as Afghanistan, Central African Republic, South Sudan and Yemen. We reaffirm that these processes should be country-owned, country-led and inclusive, preserving the achievements of the past, so that they result in lasting Peace and stability. We reiterate our collective call for the international community, particularly the United Nations, to commit to supporting conflict-affected countries to achieve Peace through genuine dialogue and reconciliation, reflecting the wishes of the citizens.

We acknowledge the generous efforts by the international community and by the host countries that help and host refugees and displaced people from war-ravaged, poverty-strickenand climate change-affected countries. However, we believe that it is not sufficient to react to the consequences of conflict and crisis by providing humanitarian assistance. There is a need to foster sustainable Peace and lasting stability in conflict-affected countries. Therefore, we call upon the international community, the United Nations, the host countries and regional powers to genuinely help to address conflicts and their root causes. The g7+, drawing on its collective wisdom and experience, reiterates its resolve to spare no efforts to supporting countries in this endeavor.

Considering that access to fair justice is an enabler of lasting peace and an important pillar of Statebuilding, we acknowledge and support the Declaration and Joint action planwhich came out of the Ministerial-Level g7+ meeting on *Access to justice for all in conflict-affectedcountries* that took place on 19-20 June 2019 in the Hague, Kingdom of the Netherlands.

We remain firm believers in the fact that resilient economic foundations are indispensable for sustaining Peace and development. Our youthful populations need to be provided with job opportunities so that they can be the source of prosperity rather than drivers of instability. We therefore call upon our Development Partners, as well as on all private actors committed to Peace, to support us in realizing our potential, becoming self-reliant and creating jobs.

Considering further that our countries are endowed with natural wealth and other resources which can be the source of economic growth and prosperity if managed effectively, we comitto establish a g7+ Ministerial-level platform on natural resource management which will facilitate the sharing of knowledge and experience in this domain.

We reaffirm our commitment to the Principles of the *New Deal*, the Agenda 2030 and the Sustaining Peace Agenda, and we pledge to enhance their effectiveness at the country level.

As a constituency of the International Dialogue on Peacebuilding and Statebuilding (IDPS), we welcomethe IDPS Peace Vision 2019-2021, and we commit to working with our partners to realize the objectives therein.

We unanimously agree for Sierra Leone to continue as the chairmanship of g7+ until the next Ministerial meeting, and appoint Afghanistan to serve as Deputy Chair until such time.

We resolve to appoint Dr. Jose Ramos Horta, Nobel Peace Laureate and former President of the Democratic Republic of Timor-Leste, as Special Envoy of the g7+.

We express our appreciation to the Democratic Republic of Timor-Leste for continuing to host the g7+ Headquarters in Dili, and to the Government of the Republic of Portugal and the Lisbon City Council for hosting the g7+'s recently-inaugurated European Hub, which will play a critical role in supporting the members states.

We endorse the decision to launch the process of seeking observer status for the g7+ at the United Nations. We entrust the g7+ Secretariat to work with the Permanent Mission of the chairing country in New York to initiate the process of submitting the application, and we call upon the support of all members of the UN throughout this process.

We commit to continuing the process of ratification of the g7+ Charter in our countriesand,with a view to consolidating the membership and sustaining the activities of the g7+, we reaffirm our commitment to meeting the voluntary contribution requirement provided for in the Charter.

We endorse the proposed strategic priorities for the year 2019-21, including the Fragile-to-Fragile Cooperation Action Plan, and we request the Secretariat to prepare a Financing Plan to that effect, while calling upon our Partners to support these priorities. We also welcome the findings of the independent review of the g7+ presented during this meeting.

As we continue on our pathway towards resilience, we look forward to celebrating the tenth anniversary of the g7+ in 2020.

ANNEX II Fragility Spectrum

	Stage 1: Crisis	Stage 2: Rebuild and Reform	Stage 3: Transition	Stage 4: Transformation	Stage 5: Resilience	Indicators to measure progress:
PSG 1: Inclusive politics	Country Description	Country Description	Country Description	Country Description	Country Description	Country Description
PSG 2: Security	Country Description	Country Description	Country Description	Country Description	Country Description	Country Description
PSG 3: Justice	Country Description	Country Description	Country Description	Country Description	Country Description	Country Description
PSG 4: Economic Foundations	Country Description	Country Description	Country Description	Country Description	Country Description	Country Description
PSG 5: Revenues & Services	Country Description	Country Description	Country Description	Country Description	Country Description	Country Description

ANNEX III g7+ Fragility Assessments

Fragility assessments and their year of completion by g7+ member countries:

Country	Year
South Sudan	2012
Sierra Leone	2012
Timor-Leste	2013
Comores	2014
Timor-Leste	2015
Guinea	2016
Guinea-Bissau	2017
Comores	2017
São Tomé e Príncipe	2017
DRC	2019

ANNEX IV Chronology of g7+'s Main Events Since 2010

CHRONOLOGY OF THE g7+

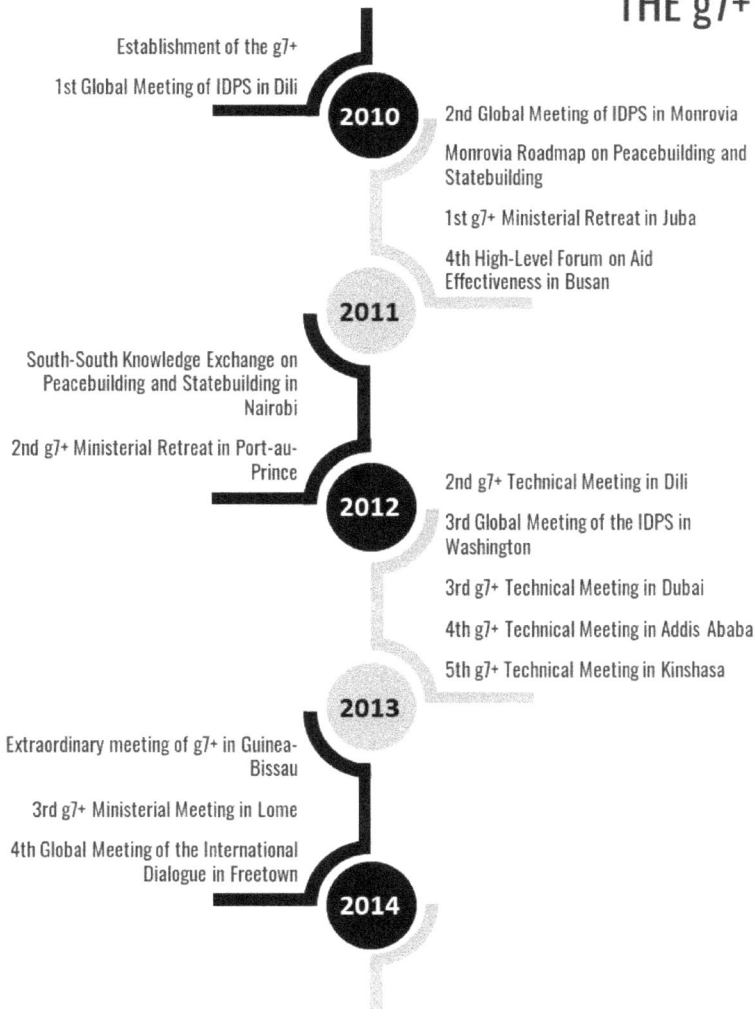

2010
- Establishment of the g7+
- 1st Global Meeting of IDPS in Dili
- 2nd Global Meeting of IDPS in Monrovia
- Monrovia Roadmap on Peacebuilding and Statebuilding
- 1st g7+ Ministerial Retreat in Juba
- 4th High-Level Forum on Aid Effectiveness in Busan

2011

2012
- South-South Knowledge Exchange on Peacebuilding and Statebuilding in Nairobi
- 2nd g7+ Ministerial Retreat in Port-au-Prince
- 2nd g7+ Technical Meeting in Dili
- 3rd Global Meeting of the IDPS in Washington
- 3rd g7+ Technical Meeting in Dubai
- 4th g7+ Technical Meeting in Addis Ababa
- 5th g7+ Technical Meeting in Kinshasa

2013

2014
- Extraordinary meeting of g7+ in Guinea-Bissau
- 3rd g7+ Ministerial Meeting in Lome
- 4th Global Meeting of the International Dialogue in Freetown

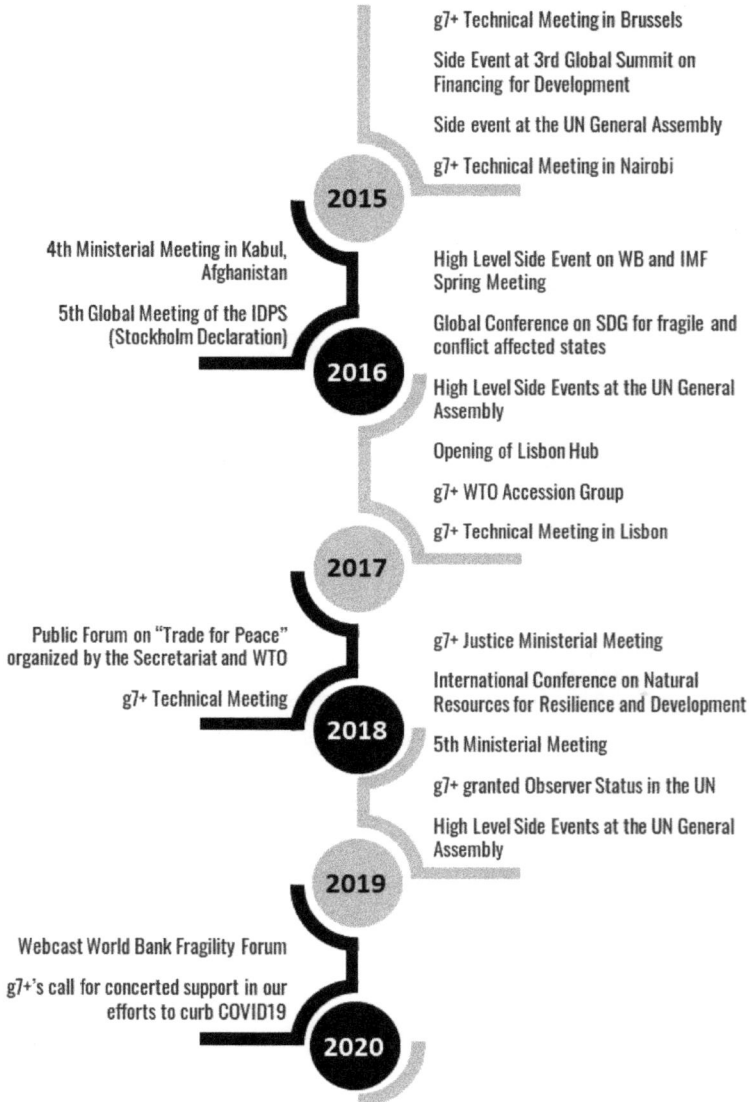

g7+ Technical Meeting in Brussels

Side Event at 3rd Global Summit on Financing for Development

Side event at the UN General Assembly

g7+ Technical Meeting in Nairobi

2015

4th Ministerial Meeting in Kabul, Afghanistan

5th Global Meeting of the IDPS (Stockholm Declaration)

High Level Side Event on WB and IMF Spring Meeting

Global Conference on SDG for fragile and conflict affected states

2016

High Level Side Events at the UN General Assembly

Opening of Lisbon Hub

g7+ WTO Accession Group

g7+ Technical Meeting in Lisbon

2017

Public Forum on "Trade for Peace" organized by the Secretariat and WTO

g7+ Technical Meeting

g7+ Justice Ministerial Meeting

International Conference on Natural Resources for Resilience and Development

2018

5th Ministerial Meeting

g7+ granted Observer Status in the UN

High Level Side Events at the UN General Assembly

2019

Webcast World Bank Fragility Forum

g7+'s call for concerted support in our efforts to curb COVID19

2020

ANNEX V 2030 Agenda
Sustainable Development Goals (SDGs)

ANNEX VI 20 TARGETS CHOSEN IN A 2016 TECHNICAL MEETING

Finalised List of Indicators at g7+ Technical Meeting in Nairobi (30–31 May 2016)

Sustainable Development Goal (SDGs)		# Indicators proposed (identified from group discussions)
SDG 1	End poverty in all its forms everywhere	1.1.1 — Proportion of population below the international poverty status and geographical location (urban/rural).
SDG 2	End hunger, achieve food security and improved nutrition and promote sustainable agriculture	(*National*) — Number of persons assisted by emergences food aid (eg. World Food Program, government).
SDG 3	Ensure healthy lives and promote well-being for all at all ages	3.2.1 — Mortality rate under 5 years (death of probability before the age of 5 per 1,000 live births).
SDG 4	Ensure inclusive and equitable quality education and promote lifelong learning opportunities for all	4.1.1. — Primary and secondary education completion rates. (*National*) — Number of persons with vocational training. (*National*) — Proportion of children with access to primary and secondary education.
SDG 5	Achieve gender equality and empower all women and girls	5.5.1 — Proportion of seats held by women in national parliament and local government. (*National*) — Number of women holding senior bureaucratic positions.
SDG 6	Ensure availability and sustainable management of water and sanitation for all	6.1.1 — Proportion of population using safely managed drinking water services

Sustainable Development Goal (SDGs)		# Indicators proposed (identified from group discussions)
SDG 7	Ensure access to affordable, reliable, sustainable and modern energy for all	*7.1.1* — Proportion of population with access to electricity
SDG 8	Promote sustained, inclusive and sustainable economic growth, full and productive employment and decent work for all	*8.b.1* — Total government spending in social protection and employment programmes as a proportion of the national budgets and GDP. *8.5.2* — Unemployment rate, by sex, age group and persons with disabilities.
SDG 9	Build resilient infrastructure, promote inclusive and sustainable industrialization and foster innovation	*(National)* — Kilometer/miles in season roads (disaggregated by regions).
SDG 10	Reduce inequality within and among countries	*10.2.1.* — Proportion of people living below 50 per cent of median income.
SDG 11	Make cities and human settlements inclusive, safe, resilient and sustainable	*11.1.1* — Proportion of urban population living in slums, informal settlements or inadequate housing.
SDG 12	Ensure sustainable consumption and production patterns	No priority indicator was defined for this especific goal
SDG 13	Take urgent action to combat climate change and its impacts (Acknowledging that the United Nations Framework Convention on Climate Change is the primary international, intergovernmental forum for negotiating the global response to climate change).	No priority indicator was defined for this especific goal
SDG 14	Conserve and sustainably use the oceans, seas and marine resources for sustainable development	No priority indicator was defined for this especific goal

Sustainable Development Goal (SDGs)		# Indicators proposed (identified from group discussions)
SDG 15	Protect, restore and promote sustainable use of terrestrial ecosystems, sustainably manage forests, combat desertification, and halt and reverse land degradation and halt biodiversity loss	No priority indicator was defined for this especific goal
SDG 16	Promote peaceful and inclusive societies for sustainable development, provide access to justice for all and build effective, accountable and inclusive institutions at all levels	*(National)* — Number of Internal Displaced Persons (IDPs) and refugees (sources). *16.3.2* — Unsentenced Detainees as % of overall prison population. *16.7.1* — Proportions of positions (by sex, age, persons with disabilities and population groups) in public institutions (national and local legislatures, public service, and judiciary) compared to national distributions.
SDG 17	Strengthen the means of implementation and revitalize the global partnership for sustainable development	*17.9.1* — Total aid per capita (see 17.9.1). *17.4.1* — Debt service as percentage of exports of goods and services.

ANNEX VII g7+ Statement of Solidarity and Cooperation: 'A call for concerted support in our efforts to curb COVID-19' (March 2020)

Statement of Solidarity and Cooperation

A call for concerted support in our efforts to curb COVID19

COVID-19 is a global threat to humanity which can only be addressed through global solidarity, cooperation, and coordination.

We the members of the g7+ group join our partners to express our profound solidarity with nations affected by COVID-19 and sympathy for the victims of this pandemic. The g7+ group is committed to curb the pandemic and contribute to international efforts to strengthen social and economic resilience globally, including through a range of partnerships and solidarity with affected countries and populations.

We express our gratitude to the healthcare professionals for their relentless services and sacrifices in treating and taking care of patients under extremely difficult conditions. We commend the efforts of the World Health Organziation (WHO) and other national and international organizations for their robust efforts to tackle the pandemic.

g7+ countries have experienced adverse social, political and economic impacts of decades-long conflicts, terrorism, disasters and extreme poverty. These countries are the most vulnerable to the pandemic as they have some of the weakest institutions, finances and human capital to cope with this crisis and its social and economic aftermath. At the same time, some of the g7+ member states have practical experiences in managing multidimensional crises, which could be brought to bear in the fight against COVID-19.

Together with our partners, we call for the following immediate steps to mitigate the impact of the pandemic on children, families and societies in the most vulnerable communities.

1. Support the UN Secretary General's Call for Global Ceasefire:
COVID-19 is a challenge that tests our care for humanity, and we support the UN Secretary General's call for a global ceasefire. This is a time to fight the common enemy, the pandemic, and save precious lives. We call upon all warring factions and parties to lay down their arms and work with governments, communities, civil society organizations and healthcare organizations to tackle the rapid spread of the disease.

2. Invest in Public Healthcare and Strengthen Institutions:

COVID-19 is putting a strain on public health systems worldwide. The Public Health Systems in fragile and conflict-affected countries are already constrained due to lack of basic equipment and inadequate personnel to address their current situation. The COVID-19 pandemic will overwhelm public health systems in g7+ countries, if the pandemic reaches a tipping point in these countries. Support from international humanitarian and development organizations to strengthen health systems in poor countries will help to save millions of lives. Noting current support, we call upon donor countries and organizations to scale up their assistance in line with the principles of New Deal *For engagement in fragile countries* to help these countries with more resilient health systems and responses to prevent, contain and recover from the pandemic.

Sharing of experiences, knowledge, good practices, and cooperation in scientific innovations, social mobilization and adaptive leadership are critical to addressing this pandemic in a diverse range of crisis-affected contexts. Therefore, we commit to serving as a platform for governments, partners, civil society and the private sector to share experiences, including "Fragile-to-Fragile cooperation" among fragile and conflict-affected countries, and as part of broader efforts for South-South and Triangular cooperation to curb the pandemic and strengthen institutions.
We reiterate our commitment to Agenda 2030 and its implementation, especially for Goals 3 and 16.

3. Care for Displaced People stranded due to Border Closures:

We commend the hospitality of societies and countries hosting displaced people and migrants who are forced to embark on difficult journeys due to wars and natural disasters. The COVID-19 induced border closures are affecting the lives and safety of countless refugees and displaced people. We call upon governments and international organizations to care for their needs and safety, as they would for their own citizens, as a gesture of human solidarity and consistent with international obligations.

4. Support for Economic Recovery, Self-reliance and the Sustaining Peace Agenda:

Fragile and conflict-affected countries are increasingly home to the world's poorest and are in critical stages of their political and development transition. These countries are already being hit the hardest by the economic downturn resulting from the COVID-19 outbreak. This has adversely affected the prospects for revenue generation in these countries, which will have a significant impact on their self-reliance. The trade and private sector are likely to be badly affected by this pandemic as experienced by the three g7+ countries during the 2014 Ebola outbreak. We welcome the announcement by the World Bank of a $12 billion response package and by the International Monetary Fund (IMF) to activate $50 billion through its rapid-disbursing emergency financing facilities. We also commend similar support by other regional Development Banks and other donors.

We call on development partners to provide sufficient resources to support the most fragile countries in their effort to contain the virus and recover from its impact.

We support the call for debt relief through waiving interest payments and using the Heavily Indebted Poor Country (HIPC) mechanisms for these countries as sustained peace and stability in conflict affected countries remain the insurance for global peace and prosperity.

Social distancing and lockdowns will be very difficult to sustain due to the lack of viable economic safety nets, underdeveloped infrastructure, and the need for citizens to sustain themselves, especially in conflict zones. Landlocked Least Developed Countries (LDCs) that depend on the uninterrupted transit of goods will be particularly affected by the closure of borders. Therefore, we urge donors and nations in those regions to address the needs of these countries through targeted investments in food security, regional cooperation, technological innovation and alternative sources of financing.

We the members of g7+ will regularly follow up and review progress on the above statement.

Index

About the Team

Alessandra Tosi was the managing editor for this book.

Lucy Barnes and Rohini Bhonsle-Allemand performed the copy-editing and proofreading. Lucy indexed the book.

Katy Saunders designed the cover. The cover was produced in InDesign using the Fontin font.

Melissa Purkiss and Luca Baffa typeset the book in InDesign and produced the paperback and hardback editions. The text font is Tex Gyre Pagella; the heading font is Californian FB.

Luca produced the EPUB, AZW3, PDF, HTML, and XML editions — the conversion is performed with open source software such as pandoc (https://pandoc.org/) created by John MacFarlane and other tools freely available on our GitHub page (https://github.com/OpenBookPublishers).

This book need not end here...

Share

All our books — including the one you have just read — are free to access online so that students, researchers and members of the public who can't afford a printed edition will have access to the same ideas. This title will be accessed online by hundreds of readers each month across the globe: why not share the link so that someone you know is one of them?

This book and additional content is available at:

https://doi.org/10.11647/OBP.0311

Donate

Open Book Publishers is an award-winning, scholar-led, not-for-profit press making knowledge freely available one book at a time. We don't charge authors to publish with us: instead, our work is supported by our library members and by donations from people who believe that research shouldn't be locked behind paywalls.

Why not join them in freeing knowledge by supporting us: https://www.openbookpublishers.com/support-us

Like Open Book Publishers

Follow @OpenBookPublish

Read more at the Open Book Publishers BLOG

You may also be interested in:

Peace and Democratic Society
Amartya Sen (ed.)

https://doi.org/10.11647/obp.0014

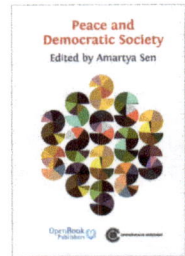

Wellbeing, Freedom and Social Justice
The Capability Approach Re-Examined
Ingrid Robeyns

https://doi.org/10.11647/obp.0130

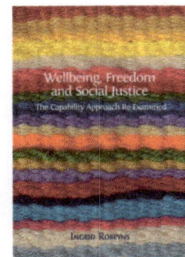

Democracy and Power
The Delhi Lectures
Noam Chomsky

https://doi.org/10.11647/obp.0050

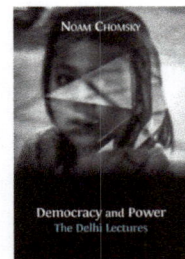